J. M. SYNGE: COLLECTED WORKS

General Editor: ROBIN SKELTON

PLAYS

BOOK I

J. M. SYNGE

COLLECTED WORKS

Volume III

PLAYS

BOOK I

EDITED BY
ANN SADDLEMYER

1982
COLIN SMYTHE
GERRARDS CROSS, BUCKS

THE CATHOLIC UNIVERSITY OF
AMERICA PRESS
WASHINGTON, D.C.

Copyright © 1968 Oxford University Press

This edition published in 1982
by Colin Smythe Limited, Gerrards Cross,
Buckinghamshire

British Library Cataloguing in Publication Data

Synge, John Millington
  The collected works of J. M. Synge
  Vol. 3: Plays. Book 1
  I. Saddlemyer, Ann
  822'.9'12   PR5530

  ISBN 0–86140–136–0
  ISBN 0–86140–060–7 Pbk.

First published in North America in 1982
by The Catholic University of America Press, Washington, D.C.

ISBN 0–8132–0567–0
ISBN 0–8132–0566–2 Pbk.
Library of Congress Catalog Card No. 82–70364

Printed in Great Britain
Set by Oxford University Press
Printed from copy supplied, and bound by
Billing & Sons Ltd., Worcester and London

TO THE MEMORY OF

NED STEPHENS

NEPHEW AND

FAITHFUL HISTORIAN OF

J. M. SYNGE

CONTENTS

INTRODUCTION

I WAS born in 1871 near Dublin—my father was a barrister and landlord. I went to various local schools and had private tutors till 1887
when I entered Trinity College Dublin, taking my degree (B.A.) in
1892. Meanwhile I had given a great deal of my time to music—I took
the scholarship of Harmony and Counterpoint in the royal Irish Aca-
demy of Music about the same time—and in 1893 I went to Germany
(partly for a holiday), but I stayed there studying music for nearly a
year. I saw that the Germans were so much more innately gifted with
the musical faculties than I was that I decided to give up music and take
to literature instead. I went back to Germany for a few months to work
at the language only, and then on the first day of 1895 I went to Paris
for six months. The next year I went to Italy and learned Italian, and
then I spent six or seven winters in Paris going back to Ireland for half
the year. In 1898 I went to the Aran Islands to learn Gaelic and lived
with the peasants. Ever since then I have spent part of my year among
the Irish speaking peasantry in various localities as I am now doing once
more. I have the MS of a book giving an account of my life on the
Aran Islands which Mr. Elkin Mathews has promised to publish
shortly. During the last 10 years I have written a certain number of
short articles and reviews for various papers, but my first real success
was with the two little plays—which I suppose you have seen or heard
of—'Riders to the Sea' and 'The Shadow of the Glen' which were
played in Dublin by our Society and also in London March, 1904,
where they were very well received. Since then I have given up Paris
and give all my time to writing for the little Theatre we have in
Dublin. I hope to have another play ready before very long. . . .

WITH these words written, appropriately, from a little country
inn in County Kerry on a wet September day in 1905,[1] Synge
summed up the achievements of thirty-four years. His corre-
spondent, Max Meyerfeld, had just completed a German translation of the third play by Synge to be produced by the Irish
National Theatre Society, *The Well of the Saints*. The new play he
mentions, *The Playboy of the Western World*, would not be ready
until January 1907, when the reaction to its first production at
the Abbey Theatre would, in the words of that arch-champion

---

[1] 1 September 1905. The letters from Synge to Meyerfeld are in the possession of the
National Library of Ireland.

William Butler Yeats, 'rock the cradle of genius' and secure Synge's fame as a dramatist.[1] Yet another play, *The Tinker's Wedding*, begun at the same time as *Riders to the Sea*, was to be finally published in 1907 but considered too dangerous to be acted at the Abbey. And in 1909, his play *Deirdre of the Sorrows* still unfinished, Synge died.

Synge's early background appears to have been less theatrical than it was linguistic and musical. His diaries during the eighteen-nineties record only two visits to the theatre, in September 1892 to see Beerbohm Tree's *Hamlet* in Dublin, and in March 1898 to see a production of Ibsen's *Ghosts* by Antoine's theatre in Paris. Evidence from his notebooks corroborates this view, for although Synge showed an interest in dramatic expression well before that fateful encounter in 1896 which Yeats describes in his Preface to *The Well of the Saints*, the early scenarios and even his first completed plays were composed far more for the reader than for the performer, despite their later theatrical success. Not until he had become a director of the Abbey Theatre and began to establish his own dramatic method do his manuscripts begin to indicate a conscious sense of stagecraft. It is significant that the first scenario illustrating his contrapuntal method of composition belongs to *The Well of the Saints*, begun in 1903 when he had seen his two one-act plays produced on the stage and had been exposed to the practical problems of direction and staging. In this first volume of his plays, then, and in the unpublished fragments and scenarios found in his notebooks, we can observe the dramatist in the making, and the surprisingly rapid evolution from musician and dilettante student of languages and literature to the practical man of the theatre.

However, although all of his plays from 1902 onwards were written for the Abbey Theatre and its small company of actors, Synge somehow managed to remain in isolation from the movement as a whole, never using the stage as a basis for experiment to the extent his co-directors, Yeats and Lady Gregory, avowedly did. This aloofness made him an excellent intermediary in times of crisis, but frequently Synge seemed too withdrawn for his more involved colleagues, who never felt completely at ease with him and at times accused him of selfishness. Similarly, although he

---

[1] Yeats actually applied these words to the storm over Sean O'Casey's *The Plough and the Stars* in 1926, but in comparison with the riots over *The Playboy*.

knew the Fays well and appreciated their talents, until he became engaged to the young actress Maire O'Neill[1] his closest friend in the theatre seems to have been the violinist Arthur Darley.

This objectivity seemed to be necessary. For months at a time he would immerse himself in Abbey Theatre affairs, directing rehearsals, accompanying the actors on tours, corresponding with his fellow directors over finances, future programmes, new plays, and replying to the unceasing complaints of the Theatre's patron, Miss Horniman. Then suddenly he would take his typewriter and notebook and depart for Kerry, the Blasket Islands, the Wicklow hills, a cousin's country home in England, or, during the last year of his life, even to old friends in Germany. If he did remain in Dublin, he would not even attend performances. During these periods of deliberate exile he would cut himself off as much as possible from theatre worries, and it was then that the incessant revising and meticulous polishing of his plays took place. When he finally reappeared, it would be to read the finished play to his colleagues—too late for any revision beyond minor verbal alterations in rehearsal. In fact, as Willie Fay has reported, by that time revision was impossible; even the suggested alteration of a single passage would upset the delicate balance of the whole.[2] In an important sense then, although Synge undoubtedly learned much from his experiences as a director of the Abbey Theatre, play-writing remained for him very much the private composition of the lyric poet or musician, writing more for the ear than for the eye, imposing a balance of mood, tone, and colour on the material he distilled from the life about him rather than allowing characterization alone to control plot. Occasionally this isolation, too, drew objections: Willie Fay complained of the consistent bad humour of the characters in *The Well of the Saints*, but Synge explained that he wanted to write 'like a monochrome painting, all in shades of one colour'[3]; actors and audience rebelled at the sharpness of his characterization in *The Shadow of the Glen*, several of the company, led by Maud Gonne, staging a public walk-out; and the riots provoked by *The Playboy of the Western World* once again emphasized the playwright's refusal to allow emotions to blur the precision of his painfully acquired technique.

---

[1] The stage name of Molly Allgood, sister to the actress Sara Allgood.
[2] W. G. Fay and Catherine Carswell, *The Fays of the Abbey Theatre* (London, Rich and Cowan, 1935), pp. 138–9.   [3] Ibid., pp. 167–8.

This restraint is all the more surprising when we examine Synge's earliest dramatic attempts and realize that while completing *Riders to the Sea* and *The Shadow of the Glen* he was at the same time floundering around with poetic drama and obstinately rewriting for the third time the argumentative outbursts of *When the Moon Has Set*. Indeed, his first compositions have a tendency towards the exaggerations of romantic opera: in May 1893 he records in his diary, 'Started words and music of an opera on Eileen Aruin'; about the same time he began a novel or play about 'A' and 'B' who love passionately but hopelessly, separated by the hero's penniless condition and the heroine's stern Victorian father. Five years later, still obsessed with the need to express the extremities of passion, he wrote *Étude Morbide* ('a morbid thing about a mad fiddler in Paris, which I hate') and was jotting down in his notebook passages later incorporated in *When the Moon Has Set*. In the meantime he had begun a novel about nurses (*Woman in White*) which he appears to have worked on intermittently from 1893 to 1899, and projected but never completed his play about a returned landlord.

Diaries for the years 1900 and 1901 are unfortunately missing from the Synge papers, but it can safely be assumed that while writing *When the Moon Has Set* Synge was experimenting also with poetry and non-dramatic prose. Furthermore, he was studying the experiments of others: Baudelaire, Flaubert, Zola, Villiers de l'Isle Adam, Pierre Loti, Maeterlinck and Oscar Wilde, Rabelais, Thomas à Kempis, and Boccaccio. It could well be that the personal involvement demanded by his lyrics and travel narratives, together with the development of his critical insight, released him from the need to dramatize his own moods and emotions. Certainly from now on there is a freedom in his choice of subject matter and, as can be seen from the sampling preserved of his scenarios and dialogues, a delight in richness and variety even before he had achieved much confidence in his dramatic abilities. To this maturing process Yeats's sponsorship seems to have acted as a catalyst, while the life Synge discovered on the Aran Islands served as an example.

Apart from the Rabelais–à Kempis dialogue, which appears to have been written in the late nineties, and *When the Moon Has Set*, which Synge brought with him on his second visit to Coole in September 1901, the bulk of the dramatic work, finished and unfinished, was conceived over a surprisingly short period. During 1902 alone, Synge began the two verse plays *A Vernal Play* and *Luasnad, Capa and Laine*, conceived the scenario of 'Magna Serenitas', revised *When the Moon Has Set*, wrote *Riders to the Sea* and *The Shadow of the Glen*, and embarked on *The Tinker's Wedding*, all this in addition to essays, reviews, and poems. Later that winter he sketched the 'Aughavanna Play' and began *The Well of the Saints*. Meanwhile he started *O'Connor's Story*, considered the 'Play of '98', and began writing *The Playboy of the Western World*. Ideas for plots flocked to his mind as he worked painstakingly at *The Playboy* and contemplated *Deirdre of the Sorrows*. The subject for *Deirdre* had interested him as early as 1901; he made his own translation of the Irish text while on Aran collecting material for his earlier work. And while at work on this last play he prepared *The Tinker's Wedding* for publication and revised *The Well of the Saints*. The letters of 1907 and 1908 from his American friend Miss Agnes Tobin repeatedly inquire after a 'Miracle Play' of which no trace remains in his notebooks, and somewhere during these years he found time to revise yet again *When the Moon Has Set*, his first completed play.

It is not surprising therefore to find close relationships in treatment of material and ideas between plays, scenarios, and dialogues while at the same time observing a natural development in choice of subject matter. Like Wilde, Synge was loath to give up a useful phrase or an appealing idea, and the drafts of *When the Moon Has Set*, for example, bear traces of much of his later work. In an early draft describing her father's death Bride anticipates Nora Burke: '. . . a little after twelve he gave a sort of a turn, and I went over and he was dead in the bed. Then I was afeard to be there and no one along with me, so I came up to see would Mrs. Byrne go down to keep me from being lonesome', and in her grief echoes old Maurya: 'I'm destroyed crying; but what good is in it. We must be satisfied, and what man at all can be living forever.' In the final draft Mary Costello repeats Maurya again in her defiance of the priests: '. . . for it's little the like of them, I was saying, knows about women or the seven sorrows of the earth', and predicts Deirdre's actions: 'There's great marrying in the world but it's late we were surely, and let yourselves not be the same.' Colm's plea for the individual's right to follow his own nature appears in all the later plays, expressed perhaps most strongly in Mary Byrne's drunken soliloquies, the Tramp's poetic invitation to the life of the road, and the Playboy's blossoming spirit; while the Douls' insistence on their illusions in the face of reality becomes an ironic comment on Sister Eileen's belief in the beneficence of faith.

When one considers the ruthlessness with which Synge perfected his later plays, however, it is difficult to appreciate his reluctance to give up a work judged inferior by both his colleagues, especially after he had raided it so freely. Furthermore, his attachment to Molly Allgood had done much to erase the pain of Cherrie Matheson's refusal on religious grounds of his offer of marriage, one of the incidents on which the play appears to have been based. Yet he clung obstinately to *When the Moon Has Set*, leaving it to be considered once more after his death. Undoubtedly Yeats and Lady Gregory were right to reject it, and Yeats's objection to the inclusion of Synge's *Manchester Guardian* articles in the 1910 collected edition adequately explains his rejection of the play:

My feeling at the time however was chiefly of anxiety lest I should allow anything undistinguished to mar the effect upon posterity of a writer whose good fortune it should be to leave behind him a mass of perfectly distinguished work. The rest of us have had to make our experiments before the world. He alone, if he escape the commercial hand, will leave behind him work as perfect as a beautiful statue.[1]

It is with reluctance, therefore, that I publish the young and immature Synge's objection to a rigidity of life and narrowness of faith he believed immoral and unjust. But it too has its place in the canon, and although his later plays far more effectively practise the belief he here preaches, *When the Moon Has Set* provides perhaps the most important clue to his transition from apprentice to playwright.

On his next visit to Coole, in September 1902, Synge brought with him *Riders to the Sea* and *The Shadow of the Glen*. We have his own word that the one-act play based on his experiences in Aran was written first,[2] but alterations seem to have been necessary. Yeats wrote to him from London on 21 December 1902,

---

[1] Letter to Joseph Hone, 6 October 1910, in the possession of the Synge Estate.
[2] Letter from Synge to Leon Brodzky (later Spencer Brodney), 12 December 1907, in the possession of Trinity College, Dublin. In the same letter he states, 'I look upon the "Aran Islands" as my first serious piece of work—it was written before any of the plays.'

'Fay's company is going to produce a play of mine at the end of January. I shall go to Dublin for that. However we will meet here, as you say and I will get you to show me your play. I thought the subject impressive and certainly it would be a fine thing for Fay if you got the play right. He is in danger of getting work which is quite articulate but also quite empty.'[1] Both plays were read aloud by Lady Gregory in her rooms at Queen Anne's Mansions in London on 20 January 1903; Synge noted in his diary that they were received 'with much approval'. A repeat performance occurred at Yeats's regular Monday gathering in Woburn Buildings on 2 February, with Chesterton and Maud Gonne in the audience. A week later Arthur Symons heard *Riders to the Sea* at Lady Gregory's and wrote to her the next day:

Wednesday

Dear Lady Gregory,

Do you think Mr. Sing would like to publish his play in the Fortnightly before issuing it as a book? I feel almost sure that ⟨Courtney?⟩ would take it, and if you do not know him I will send it and warmly recommend it myself. One advantage if he took it, would be that it would bring in double money for the writer, who, I gather, would find that useful. Let me know if you think it worth trying.

Sincerely yours,
Arthur Symons

But *Riders to the Sea* came back from the *Fortnightly Review* 'as not suitable for their purposes', and was not published until September 1903 in Yeats's *Samhain*. The players, too, had some reservations; Willie Fay as stage manager wrote to Synge that the reading committee thought it 'wanted more speed towards the end, after the body is brought in'. Fay himself, Lady Gregory reported, 'is longing to act the poor drowned man in it. "He knows he could make the audience shiver by the way he would hang his head over the side of the table"!' And finally, on 25 February 1904, it was produced. *The Shadow of the Glen*, on the other hand, was accepted immediately when read to the company by Lady Gregory. Although Yeats did not publish it until the December 1904 issue of *Samhain*, it was produced by the Irish National Theatre Society on 8 October 1903, and with that production the long battle between Synge and the Irish nationalists began.

[1] Unless otherwise stated, all letters quoted are in the possession of the Synge Estate.

The story of Synge's—or rather Yeats's, for Synge did not actively participate[1]—struggle with the press over *The Shadow of the Glen* has been fully described by David H. Greene and Edward M. Stephens in their detailed biography of Synge, and need not be retold here.[2] It seems likely, as Yeats and Lady Gregory always suspected, that the criticism was part of a premeditated attack on the entire theatre movement, which began over *The Countess Cathleen* in 1899 and was to flare up again over *The Playboy of the Western World* in 1907. But it is clear also that the audience, trained on traditional melodrama at the Queen's Theatre and led to expect another 'Celtic' play in the Yeatsian tradition, were hardly prepared for the shock of reality to which Synge subjected them. Furthermore, the production emphasized the reality of the life he depicted. Dan Burke's cottage was scrupulously copied from life, and Synge, who knew well the actual building and site (Harney's cottage in Glenmalure, County Wicklow), could describe to Willie Fay the exact setting:

His power of visualisation was perfect. I would work out a scale plan of the stage and furniture, and he would say, 'That is just the way I saw the room as I was writing the play.' It was very lucky that there seemed to be a sort of pre-established harmony between my mind and his, for I always wanted to produce his plays as nearly as possible as he saw them. If I asked him, 'Was Dan standing where he is on the right, behind the table, when he said these lines?' he would say, 'No, he was on the right-hand side of the table with his hand on it.' He was a great joy to work with, for he had a keen sense of humour and plenty of patience, and above all he knew what he wanted, and when he got it said so.[3]

Similarly, *Riders to the Sea* was produced with as much authenticity as possible. Micheal Costello of Inisheer forwarded *pampooties*, the traditional Aran footgear, and replied to Synge's queries, 'I herewith enclose patterns of the flannel usually worn by the native men here and also in Inishmaan there is no difference

---

[1] Except for a brief note to the *United Irishman* enclosing the original story as he heard it on Aran (see Appendix B).

[2] *J. M. Synge 1871–1909* (New York, Macmillan, 1959). See also David Greene, 'The Shadow of the Glen and the Widow of Ephesus' (*P.M.L.A.*) (March 1947), pp. 233–8. Two of the most interesting contributions to the press during the controversy were a letter by J. B. Yeats on Ireland's loveless marriages and a brief play by 'Conn', 'In a Real Wicklow Glen'.

[3] *The Fays of the Abbey Theatre*, pp. 138–9.

in dress between the two Islands. This kind of thick flannel was spun on the woollen wheel by hand and woven in Aranmore. . . .' When the company visited London in 1904 Synge anxiously wrote to George Roberts, secretary of the Irish National Theatre Society, 'I suppose you will take over the spinning wheel, it helps the scene so much.' (Several years later he was urging that Molly Allgood be taught to spin 'so that there be no fake about the show'.[1])

This fidelity to detail and simplicity of design, developed for the most part in Synge's two one-act plays, was emphasized by Willie Fay's experience with amateur 'fit-ups' and Frank Fay's pedantry concerning voice production, and helped not a little by the nationalist fervour of the first company of players. Defended and outlined by Yeats in lectures and essays, these elements combined to create the style of acting and production which became known as 'the Abbey method'. A brochure prepared for the players' first extensive tour in 1906 explains the theory behind this method:

The Folk Play needs a special kind of acting, and the Company selected to interpret the programme are all familiar with the ways of the Irish peasantry, and in their acting take care to keep close to the actual movements and gestures of the people. Their costumes and their properties are not the haphazard collection from the theatre store, but thoroughly appropriate and accurate, while the scenes in which they play are actual replicas of some carefully chosen original; forasmuch as these plays are portions of Irish life, so are they put upon the stage with a care and accuracy of detail that has hardly been attempted before.[2]

Although Lady Gregory was to make far more use of 'the Folk Play' than Synge, clearly his two one-act plays were the inspiration as much as they were the product of the new movement in Irish drama. And it is hardly surprising, therefore, that the audience, taken off guard by the realism of the production in front of them, should take the next step and accept literally the words and situation presented there.

The reception given to *Riders to the Sea* on its first performance

[1] Synge's letter to Roberts and the one following to Lady Gregory are in the Berg Collection of the New York Public Library. Maire Nic Shiubhlaigh reproduces the keen used in *Riders to the Sea* in her book *The Splendid Years* (Dublin, Duffy, 1955), p. 56.

[2] A copy of this brochure is preserved in the W. A. Henderson collection, National Library of Ireland.

was less argumentative but still unsympathetic, and it was not until the company paid its second visit to London on 26 March 1904 that Synge's two plays were received with appreciation by audience and critics alike. By this time, also, Synge was becoming aware of the significance of production. After the first performance of *Riders to the Sea* he wrote to Frank Fay, 'I regret endlessly to have had to miss the two other performances as there were many things I wanted to consider with a view to London. It can't be helped and it is well I saw one.' After the London visit he wrote again on 10 April, in response to Fay's request for criticism of the acting, 'Again all our women are too young; where else will you see such girls holding an audience—as they did after all— in serious drama? It was worst in the Shadow of the Glen, Miss W. ⟨Walker, who acted under her Irish name, Maire Nic Shiubhlaigh⟩ is clever and charming in the part, but your brother is so strong he dominates the play—unconsciously and inevitably —and of course the woman should dominate.'[1] From now on he wrote with a knowledge of the actors who would be called upon to interpret his roles.[2]

But even before he had seen *Riders to the Sea* on stage, and perhaps as early as the first rehearsals of *The Shadow of the Glen*, Synge had begun work on his next play. In a letter to Lady Gregory on 16 December 1903 he remarks, 'I was getting on well with the blind people till about a month ago when I suddenly got ill with influenza and a nasty attack on my lung. I am getting better now but I cannot work yet satisfactorily so I hardly know when the play is likely to be finished. There is no use trying to hurry on with a thing of that kind when one is not in the mood.' His letter to Frank Fay from London on 10 April 1904 continues, 'I am very well but in agony and horror over my play with the blind people. It is exceedingly difficult to make it work out.' The following month, back in Dublin, he reported to Lady Gregory in his capacity as a member of the reading committee, and added, 'I am hard at work overhauling my play and generally sharpening

[1] Original letter in the Fay Papers, National Library of Ireland. Gerard Fay quotes the letter in full in *The Abbey Theatre: Cradle of Genius* (Dublin, Clonmore and Reynolds, 1958), pp. 75-77.

[2] On 10 March 1906 he wrote to Lady Gregory, 'I have just performed the delicate operation of getting Sara Allgood out of Nora Burke's part—where she was impossible— and getting Molly Allgood in. Molly A.'s voice is too young for the part but she feels it, and has some expression.' Letter in the Berg Collection, New York Public Library.

the dialogue, but the more I do the more there seems to be done.'[1] Finally early in July 1904 he handed over the completed play to Willie Fay and escaped to County Kerry, stopping only long enough at Coole to help Lady Gregory revise her folk-history play, *Kincora*.

But by now Synge's fortunes were tied to the small company in Dublin. The English heiress Miss Horniman, in sympathy with Yeats's ambition to create a theatre of poetry, had offered the Irish National Theatre Society a permanent home on Lower Abbey Street; Yeats, Lady Gregory, and Synge gained more power and responsibility. Concern over details of production became more anxious as the decision over the opening programme drew near. On 21 August 1904, having just returned from the hearings over the Abbey Theatre patent, Yeats dictated the following letter from Coole:

I saw your play rehearsed in Dublin, or rather I saw the first act several times. Of course it was imaginative and original from the very first, but at first I was inclined to think that it would lack climax, gradual and growing interest. Then I forced myself to attend to the picture of the eye, the bell in the girl's hand, the cloak, the withered faces of the old people, and I saw that these things made all the difference. It will be very curious, beautiful and I think exciting.

One or two criticisms occurred to me. There is a place where you make the saint say that some one of the characters has a low voice or should have a low voice, and that this is a good thing in women. This suggests that he has been reading King Lear, where Cordelia's voice is described as low 'an excellent thing in woman'. I think this is a wrong association in the mind. I do not object to another passage about the spells of smiths and women which suggests that he has been reading S. Patrick's hymn. He might naturally have done so. The point is not however very important. But I do think it of some importance that you should cross out a number of the Almighty Gods. I do not object to them on the ground that they are likely to shock people but because the phrase occurs so often that it may weary and irritate the ear. I remember the disastrous effect of the repetition of the word beauty in the last act of Edward Martyn's Maeve. I daresay the people do repeat the word very often, but unhappily the stage has its laws which are not those of life. Fay told me that you gave him leave to cross out what he will, but though he is very anxious to reduce the number of the God Almightys

---

[1] The original letters to Lady Gregory are in the Berg Collection, New York Public Library.

he does not like to do it of himself. He wants you to do it. . . . I think William Fay will be as fine as possible in your play if I can judge by the first act. Frank Fay will be good as the saint. I like the women rather less. . . .

On his return to Dublin Synge himself joined the rehearsals, and reported to Lady Gregory on 11 September 1904:

I have seen about four rehearsals since I came up, which include two or three of the first act of Kincora. It works out, I think, as a thoroughly sound healthy act, but I cannot say so much for the cast. . . . A few evenings ago Russell ⟨Æ⟩ raised the question of the opening programme and there was a somewhat violent discussion. W. Fay is very reasonable, but F. F. is as mad as a March hare. AE and myself urged W. Fay—and I am sure you will agree—to rehearse Kincora as hard as he could for some weeks, and then, if he found it impossible to get a satisfactory show out of his cast, to reconsider his opening programme. The difficulty is that F. F. is dead against my play or Cuchulain ⟨Yeats's *On Baile's Strand*⟩ so one does not know what to suggest.[1] He says my work is only addressed to the blasé town-dwelling theatre-goers, that as long as we play that sort of work we are only doing what Antoine does in Paris and doing it worse, that he wants a National Theatre that will draw the people etc. etc. etc. He's got Brian Boru on the brain it seems. I do not know whether all this is his own feeling only—in which case it is of no consequence—or whether there is a Neo-patriotic-Catholic clique growing which might be serious. Colum finds my play unsatisfactory because the Saint is really a Protestant! . . .

They have very little to show for the two months work they have given my play. F. F. and Miss Esposito are the only ones who know their parts at all beyond the first act. I think W. F. will be very good though ⟨it⟩ is not easy to judge him all through yet, as he is so much taken up with the words. Miss Esposito is better than I expected, Miss Allgood much worse, Roberts is very middling, and I don't quite like F. F. though he is always adequate. So you see my prospects are not very golden either. F. F. sits in the corner during my rehearsals muttering he'd like 'to cut their $\frac{\text{(bloody)}}{}$ throats'.[2]

Synge did his best to explain his play to the company, and among the Fay papers are the following notes evidently intended for Willie Fay:

[1] The opening programme at the Abbey Theatre on 27 December 1904 was *On Baile's Strand* by Yeats and *Spreading the News* by Lady Gregory. On 22 September 1905 a meeting was held to reorganize the society, which became the Irish National Theatre Society, Limited, with Yeats, Lady Gregory, and Synge given complete control as the Directors.

[2] Original letter in the Berg Collection, New York Public Library.

If it is possible—Timmy, Molly should be got to show that in all their relations with Martin & Mary—friendly as they are—they feel their own superiority—for this reason Timmy's slapping Martin on back etc. is better left out.

Timmy's key-note is that he's always telling queer things and the lot of them nothing at all—thus he runs up before all the others to tell the news—when the saint appears he comes forward with a long speech about Martin & M. and so on—He is a good-natured, naive, busy-body with a hot temper—i.e. that is how I felt him, but of course it is quite possible that in the necessarily slight sketch of him this did not come out strongly enough to tell on stage—

Entr. of Molly carrying things like eggs in her bib—

Position of Mary Doul and men while saint is in the church

Men crying out Try again Martin try again etc. must not sound as if they were repeating a chorus—

A marked difference of voice and bearing should be felt when the saint goes into church and the people are left to themselves.

Following these last notes is an additional comment in Frank Fay's hand but probably again a direction from Synge:

Getting up in the morning & eating her food etc. pianissimo & slow from that crescendo up to where he goes blind & stay up till he gets near end of curse when it dies off a little the feeling having become so intense that it cannot be spoken.

But he would not alter his play to conform to Yeats's view of art or anyone else's, as he explained about the same time:

Thursday night

Dear Mr. Fay

I have just come home from our long day in the country and found your letter waiting for me. Miss G⟨arvey⟩ mentioned the matter of the speech about priest to me directly but I had not time to go into matter fully with her and see what she meant. In your letter you quote your objector as saying *these things are not true*. What put the simile into my head was a scene I saw not long ago in Galway when I saw a young man behaving most indecently to a girl on the roadside while two priests sat near by on a seat looking out to sea and pretending not to see what was going on. The girl, of course, was perfectly well able to take care of herself and stoned the unfortunate man half a mile into Galway. The way the two priests sat stolidly looking out to sea with this screaming row going on at their elbows tickled my fancy and seemed to me rather typical of many attitudes of the Irish church party. Further though it is true—I am sorry to say—that priests do beat their *parishioners*, the man in question—in my play—may have been a tinker, stranger, sailor, cattle-drover—God knows what—types with which no priest would dream of interfering. Tell Miss G.—or whoever it may be—that what I write of Irish country life I know to be true and I most emphatically will not change a syllable of it because A. B. or C. may think they know better than I do. The other speech you refer to is not fresh in my mind, we can discuss it when we meet. You understand my position: I am *quite ready* to avoid hurting people's feelings needlessly, but I will *not* falsify what I believe to be true for anybody. If one began that where would one end? I would rather drop play-writing altogether.

I told Miss G. today, on the spur of the moment, that the said man in the side ditch was a Protestant and that if the priest had touched him he would have got six months with hard labour for common assault—perhaps as good an answer as any. She seems to have thought that I was sneering at the priest for not doing his obvious duty, an idea which of course never entered my head.

If there are passages in the saint's role that give unnecessary trouble, I will do what I can to make them better if the reading committee—or if that is not possible—you yourself—will point them out to me.

Excuse scrawl and believe me very sincerely yours

J. M. Synge.

P.S. Don't imagine for a moment that I am in any way annoyed at your note on the contrary I am glad to know what is thought.[1]

Anticipating an even stronger reaction on the part of the audience, Yeats wrote in the December issue of *Samhain*, 'Mr. Synge has written us a play in three acts called *The Well of the Saints* full, as few works of our time are, with temperament, and of a true and yet bizarre beauty.' But when the unveiling came in February, the critics though hostile were brief: Arthur Griffith had renewed his attack on *The Shadow of the Glen*, and the audience on the whole simply stayed away. Yeats wrote to the American patron and collector John Quinn,

We will have a hard fight in Ireland before we get the right for every man to see the world in his own way admitted. Synge is invaluable to us because he has that kind of intense narrow personality which necessarily raises the whole issue. It will be very curious to notice the effect of his new play. He will start next time with many enemies but with

[1] Original letter in the Fay papers, National Library of Ireland.

many admirers. It will be a fight like that over the first realistic plays of Ibsen.[1]

Nor was Synge himself satisfied. He experimented with the dialogue in his own copy of the play, and when the play was revived in the spring of 1908 with a new stage design by Charles Ricketts, he revised the third act.

Oddly enough, it was defence from an unexpected quarter which led to Synge's reputation on the Continent. On 13 February 1905 a letter praising the recent production appeared in the *Irish Times*. It was signed by George Moore, who lauded 'the abundance and the beauty of the dialogue' and admired the interpretation. 'Mr. Synge has discovered great literature in barbarous idiom as gold is discovered in quartz, and to do such a thing is surely a rare literary achievement.' A French friend of Synge's, Henry LeBeau, wrote an article on the production and 'la langue toute spéciale dans laquelle est écrite la pièce' for the *Revue de l'art dramatique*; it was reprinted in the April 1905 issue of *Dana* and Moore promptly sent a copy of the magazine to a German friend of his, Max Meyerfeld. Meyerfeld's translation of *The Well of the Saints* was produced in Berlin on 12 January 1906 and so, thanks to George Moore, who had left the dramatic movement before Synge entered it, Synge's fame spread. On 7 February 1906 a Czech translation of *The Shadow of the Glen* was produced in Prague, under the direction of the translator Karl Musek.

Other translations of Synge's plays followed, including an Italian translation of *Riders to the Sea* by James Joyce.[2] And the same play has been made into an opera by Vaughan Williams. But although Synge's reputation gained outside Ireland, he remained suspect in his own country, a fact which doubtless played its part in the reaction to *The Playboy*.

Nor were English publishers eager to risk his work. It was only after constant efforts on the part of Yeats and Lady Gregory that *The Aran Islands* was published in 1907, five years after the manuscript was completed; and during that time they campaigned also for his plays. John Masefield was drawn into the battle, and wrote to Synge on 18 December 1903:

[1] *The Letters of W. B. Yeats*, ed. Allan Wade (London, Rupert Hart-Davis, 1954), pp. 447–8.

[2] The manuscript of the translation by Joyce and Nicolo Vidacovich is in the possession of the University of Texas.

I've seen Mathews about the plays, and he seems eager, on the strength of the Samhain tragedy, to publish all three in one of his Vigo editions. I send a specimen (it's a grisly thing in its way) which will show you the size and shape of the series. You can choose any colour you like for a cover. The reprint of The Tables of the Law will appear in this series.

Mathews thought of putting the plays on his spring list, and publishing them in May, to act as a sort of John the Baptist to the Aran book appearing later in the year. We could all join in showing the book through that part of the press we can command and I am sure the things would go.

. . . After Xmas sometime will you send me a fair copy of the plays that I may give to Mathews. By all means add the abortive wedding play. . . .

Elkin Mathews himself wrote to Yeats on 19 July 1904:

Now with regard to Mr. Synge's work, I think I did hint to Mr. Dermot Freyer that I was a bit doubtful about issuing the Aran book this year but I don't think I included the Plays in the doubt, anyhow in view of what you say I will certainly bring them on in the autumn in the Vigo Series. I understood from Masefield that either you or Lady Gregory will write a Preface. . . .

When Synge finally entered into the discussion he decided to hold over The Tinker's Wedding ('a character . . . is likely to displease a good many of our Dublin friends and would perhaps hinder the sale of the book in Ireland'). He also rejected the idea of a Preface: 'Mr. Yeats . . . ⟨has⟩ spoken favourably of my work in Samhain and also in a short preface he has done for the new play in three acts which Mr. Bullen is bringing out, so I fear if I get any more introductions people will cry out that we are log-rolling!' And so the two plays appeared in May 1905 as part of the Vigo Cabinet series, with apology from neither Yeats nor the author. In January 1909 Synge wrote to Elkin Mathews concerning a proposed American edition of his plays in one volume, but their next appearance was in the collected edition published by Maunsel and Company after his death.

Meanwhile Yeats was busy peddling The Well of the Saints, and received the following reply from A. H. Bullen on 9 November 1904:

I shall be very willing to publish Mr. Synge's play on your recommendation and pay him a royalty of 15% of the published price. You may remember that I have not yet seen the play in MS. or on the stage. As your brother is designing the scenery, I think that two or three illustrations from his designs would be an interesting feature.

But Jack Yeats did not design the setting for *The Well of the Saints* after all, and when the play was offered on sale in the theatre as the first of the Abbey Theatre Series it appeared ungarnished. Several months later, however, the next issue appeared with an introduction by Yeats. By now Synge had learned to judge his reading audience also, and by the end of 1905 we find him suggesting to Elkin Mathews that *The Aran Islands* be published in Dublin by Maunsel: 'One or two of my plays have made me very unpopular with a section of our Irish Catholic public and I feel that it will be a great advantage to me, to have the book published and printed in Dublin on Irish paper—small matters that are nevertheless thought a good deal of over here.' The rest of his work appeared first in Ireland.

Partly through temperament, partly through his experience with the critics and actors, Synge gradually developed a theory of the drama which, once formed, became the groundwork for the subject and structure of his plays. It can be seen as early as his lengthy letter to Frank Fay in April 1904, when he commented on the London performances:

We have indeed had a great success with our show, and a good deal of our criticism has been most interesting although I still believe—as I once said to you—that our real critics must come from Dublin. It is only where an art is native, I think, that all its distinctions all its slight gradations, are fully understood. For instance most of our recent London critics have spoken well of the two plays we gave them that were perfectly obvious—I mean 'Riders to the Sea', and the 'Pot of Broth', but most of them failed to grasp 'Seanchan' ⟨Yeats's *The King's Threshold*⟩, and the 'Shadow of the Glen', both of which demand an intellectual effort to make them comprehensible, or at least a repeated hearing. . . . The whole interest of our movement is that our little plays try to be literature first—i.e. to be personal, sincere, and beautiful—and drama afterwards.

Rough notes written for the *Manchester Guardian* during the 1906 tour (but apparently never published) further stress Synge's view of the Irish dramatic movement as part of a necessary search for a new dramatic form, making use of new material. Tracing the early history of the Irish Literary Theatre, he singled out

Douglas Hyde's Irish one-act comedy, *The Twisting of the Rope*, as 'in some ways the most important of all those produced by the Irish Literary Theatre, as it alone has had an influence ⟨on⟩ the plays that have been written since and have built up the present movement'. Since the discovery of Willie Fay's company of Irish actors, he continued, 'actors, writers and a part at least of the audience have been intimately related and the movement has lost, it is hoped, all resemblance to the movements fostered by purely artistic cliques in London and Paris'. And he concluded his comments with an emphasis on the 'tendency and differen⟨ce⟩' he saw guiding the movement as a whole and essential to his own theory of drama, the 'eternal problem . . . in all the greater arts', of 'finding a universal expression for the particular emotions and ideas of the personality of the artist himself'.[1]

But while pleading for the freedom required by each writer individually, Synge did not hesitate to speak in his capacity as Director for the 'tendencies' he thought advisable. When in 1906 Yeats suggested developing the company along the lines of a continental municipal theatre, Synge wrote a three-page rejoinder.[2] During his period of management of 1907, when Yeats and Lady Gregory were in Italy, he objected to the starring of an actress while on tour ('We go to the cultured people of these places to show them something that is new to them—our plays and the ensemble acting of our little company'), and criticized the first effort of their new producer, brought in from England by Miss Horniman ('it came out as a bastard literary pantomime, put on with many of the worst tricks of the English stage. That is the end of all the Samhain principles and this new tradition we were to lay down!! I felt inclined to walk out of the Abbey and go back no more'). The following year he felt compelled to write to W. B. Yeats of Lady Gregory's play, 'I do not like the Canavans myself and I have not met anyone who does, except you.'

But his severest criticism he reserved for himself. As can be seen most clearly in his longer plays, he rewrote each scene over and over again, polishing the phrasing, balancing the dialogue, clarifying the action, until he had achieved the strong stage play he required. '. . . *strong* and good dramas only will bring us people who are interested in the drama', he had written to Frank Fay in

[1] This manuscript is now in the Berg Collection, New York Public Library.
[2] See Greene and Stephens, *J. M. Synge*, pp. 233–4.

1904, and he could be satisfied with no less. Among the Estate papers, for example, there exist six full drafts of Act I of *The Well of the Saints*, six of Act II, and five of Act III, not counting the full draft at the University of Texas or the innumerable remnants from other versions he destroyed as he went along. It is obvious that he spoke from experience when he wrote to Lady Gregory in 1907, 'I think your suggestion about Yeats writing an acting version in prose ⟨of Yeats's *Deirdre*⟩ is excellent. It might be of use to him also as he could then make the alterations he thought necessary in the prose version without the worry of continually re-writing the verse.'[1]

Much of his own problem was, indeed, the problem of poetry, for in his dialogue Synge was trying to achieve the melodic quality of poetry while at the same time preserving the strong base of prose. And although in his folk plays he wished to re-produce the peculiar characteristics of a peasantry who spoke in one language while thinking in another, it is clear from his experiments with 'poems in prose' that the practical had a basis in theory also. In an early notebook (No. 15, 1896–9) we find the rough notes of a dialogue which indicate that the ideas expressed in the 1909 preface to *Poems and Translations* were formed even before he wrote his plays:

The folk melody is complete in itself; the folk poems need a music which must be drawn from the words by the reader or reciter. In primitive time every poet recited his own poem with the music that he conceived with the words in his moment of excitement. Any of his hearers who admired the work repeated it with the exact music of the poet. This is still done among the Aran islanders. An old man who could not read has drawn tears to my eyes by reciting verse in Gaelic I did not fully understand. The modern poet composes his poems with often extremely subtle and individual intonations which few of his readers ever interpret adequately. . . . I have often thought of a collection of pressed flowers, when listening to ordinary reading dealing with poetry. The flower is there but its perspective and perfume are lost. . . . Sometimes in my MS I have marked all the intonations ff. rall. etc. but it has a certain affectation and what is worse would become mechanical with the reader. . . . Perhaps in a few years a perfected science will render the poet's voice again immortal.

[1] These three letters to Lady Gregory are in the Berg Collection, New York Public Library.

It may not be too fanciful to see in Synge's careful and deliberate artistry an attempt to perfect that science of immortality. For, as the actors themselves have testified, this was speech that did not trip easily off the tongue; Willie Fay has stated that Synge himself could not speak it. 'They had what I call a balance of their own, and went with a kind of lilt.'[1]

Synge's concern with a musical notation for his plays explains the care he took also with punctuation. Like Bernard Shaw, he punctuated as much for rhythm and sound as for sense; consequently in this edition far more attention is paid to such variants than may at first appear necessary. This is especially important for his first two plays, before he learned to take full responsibility for printing and proof-reading. All editions during his lifetime are therefore collated in detail, in an attempt to aid the student of his plays to find the appropriate 'kind of lilt'.

It will be evident from the appendixes and notes that collation has also been made with all manuscript material known to exist. Although Synge once complained to Yeats that he could not write letters on the typewriter, he did type many of the drafts of his plays, and there exists an impressive bundle of typescript pages for each play, almost every page with manuscript emendations. In addition, he frequently jotted down passages of dialogue in the notebook he always carried with him, and noted in his diary the day's work and reading. With these three sources, therefore, it is possible to present not only a definitive text for each play but a reproduction of his working method and the 'atmosphere of creation' surrounding it. As Mr. Skelton and Dr. Price have both indicated,[2] Synge's cavalier use of his diaries and notebooks (especially disconcerting when one contemplates the scrupulousness with which he preserved and lettered his typescripts) causes much agony in assigning dates. Inevitably an editorial decision is followed by a period of uncertainty as more conflicting proofs turn up. This is especially true of his unpublished work where no lettered typescript drafts are available for guidance. And occasionally the lettering on the typescripts is inaccurate. In each case where the date must remain questionable, an effort has been

---

[1] *The Fays of the Abbey Theatre*, pp. 137–8. See also Maire Nic Shiubhlaigh, *The Splendid Years*, pp. 42–3.

[2] J. M. Synge, *Collected Works, Poems*, ed. Robin Skelton (Oxford University Press, 1962), p. xxv; *Prose*, ed. Alan Price (Oxford University Press, 1966), p. xv. Unless otherwise stated, all notebooks and diaries are in the possession of the Synge Estate.

made to place the composition in order of subject to give some
indication of Synge's development. In this context the words
'early', 'middle', and 'late' indicate the approximate order I
have assigned to this undated material.

With work and working methods so variable, each play has
involved its own editorial problems. On the whole, however, I
have tried to abide by certain guiding principles. In preparing
the text, every draft has been consulted, but the notes offer selected examples only from the earlier drafts, with emphasis placed
upon later versions. The notes themselves have been restricted to
textual variants and comments by Synge; detailed description of
the manuscript material is included in the appendix to each play,
where the evolution from notebook to typescript to printed text
is traced and additional commentary by Synge is given. Although
the history of the play ends with the final text, an attempt has
been made to indicate Synge's attitude towards production by
noting any variant or interesting stage directions. The idio-
syncrasies of Synge's spelling (or typing) have been modified in
the interests of consistency, with any alterations in names of persons and places noted. So, too, with the unpublished material
a standard form of presentation has been imposed, with dialogue and directions set out as in the finished texts to facilitate
comparison. Angular brackets indicate editorial emendations; bold
type signifies a conflation of manuscripts. Fortunately Synge
thoroughly explained Irish pronunciation in his notes to Max
Meyerfeld (see Appendix C) with the exception of 'Samhain'
(*sow'in*) which occurs in *Riders to the Sea*.

ACKNOWLEDGEMENTS

WITH an edition which has been 'in progress' for over six years and has involved people and libraries on two continents it is impossible for me to thank individually all those who have graciously and generously given of their time, knowledge, and materials. Mrs. Lilo Stephens gave me a home in Dublin and, together with the Synge family and officials of the National City Bank of Dublin, made available to me all the papers held by the J. M. Synge Estate. Mrs. W. B. Yeats gave freely of advice and material in her possession; Miss Anne Yeats enhanced my work by 'discovering' some new drawings of Synge by Jack B. Yeats; Mr. Alf MacLochlainn of the National Library of Ireland gave his invaluable help in searching out missing information; Mr. Gerard Fay and Professor David Greene provided much needed advice, Mr. Fay directing me to the Fay Papers, while the Greene and Stephens biography of Synge has been an indispensable aid.

Further material was provided by the Academic Center Library, University of Texas; the Trustees and Librarian of Houghton Library, Harvard University; the Trustees of the New York Public Library and Dr. John Gordan, Curator of the Berg Collection; the Trustees of the National Library of Ireland; and the Fellows of Trinity College, Dublin, and Mr. F. J. Hurst, Librarian. I am indeed grateful to all these institutions for their generous help.

Permission to quote has graciously been given by Dr. John Masefield for his letter to Synge; Mr. H. F. Read for Arthur Symons's letter to Lady Gregory; Mrs. W. B. Yeats for her husband's letters to Synge, Joseph Hone, and the Synge executors; Major Richard Gregory for Lady Gregory's letters to Synge and to W. B. Yeats; Messrs. Allen and Unwin Ltd. for Elkin Mathews's letters to Synge; Messrs. James Duffy and Co. Ltd. for excerpts from *The Splendid Years*, by Maire Nic Shiubhlaigh and Edward Kenny; Messrs. Rupert Hart-Davis for excerpts from *The Letters of W. B. Yeats*, edited by Allan Wade; Mr. M. B. Yeats and Macmillan & Co. Ltd. for W. B. Yeats's Preface to *The Well of the Saints* from *Essays and Introductions*, and excerpts from *Autobiographies* and *Essays and Introductions* and, in the U.S.A., The Macmillan Company for excerpts from *The Cutting of an Agate* (copyright 1912 by The Macmillan Company, copyright renewed 1939 by Bertha Georgie Yeats).

Financial aid has been given me by the Canada Council and the University of Victoria and I wish here to express my appreciation to both institutions.

Finally, my gratitude to Mr. Robin Skelton for his unfailing encouragement; to the staff of the National City Bank, Dublin, for their patience and courtesy; and to Miss Joan Coldwell for her careful criticism and help with research and translation.

ANN SADDLEMYER

University of Victoria,
Victoria, British Columbia,
Canada

RIDERS TO THE SEA

A PLAY IN ONE ACT

PERSONS

MAURYA,[1] an old woman
BARTLEY, her son
CATHLEEN,[2] her daughter
NORA, a younger daughter
MEN AND WOMEN

SCENE

An Island off the West of Ireland

---

[1] Houghton TS. and pp. 1–5, 13–14 of Box File E TS. read 'Maura'. The top of p. 1 of Box File E TS. reads, in Synge's hand, 'In small type version Cailteen is the old woman Maura the elder daughter.' In all the MS. versions Maur(y)a is the elder daughter and the mother's name is Bride. For detailed description of MSS. see Appendix A.

[2] Pp. 1–5, 13–14 of Box File E TS. read 'Cailteen', while pp. 6–12 and 15–16 read 'Cathleen' and 'Maurya'.

1 *Samhain* alone has semicolon instead of comma after 'down'.

2 Vigo edition alone reads 'may be'. Berg, Houghton, and Box File E TSS. do not have comma after 'sleeping', and this reading may be more suitable to the rhythm of the line.

3 Houghton TS. adds direction *whispers*. Box File E TS. reads [CATHLEEN *catches her wheel and stops it.* NORA *leans out and whispers.*]

4 Berg, Houghton, and Box File E TSS. give the Irish spelling 'Micheal' throughout. Both earlier TSS. also omit comma after 'are'.

5 Berg, Houghton, and Box File E TSS. give question mark here, but this appears to alter the intonation of the line too drastically.

6 *Samhain* and Berg TS. indicate a pause here which Synge strikes out.

7 Houghton TS. reads 'If they're Micheal's' for 'If it's Michael's they are'.

8 Box File E TS. adds comma after 'burial'.

9 Houghton TS. omits 'if'. Vigo edition alone adds comma after 'his'.

10 The words *behind her* occur in all versions except Vigo edition.

11 In his own copy of *Samhain* Synge strikes out 'to Connemara' and adds 'with the horses to the Galway fair'.

12 Houghton TS. omits phrase 'says he'.

Cottage kitchen, with nets, oil-skins, spinning wheel, some new boards standing by the wall, etc. CATHLEEN, *a girl of about twenty, finishes kneading cake, and puts it down in the pot-oven by the fire; then wipes her hands, and begins to spin at the wheel.* NORA, *a young girl, puts her head in at the door.*

NORA [*in a low voice*]. Where is she?

CATHLEEN. She's lying down,[1] God help her, and maybe sleeping,[2] if she's able.

[NORA *comes in softly, and takes a bundle from under her shawl.*]

CATHLEEN [*spinning the wheel rapidly*]. What is it you have?

NORA. The young priest is after bringing them. It's a shirt and a plain stocking were got off a drowned man in Donegal.

[CATHLEEN *stops her wheel with a sudden movement, and leans out to listen.*]

NORA.[3] We're to find out if it's Michael's they are,[4] some time herself will be down looking by the sea.

CATHLEEN. How would they be Michael's, Nora.[5] How would he go the length of that way to the far north?

NORA. The young priest says he's known the like of it.[6] 'If it's Michael's they are,'[7] says he, 'you can tell herself he's got a clean burial[8] by the grace of God, and if they're not his,[9] let no one say a word about them, for she'll be getting her death,' says he, 'with crying and lamenting.'

[*The door which* NORA *half closed behind her*[10] *is blown open by a gust of wind.*]

CATHLEEN [*looking out anxiously*]. Did you ask him would he stop Bartley going this day with the horses to the Galway fair?[11]

NORA. 'I won't stop him,' says he, 'but let you not be afraid. Herself does be saying prayers half through the night, and the Almighty God won't leave her destitute,' says he,[12] 'with no son living.'

CATHLEEN. Is the sea bad by the white rocks, Nora?

1 Box File E. TS. omits 'getting'.

2 Berg and Houghton TSS. use early form 'she'ld'.

3 Berg, Houghton, and Box File E TSS. omit comma after 'we'll be'.

4 Berg, Houghton, and Box File E TSS. add dots to indicate pause after 'bed'.

5 Box File E TS. omits commas after 'ladder' and 'turf-loft'. Houghton TS. omits commas after 'ladder' and 'at all'. Berg TS. omits comma after 'ladder'.

6 In his own copy of *Samhain* Synge strikes out the directions . . . CATHLEEN *goes up under the thatch with the bundle in her hand* and the phrase *the old woman* after MAURYA.

7 Box File E TS. has ink insertion 'by the fire'.

8 Houghton TS. omits 'and'.

9 Houghton and Box File E TSS. read 'in' for 'from'.

10 All TSS. omit comma after 'day'.

11 Berg, Houghton, and Box File E TSS. add commas after 'Simon' and 'Pheety'. Box File E TS. reads 'Phetty' for 'Pheety'.

12 Berg, Houghton, and Box File E TSS. omit comma after 'now'.

13 MS. emendation in Box File E TS. reads 'hooker is' for 'hooker's'.

14 In his own copy of *Samhain* Synge strikes out 'is' before 'in a hurry'.

NORA. Middling bad, God help us. There's a great roaring in the west, and it's worse it'll be getting[1] when the tide's turned to the wind. [*She goes over to the table with the bundle.*] Shall I open it now?

CATHLEEN. Maybe she'd[2] wake up on us, and come in before we'd done [*coming to the table*]. It's a long time we'll be,[3] and the two of us crying.

NORA [*goes to the inner door and listens*]. She's moving about on the bed.[4] She'll be coming in a minute.

CATHLEEN. Give me the ladder, and I'll put them up in the turf-loft, the way she won't know of them at all,[5] and maybe when the tide turns she'll be going down to see would he be floating from the east.

[*They put the ladder against the gable of the chimney;* CATHLEEN *goes up a few steps and hides the bundle in the turf-loft.* MAURYA[6] *comes from the inner room.*]

MAURYA [*looking up at* CATHLEEN *and speaking querulously*]. Isn't it turf enough you have for this day and evening?

CATHLEEN. There's a cake baking at the fire[7] for a short space [*throwing down the turf*], and[8] Bartley will want it when the tide turns if he goes to Connemara.

[NORA *picks up the turf and puts it round the pot-oven.*]

MAURYA [*sitting down on a stool at the fire*]. He won't go this day with the wind rising from[9] the south and west. He won't go this day,[10] for the young priest will stop him surely.

NORA. He'll not stop him, mother, and I heard Eamon Simon and Stephen Pheety and Colum Shawn[11] saying he would go.

MAURYA. Where is he itself?

NORA. He went down to see would there be another boat sailing in the week, and I'm thinking it won't be long till he's here now,[12] for the tide's turning at the green head, and the hooker's[13] tacking from the east.

CATHLEEN. I hear some one passing the big stones.

NORA [*looking out*]. He's coming now, and he in a hurry.[14]

1 Houghton TS. omits *and quietly*; Box File E adds it in MS.

2 Berg, Houghton, and Box File E TSS. all have comma instead of semicolon after 'Nora' and omit comma after 'morning'. Box File E TS. reads 'snout' for 'feet', in ink MS. addition.

3 Stage direction from Box File E TS.

4 Here and throughout the remainder of the play, all versions use Synge's earlier form, 'You'ld', which he altered for the final drafts of his later plays.

5 Houghton TS. omits 'Bartley'; Box File E TS. omits comma after 'Bartley'.

6 Vigo edition alone includes 'for horses' which Synge adds to his own copy of *Samhain*. Box File E TS. adds comma after 'fair'.

7 Houghton and Box File E TSS. add comma after 'up' and read 'there is' for 'there's'.

8 Vigo edition reads 'flowing' for 'blowing', apparently a misprint.

9 Box File E TS. omits comma after 'itself'.

10 Berg, Houghton, and Box File E TSS. omit comma after 'moon'.

11 Houghton and Box File E TSS. read 'there's' for 'there is'.

12 Houghton TS. alone reads 'stack' for 'cock', conceivably an alteration for American audiences, or by an American typist. In his copy of *Samhain* Synge strikes out dots indicating pause after 'kelp'.

13 Houghton and Box File E TSS. add comma after 'this day'.

BARTLEY [*comes in and looks round the room; speaking sadly and quietly*].[1] Where is the bit of new rope, Cathleen, was bought in Connemara?

CATHLEEN [*coming down*]. Give it to him, Nora; it's on a nail by the white boards. I hung it up this morning, for the pig with the black feet[2] was eating it.

NORA [*giving him a rope*]. Is that it, Bartley?

MAURYA ⟨[*as before*]⟩[3] You'd[4] do right to leave that rope, Bartley,[5] hanging by the boards. [BARTLEY *takes the rope*.] It will be wanting in this place, I'm telling you, if Michael is washed up tomorrow morning, or the next morning, or any morning in the week, for it's a deep grave we'll make him by the grace of God.

BARTLEY [*beginning to work with the rope*]. I've no halter the way I can ride down on the mare, and I must go now quickly. This is the one boat going for two weeks or beyond it, and the fair will be a good fair for horses[6] I heard them saying below.

MAURYA. It's a hard thing they'll be saying below if the body is washed up and there's[7] no man in it to make the coffin, and I after giving a big price for the finest white boards you'd find in Connemara. [*She looks round at the boards*.]

BARTLEY. How would it be washed up, and we after looking each day for nine days, and a strong wind blowing[8] a while back from the west and south?

MAURYA. If it isn't found itself,[9] that wind is raising the sea, and there was a star up against the moon,[10] and it rising in the night. If it was a hundred horses, or a thousand horses you had itself, what is the price of a thousand horses against a son where there is[11] one son only?

BARTLEY [*working at the halter, to* CATHLEEN]. Let you go down each day, and see the sheep aren't jumping in on the rye, and if the jobber comes you can sell the pig with the black feet if there is a good price going.

MAURYA. How would the like of her get a good price for a pig?

BARTLEY [*to* CATHLEEN]. If the west wind holds with the last bit of the moon let you and Nora get up weed enough for another cock for the kelp.[12] It's hard set we'll be from this day[13] with no one in it but one man to work.

[1] Houghton and Box File E TSS. do not abbreviate 'drowned'.

[2] Houghton TS. runs these two sentences into one without any punctuation after 'rest' and no capitalizing of 'What'; also omits comma after 'me', as does the Berg TS.

[3] Houghton and Box File E TSS. add comma after 'green head'.

[4] Houghton TS. adds comma after 'coming again'. In his copy of *Samhain* Synge strikes out dots which indicated pause at the end of Bartley's speech.

[5] Houghton TS. adds comma after 'man'.
[6] Box File E and Berg TSS. omit comma after 'woman'.

[7] Houghton and Box File E TSS. omit 'down'.
[8] Box File E TS. omits comma after 'mare'.

[9] *Samhain* omits comma after 'now'.
[10] Houghton and Box File E TSS. read 'when the black night is in it'.
[11] Houghton TS. reads 'no son living' for 'no son left me'.

[12] Houghton TS. reads 'back' for 'round'.

[13] Houghton and Box File E TSS. omit stage direction.

[14] Box File E TS. reads 'till the dark night'.

MAURYA. It's hard set we'll be surely the day you're drown'd[1] with the rest. What way will I live and the girls with me,[2] and I an old woman looking for the grave?

[BARTLEY *lays down the halter, takes off his old coat, and puts on a newer one of the same flannel.*]

BARTLEY [*to* NORA]. Is she coming to the pier?

NORA [*looking out*]. She's passing the green head[3] and letting fall her sails.

BARTLEY [*getting his purse and tobacco*]. I'll have half an hour to go down, and you'll see me coming again in two days, or in three days, or maybe in four days if the wind is bad.[4]

MAURYA [*turning round to the fire, and putting her shawl over her head*]. Isn't it a hard and cruel man[5] won't hear a word from an old woman,[6] and she holding him from the sea?

CATHLEEN. It's the life of a young man to be going on the sea, and who would listen to an old woman with one thing and she saying it over?

BARTLEY [*taking the halter*]. I must go now quickly. I'll ride down[7] on the red mare,[8] and the grey pony'll run behind me. . . . The blessing of God on you. [*He goes out.*]

MAURYA [*crying out as he is in the door⟨way⟩*]. He's gone now, God spare us, and we'll not see him again. He's gone now,[9] and when the black night is falling[10] I'll have no son left me[11] in the world.

CATHLEEN. Why wouldn't you give him your blessing and he looking round[12] in the door? Isn't it sorrow enough is on every one in this house without your sending him out with an unlucky word behind him, and a hard word in his ear?

[MAURYA *takes up the tongs and begins raking the fire aimlessly without looking round.*]

NORA [*turning towards her.*][13] You're taking away the turf from the cake.

CATHLEEN [*crying out*]. The Son of God forgive us, Nora, we're after forgetting his bit of bread. [*She comes over to the fire.*]

NORA. And it's destroyed he'll be going till[14] dark night, and he after eating nothing since the sun went up.

¹ Berg, Houghton, and Box File E TSS. omit comma after 'be'. In his own copy of *Samhain* Synge strikes out dots indicating pause after 'surely'.

² Houghton TS. reads 'There is' for 'There's'.

³ Vigo edition alone gives this as two words, 'for ever'.

⁴ Houghton TS. omits comma after 'God speed you'. 'God bless and speed you' is struck out of Berg TS.

⁵ Houghton and Box File E TSS. read 'she'd' for 'she'll'; Berg TS. reads 'she'ld'.

⁶ Box File E TS. reads 'behind' for 'after'.

⁷ Box File E TS. omits comma after 'children'.

⁸ Box File E TS. omits comma after 'Wait'. Houghton TS. reads 'Wait, Nora. . Maybe' etc.

⁹ Box File E and Berg TSS. omit comma after 'sorry'.

¹⁰ Berg, Houghton, and Box File E TSS. add dots indicating pause after 'now'.

¹¹ Box File E TS. omits comma after 'quickly'. Berg TS. adds 'for' in MS.

¹² Berg, Houghton, and Box File E TSS. read 'he'ld' for 'he'd'.

¹³ Houghton TS. adds comma after 'below'. Box File E TS. reads 'speak with below if' etc.

¹⁴ Additional stage direction from Houghton TS.

¹⁵ Houghton TS. alone omits comma after 'crowed'.

CATHLEEN [*turning the cake out of the oven*]. It's destroyed he'll be, surely.[1] There's[2] no sense left on any person in a house where an old woman will be talking forever.[3]

[MAURYA *sways herself on her stool.*]

CATHLEEN [*cutting off some of the bread and rolling it in a cloth, to* MAURYA]. Let you go down now to the spring well and give him this and he passing. You'll see him then and the dark word will be broken, and you can say 'God speed you',[4] the way he'll be easy in his mind.

MAURYA [*taking the bread*]. Will I be in it as soon as himself?

CATHLEEN. If you go now quickly.

MAURYA [*standing up unsteadily*]. It's hard set I am to walk.

CATHLEEN [*looking at her anxiously*]. Give her the stick, Nora, or maybe she'll[5] slip on the big stones.

NORA. What stick?

CATHLEEN. The stick Michael brought from Connemara.

MAURYA [*taking a stick* NORA *gives her*]. In the big world the old people do be leaving things after[6] them for their sons and children,[7] but in this place it is the young men do be leaving things behind for them that do be old. [*She goes out slowly.*]

[NORA *goes over to the ladder.*]

CATHLEEN. Wait, Nora,[8] maybe she'd turn back quickly. She's that sorry,[9] God help her, you wouldn't know the thing she'd do.

NORA. Is she gone round by the bush?

CATHLEEN [*looking out*]. She's gone now.[10] Throw it down quickly,[11] for the Lord knows when she'll be out of it again.

NORA [*getting the bundle from the loft*]. The young priest said he'd[12] be passing tomorrow, and we might go down and speak to him below[13] if it's Michael's they are surely.

CATHLEEN [*taking the bundle ⟨from* NORA⟩].[14] Did he say what way they were found?

NORA [*coming down*]. 'There were two men,' says he, 'and they rowing round with poteen before the cocks crowed,[15] and the oar of one of

¹ Vigo edition alone gives comma after 'beyond'.
² Houghton TS. reads 'nine days'.

³ Vigo edition alone gives comma after 'take'.

⁴ Vigo edition omits *a shirt and*.

⁵ *Samhain* reads 'The Lord spares us, Nora; isn't is' ⟨*sic*⟩ etc. Berg and Houghton TSS. read 'The Lord spare us, Nora, isn't it' etc. Box File E TS. reads 'The Lord spare us Nora, it's a' etc. and omits question mark at the end.
⁶ Houghton TS. alone adds comma after 'hook'.
⁷ Box File E TS. omits 'the' before 'one flannel'.

⁸ Box File E TS. reads 'this morning'.

⁹ Berg, Houghton, and Box File E TSS. give comma after 'Nora'.
¹⁰ *Samhain* adds comma after 'itself'.

¹¹ Houghton TS. omits comma after 'Galway' and reads 'and it's many another' etc., omitting question mark at end.

¹² *Samhain* corresponds to Vigo edition. Houghton TS. reads 'It's Micheal, Cailleen. It's Micheal, may God spare his soul, and what will' etc. Box File E TS. reads 'It's Micheal, Cathleen, It's Micheal, God spare his soul and what will' etc. Berg TS. corresponds to Box File E TS. and adds comma after 'soul'.

¹³ Vigo edition alone adds comma after 'story'. Houghton TS. ends with full point instead of question mark.

¹⁴ Berg TS. and *Samhain* correspond to Vigo edition. Houghton TS. reads '. . . I knitted, and I put up three score stitches and dropped four of them.' Box File E TS. reads '. . . I knitted. I put up three score stitches and I dropped four of them.'

them caught the body, and they passing the black cliffs of the north.'

CATHLEEN [*trying to open the bundle*]. Give me a knife, Nora, the string's perished with the salt water, and there's a black knot on it you wouldn't loosen in a week.

NORA [*giving her a knife*]. I've heard tell it was a long way to Donegal.

CATHLEEN [*cutting the string*]. It is surely. There was a man in here a while ago—the man sold us that knife—and he said if you set off walking from the rocks beyond,[1] it would be in seven[2] days you'd be in Donegal.

NORA. And what time would a man take,[3] and he floating?

[CATHLEEN *opens the bundle and takes out a bit of a shirt and*[4] *a stocking. They look at them eagerly.*]

CATHLEEN [*in a low voice*]. The Lord spare us, Nora! Isn't it a queer hard thing to say if it's his they are surely?[5]

NORA. I'll get his shirt off the hook[6] the way we can put the one[7] flannel on the other. [*She looks through some clothes hanging in the corner.*] It's not with them, Cathleen, and where will it be?

CATHLEEN. I'm thinking Bartley put it on him in the morning,[8] for his own shirt was heavy with the salt in it. [*Pointing to the corner.*] There's a bit of a sleeve was of the same stuff. Give me that and it will do.

[NORA *brings it to her and they compare the flannel.*]

CATHLEEN. It's the same stuff, Nora;[9] but if it is itself[10] aren't there great rolls of it in the shops of Galway, and isn't it many another man may have a shirt of it as well as Michael himself?[11]

NORA [*who has taken up the stocking and counted the stitches, crying out*]. It's Michael, Cathleen, it's Michael; God spare his soul, and what will[12] herself say when she hears this story, and Bartley on the sea?[13]

CATHLEEN [*taking the stocking*]. It's a plain stocking.

NORA. It's the second one of the third pair I knitted, and I put up three score stitches, and I dropped four of them.[14]

¹ Houghton and Box File E TSS. read 'are in it'. Houghton TS. appears to have exclamation mark.

² Box File E TS. reads 'a pitiful thing'.

³ Houghton TS. reads 'that way to the far North and no-one to keen him, but', etc.

⁴ Berg, Houghton, and Box File E TSS. omit 'that'.

⁵ Box File E TS. reads [*swaying herself round and throwing her arm out*]. *Samhain*, Berg, and Houghton TSS. read *arm* for *arms*.

⁶ Box File E TS. omits comma after 'fisher'.

⁷ Vigo edition alone gives question mark, Berg TS. gives comma. In Houghton TS. the next four speeches vary considerably from the other versions, see below.

⁸ Box File E TS. reads 'those'.

⁹ These four speeches in Houghton TS. read as follows:

C [*after a moment*]. I hear something on the path, Put those things away quickly before herself will come in. Maybe it's easier she'll be after giving her blessing to Bartley, and we won't let on we've heard anything the time he is on the sea.

N [*looking out as they are bundling up the things*]. She's at the door now, we must put them here in the corner.

—[*they put them in with some other things in a hole in the chimney corner.*]

¹⁰ *Samhain* corresponds to Vigo edition, as does Houghton TS. with addition of comma after 'door'. Box File E TS. reads 'Keep your back turned round to the door, the way the light'll not be on you.'

¹¹ Houghton TS. omits stage direction.

¹² Box File E TS. reads *without looking round.*

¹³ Berg, Houghton, and Box File E TS. omit semicolon.

¹⁴ In his own copy of *Samhain* Synge strikes out ''ve' after 'you', as in Berg and Box File E TSS. Houghton TS. reads 'and tell us what you've seen than' etc.

¹⁵ Berg, Houghton, and Box File E TSS. add dots indicating pause.

¹⁶ Houghton TS. adds question mark. Box File E TS. as in Vigo and *Samhain* but no comma after 'Bartley'.

CATHLEEN [*counts the stitches*]. It's that number is in it.[1] [*Crying out.*] Ah, Nora, isn't it a bitter thing[2] to think of him floating that way to the far north, and no one to keen him but[3] the black hags that[4] do be flying on the sea?

NORA [*swinging herself round and throwing out her arms[5] on the clothes*]. And isn't it a pitiful thing when there is nothing left of a man who was a great rower and fisher,[6] but a bit of an old shirt and a plain stocking?

CATHLEEN [*after an instant*]. Tell me is herself coming, Nora?[7] I hear a little sound on the path.

NORA [*looking out*]. She is, Cathleen. She's coming up to the door.

CATHLEEN. Put these[8] things away before she'll come in. Maybe it's easier she'll be after giving her blessing to Bartley, and we won't let on we've heard anything the time he's on the sea.

NORA [*helping* CATHLEEN *to close the bundle*]. We'll put them here in the corner. [*They put them into a hole in the chimney corner.[9]* CATHLEEN *goes back to the spinning-wheel.*]

NORA. Will she see it was crying I was?

CATHLEEN. Keep your back to the door the way[10] the light'll not be on you.

[NORA *sits down at the chimney corner, with her back to the door.* MAURYA *comes in very slowly, without looking at the girls, and goes over to her stool at the other side of the fire. The cloth with the bread is still in her hand. The girls look at each other, and* NORA *points to the bundle of bread.*]

CATHLEEN [*after spinning for a moment*].[11] You didn't give him his bit of bread?

[MAURYA *begins to keen softly, without turning[12] round.*]

CATHLEEN. Did you see him riding down?

[MAURYA *goes on keening.*]

CATHLEEN [*a little impatiently*]. God forgive you;[13] isn't it a better thing to raise your voice and tell what you seen,[14] than to be making lamentation for a thing that's done?[15] Did you see Bartley, I'm saying to you.[16]

[1] Berg and Houghton TSS. add dots indicating pause.

[2] *Samhain* corresponds to Vigo edition, as do Berg and Houghton TSS. with omission of semicolon after 'forgive you'. Box File E TS. reads 'God forgive you, there he is now riding the mare over the green head and' etc.

[3] Houghton TS. adds exclamation mark after dots.

[4] Berg, Houghton, and Box File E TSS. omit comma after 'ails you'.

[5] Box File E TS. omits comma after 'has seen'; Houghton TS. replaces comma with dots to indicate pause.
[6] In his own copy of *Samhain* Synge strikes out 'saw' and writes 'seen'.
[7] Berg, Houghton, and Box File E TSS. add dots to indicate pause.

[8] Houghton TS. reads 'Tell us what it is you're after seeing.'

[9] Berg and Houghton TSS. alone omit comma after 'well'.
[10] Berg, Houghton, and Box File E TSS. add dots after 'myself'.
[11] Houghton TS. alone omits comma after 'along', which is added to Berg TS. in ink.
[12] Berg, Houghton, and Box File E TSS. add dots after 'behind him'.
[13] *Samhain* corresponds to Vigo edition. Stage direction in Houghton TS. reads *puts out her hand*; Berg and Box File E TSS. read *puts up her hand* etc.
[14] *Samhain* reads '. . . spare us, Nora.' Berg, Houghton, and Box File E TSS. add dots at end to indicate pause; Houghton TS. omits comma after 'us'.
[15] Houghton TS. adds stage direction [*half sobbing*]. Berg TS. adds dots after 'himself'.

[16] Berg, Houghton, and Box File E TSS. give comma instead of semicolon after 'mother'. Box File E TS. reads 'isn't' for 'wasn't'. Box File E TS. omits comma before 'mother'.
[17] Houghton and Box File E TSS. omit comma after 'seen'.
[18] Berg and Box File E TSS. omit comma after 'day'.
[19] Berg, Houghton, and Box File E TSS. add dots after 'galloping'.
[20] Houghton TS. omits semicolon after 'mare'; Berg and Box File E TSS. replace it with comma.
[21] Box File E TS. reads 'God Bless you'.
[22] Berg, Houghton, and Box File E TSS. give comma instead of semicolon after 'quickly'.
[23] Houghton TS. omits comma after 'on you'.
[24] Berg and Box File E TSS. omit dash after 'upon it'; Houghton TS. replaces it with comma.
[25] Houghton and Box File E TSS. omit comma between 'destroyed' and 'surely'. Houghton TS. replaces full point after 'from this day' with comma, and adds dots at end of sentence to indicate pause.

MAURYA [*with a weak voice*]. My heart's broken from this day.

CATHLEEN [*as before*]. Did you see Bartley?

MAURYA. I seen the fearfullest thing.[1]

CATHLEEN [*leaves her wheel and looks out*]. God forgive you; he's riding the mare now over the green head, and[2] the grey pony behind him.

MAURYA [*starts, so that her shawl falls back from her head and shows her white tossed hair. With a frightened voice*]. The grey pony behind him . . .[3]

CATHLEEN [*coming to the fire*]. What is it ails you,[4] at all?

MAURYA [*speaking very slowly*]. I've seen the fearfullest thing any person has seen,[5] since the day Bride Dara seen[6] the dead man with the child in his arms.[7]

CATHLEEN and NORA. Uah. [*They crouch down in front of the old woman at the fire.*]

NORA. Tell us what it is you seen.[8]

MAURYA. I went down to the spring well,[9] and I stood there saying a prayer to myself.[10] Then Bartley came along,[11] and he riding on the red mare with the grey pony behind him[12] [*she puts up her hands,[13] as if to hide something from her eyes*]. The Son of God spare us, Nora![14]

CATHLEEN. What is it you seen?

MAURYA.[15] I seen Michael himself.

CATHLEEN [*speaking softly*]. You did not, mother; it wasn't[16] Michael you seen,[17] for his body is after being found in the far north, and he's got a clean burial by the grace of God.

MAURYA [*a little defiantly*]. I'm after seeing him this day,[18] and he riding and galloping.[19] Bartley came first on the red mare;[20] and I tried to say 'God speed you,'[21] but something choked the words in my throat. He went by quickly;[22] and 'the blessing of God on you,'[23] says he, and I could say nothing. I looked up then, and I crying, at the grey pony, and there was Michael upon it—[24] with fine clothes on him, and new shoes on his feet.

CATHLEEN [*begins to keen*]. It's destroyed we are from this day. It's destroyed, surely.[25]

¹ Berg and Houghton TSS. omit comma after 'now'.

² Houghton and Box File E TSS. both omit comma after 'men'.
³ Box File E TS. reads 'them' for 'they'.
⁴ In his own copy of *Samhain* Synge strikes out 'there were' before 'some of them'.
⁵ Berg and Box File E TSS. omit comma after 'found'.
⁶ Houghton TS. reads 'was' for 'were'.
⁷ Box File E TS. reads 'lone' for 'lost'.
⁸ Houghton TS. alone omits comma after 'wind'.
⁹ Houghton TS. adds comma after 'up'; Box File E TS. adds the word 'here' after 'up'.
¹⁰ Berg and Box File E TSS. omit comma after 'plank'.
¹¹ Box File E TS. reads 'through' for 'by'.

¹² Houghton and Box File E TSS. omit comma after 'that'.

¹³ Houghton TS. reads 'There is' for 'There's'.

¹⁴ Box File E TS. omits comma after 'father'; Houghton TS. adds comma after 'Sheamus'.
¹⁵ In his own copy of *Samhain* Synge strikes out dots after 'up'.

¹⁶ Houghton TS. has comma after 'baby' struck out in ink. Box File E TS. omits comma and 'lying'.
¹⁷ In his own copy of *Samhain* Synge alters 'saw' to 'seen'.
¹⁸ Box File E TS. omits 'coming' after 'four women'.
¹⁹ Houghton TS. omits comma after 'themselves'.
²⁰ In his own copy of *Samhain* Synge strikes out dots after 'word'.
²¹ Houghton TS. omits comma after 'then'.
²² Box File E TS. omits 'coming' after 'men'.

²³ The stage directions in *Samhain* and Berg, Houghton, and Box File E TSS. are all more explicit here: . . . *and kneeling down in front of the stage with their backs to the people, and the white waist-bands of the red petticoats they wear over their heads just seen from behind.*] Synge altered his own copy of *Samhain* to the final version.

NORA. Didn't the young priest say the Almighty God won't leave her destitute with no son living?

MAURYA [*in a low voice, but clearly*]. It's little the like of him knows of the sea. . . . Bartley will be lost now,[1] and let you call in Eamon and make me a good coffin out of the white boards, for I won't live after them. I've had a husband, and a husband's father, and six sons in this house—six fine men,[2] though it was a hard birth I had with every one of them and they[3] coming to the world—and some[4] of them were found and some of them were not found,[5] but they're gone now the lot of them. . . . There were[6] Stephen, and Shawn, were lost[7] in the great wind,[8] and found after in the Bay of Gregory of the Golden Mouth, and carried up[9] the two of them on one plank,[10] and in by[11] that door.

[*She pauses for a moment; the girls start as if they heard something through the door that is half open behind them.*]

NORA [*in a whisper*]. Did you hear that, Cathleen?[12] Did you hear a noise in the north-east?

CATHLEEN [*in a whisper*]. There's[13] some one after crying out by the seashore.

MAURYA [*continues without hearing anything*]. There was Sheamus and his father,[14] and his own father again, were lost in a dark night, and not a stick or sign was seen of them when the sun went up.[15] There was Patch after was drowned out of a curagh that turned over. I was sitting here with Bartley, and he a baby, lying[16] on my two knees, and I seen[17] two women, and three women, and four women coming in,[18] and they crossing themselves,[19] and not saying a word.[20] I looked out then,[21] and there were men coming[22] after them, and they holding a thing in the half of a red sail, and water dripping out of it—it was a dry day, Nora—and leaving a track to the door.

[*She pauses again with her hand stretched out towards the door. It opens softly and old women begin to come in, crossing themselves on the threshold, and kneeling down in front of the stage with red petticoats over their heads.*][23]

MAURYA [*half in a dream, to* CATHLEEN]. Is it Patch, or Michael, or what is it at all?

[1] Houghton and Box File E TSS. omit comma after 'had'.

[2] *Samhain* and Berg, Houghton, and Box File E TSS. all read 'a wind' for 'the wind'; Box File E TS. omits comma after 'sea'.

[3] Houghton and Box File E TSS. omit comma after 'blowing'.

[4] A slip inserted in Box File E TS. reads 'It's Micheal it was, God' etc.

[5] The slip inserted in Box File E TS., and evidently prepared for the printer, reads [*she gives the bits of clothes to* MAURA]—
    —[*the old woman stands up and takes them into her hand,* NORA *stands up also nearer the door*]—. Berg TS. adds dots before NORA *looks out.*

[6] Houghton TS. alone adds comma after 'them'.

[7] *Samhain*, Berg, and Houghton TSS. add dots after 'stones' to indicate pause.

[8] Synge alters the wording in his own copy of *Samhain*, which read 'It is Bartley it is?'

[9] Houghton and Box File E TSS. assign this speech and the later speech to the women in general.

[10] Box File E TS. reads 'What way was he drowned, God spare his soul?'

[11] Houghton TS. reads 'echo' for 'stir'; Box File E TS. has 'echo' struck out in Synge's ink MS. and 'stir' written above.

CATHLEEN. Michael is after being found in the far north, and when he is found there how could he be here in this place?

MAURYA. There does be a power of young men floating round in the sea, and what way would they know if it was Michael they had,[1] or another man like him, for when a man is nine days in the sea, and the[2] wind blowing,[3] it's hard set his own mother would be to say what man was in it.

CATHLEEN. It's Michael,[4] God spare him, for they're after sending us a bit of his clothes from the far north.

[*She reaches out and hands* MAURYA *the clothes that belonged to Michael.* MAURYA *stands up slowly, and takes them in her hands.* NORA *looks out.*][5]

NORA. They're carrying a thing among them[6] and there's water dripping out of it and leaving a track by the big stones.[7]

CATHLEEN [*in a whisper to the women who have come in*]. Is it Bartley it is?[8]

ONE OF THE WOMEN.[9] It is surely, God rest his soul.

[*Two younger women come in and pull out the table. Then men carry in the body of* BARTLEY, *laid on a plank, with a bit of a sail over it, and lay it on the table.*]

CATHLEEN [*to the women, as they are doing so*]. What way was he drowned?[10]

ONE OF THE WOMEN. The grey pony knocked him over into the sea, and he was washed out where there is a great surf on the white rocks.

[MAURYA *has gone over and knelt down at the head of the table. The women are keening softly and swaying themselves with a slow movement.* CATHLEEN *and* NORA *kneel at the other end of the table. The men kneel near the door.*]

MAURYA [*raising her head and speaking as if she did not see the people around her*]. They're all gone now, and there isn't anything more the sea can do to me. . . . I'll have no call now to be up crying and praying when the wind breaks from the south, and you can hear the surf is in the east, and the surf is in the west, making a great stir[11] with the

[1] Berg and Box File E TSS. omit comma after 'noises'.

[2] In his own copy of *Samhain* Synge strikes out dots which indicated pause here.

[3] Houghton TS. omits comma after 'Water'.

[4] Box File E TS. simply gives as the stage directions [*scattering it on the body*], omitting any reference to Michael's clothes. All versions break Maurya's speech here into two separate speeches, presumably to indicate the pause for the action, which is here indicated by adding four dots, in order to be consistent with Synge's later practice, while at the same time making the rhythm of the entire speech more obvious to the reader.

[5] Houghton and Box File E TSS. replace semicolon with comma after 'saying'. Vigo edition, *Samhain*, and Berg and Houghton TSS. all read 'I'ld' for 'I'd'.

[6] In his own copy of *Samhain* Synge strikes out dots here which indicated pause.

[7] Berg and Box File E TSS. omit comma after 'now'.

[8] The emended stage directions in Box File E TS. are of interest here as they may indicate the type of alteration suggested by Willie Fay:

saying prayers under her breath,
—[*she kneels down again with her head in her hands,* ~~the other old women~~ *and the men begin to cross themselves with the holy water and go out one after the other.*
to one of   who
Cailteen ~~stops one of~~ *the men* ~~as he~~ *is* ~~going.~~]—*kneeling near her.*]——

[9] Houghton TS. here follows emendations of Box File E TS., reading [*to one of the men who is kneeling near her*]. In his own copy of *Samhain* Synge alters *one of the men* to *an old man*.

[10] Houghton and Box File E TSS. add introductory clause 'The priest will be over in the morning, and maybe' etc. This is struck out of Berg TS.

[11] In his own copy of *Samhain* Synge alters THE MAN to THE OLD MAN.

[12] Berg, Houghton, and Box File E TSS. have comma instead of semicolon after 'Colum'.

[13] Houghton TS. apparently gives this speech to the same man; Berg and Box File E TSS. differentiate by saying ANOTHER MAN.

[14] Box File E TS. reads 'them' for 'the nails' and omits comma.

[15] *Samhain* and Box File E TS. omit comma after 'is'. Houghton TS. is much more defensive in tone: 'Isn't it getting old she is and broken?' This is altered in ink in the Berg TS. to the *Samhain* version.

[16] Berg, Houghton, and Box File E TSS. give comma instead of semicolon after 'easy'.

[17] Box File E TS. reads 'found' for 'drowned'.

[18] Berg, Houghton, and Box File E TSS. add dots here, but a pause seems unnecessary to the sense of the speech.

[19] Houghton TS. alone omits comma after 'Micheal'.

[20] *Samhain* and Berg and Houghton TSS. make 'anyone' one word, which may somewhat alter the emphasis.

[21] Box File E TS. alone omits comma after 'do', as well as stage direction.

[22] The Vigo edition omits comma after 'crying'.

[23] Berg, Houghton, and Box File E TSS. omit comma after 'time'.

two noises,[1] and they hitting one on the other. I'll have no call now to be going down and getting Holy Water in the dark nights after Samhain, and I won't care what way the sea is when the other women will be keening.[2] [*To* NORA.] Give me the Holy Water,[3] Nora, there's a small sup still on the dresser. [NORA *gives it to her.* MAURYA *drops Michael's clothes across* BARTLEY'S *feet, and sprinkles the Holy Water over him.*]. . . .[4] It isn't that I haven't prayed for you, Bartley, to the Almighty God. It isn't that I haven't said prayers in the dark night till you wouldn't know what I'd be saying;[5] but it's a great rest I'll have now, and it's time surely.[6] It's a great rest I'll have now,[7] and great sleeping in the long nights after Samhain, if it's only a bit of wet flour we do have to eat, and maybe a fish that would be stinking. [*She kneels down again, crossing herself, and saying prayers under her breath.*][8]

CATHLEEN [*to an old man ⟨kneeling near her⟩*].[9] Maybe[10] yourself and Eamon would make a coffin when the sun rises. We have fine white boards herself bought, God help her, thinking Michael would be found, and I have a new cake you can eat while you'll be working.

THE OLD MAN[11] [*looking at the boards*]. Are there nails with them?

CATHLEEN. There are not, Colum;[12] we didn't think of the nails.

ANOTHER MAN.[13] It's a great wonder she wouldn't think of the nails,[14] and all the coffins she's seen made already.

CATHLEEN. It's getting old she is, and broken.[15]

[MAURYA *stands up again very slowly and spreads out the pieces of Michael's clothes beside the body, sprinkling them with the last of the Holy Water.*]

NORA [*in a whisper to* CATHLEEN]. She's quiet now and easy;[16] but the day Michael was drowned[17] you could hear her crying out from this to the spring well.[18] It's fonder she was of Michael,[19] and would any one[20] have thought that?

CATHLEEN [*slowly and clearly*]. An old woman will soon be tired with anything she will do,[21] and isn't it nine days herself is after crying,[22] and keening, and making great sorrow in the house?

MAURYA [*puts the empty cup mouth downwards on the table, and lays her hands together on* BARTLEY'S *feet.*] They're all together this time,[23]

1 Berg, Houghton, and Box File E TSS. add dots here to indicate pause, which seems rather too early in the speech.

2 Houghton TS. alone omits comma after 'Bartley's soul'. Box File E TS. adds comma after 'God'.

3 Houghton TS. omits 'on' before 'Micheal's'.

4 *Samhain* and Berg and Box File E TSS. include commas after 'Sheamus' and 'Stephen', which seem to destroy the rhythm; Houghton TS. adds comma after 'Stephen'.

5 Here Houghton and Box File E TSS. are followed in including dots to indicate an obvious pause.

6 Box File E TS. reads 'souls'.

7 Again, in order to illustrate the full rhythmic flow of this final paean, Maurya's speech is not broken into two parts as in the other versions.

8 Berg, Houghton, and Box File E TSS. omit comma after 'north'.

9 Houghton TS. alone adds dots after 'Almighty God' to indicate pause.

10 Here Berg, Houghton, and Box File E TSS. are followed in indicating pause.

11 Berg and Box File E TSS. are followed here to indicate pause.

12 Berg and Box File E TSS. give 'forever' as one word.

and the end is come.[1] May the Almighty God have mercy on Bartley's soul,[2] and on[3] Michael's soul, and on the souls of Sheamus and Patch, and Stephen[4] and Shawn [*bending her head*]. . . .[5] and may He have mercy on my soul, Nora, and on the soul[6] of every-one is left living in the world. [*She pauses, and the keen rises a little more loudly from the women, then sinks away. Continuing.*][7] Michael has a clean burial in the far north,[8] by the grace of the Almighty God.[9] Bartley will have a fine coffin out of the white boards, and a deep grave surely. . . .[10] What more can we want than that? . . .[11] No man at all can be living for ever,[12] and we must be satisfied.

[*She kneels down again and the curtain falls slowly.*]

THE END

THE SHADOW OF THE GLEN[1]

A PLAY IN ONE ACT

---

[1] Vigo edition and Box File E draft give title as above; Texas TS. and *Samhain* give *In the Shadow of the Glen*; TS. 'H' has both versions and an earlier one still, *In the Glen*.

PERSONS

DAN BURKE, farmer and herd
NORA BURKE, his wife[1]
MICHAEL DARA, a young herd[2]
A TRAMP

SCENE

*The last cottage at the head of a
long glen in County Wicklow*

---

[1] Texas TS. adds description 'a much younger woman'.
[2] Although all editions during Synge's lifetime give the Irish spelling of 'Micheal', it seems better to follow his later practice of anglicizing the name.

1 *Samhain* includes direction: *Then she goes over and looks at a small clock near the chimney.*

2 Phrase *on the left* taken from Texas TS.

3 Here punctuation of *Samhain*, Texas TS., and Box File E draft appears preferable to Vigo edition: 'Good evening, kindly stranger, it's' etc.

4 Wording of Texas TS. here seems more appropriate than Vigo edition's *and sees the dead man.* TS. 'H' gives earliest version of this stage direction: [*She has left the corner of the sheet turned back showing a man's face.*]

5 By indicating 'any way' as two words, Texas TS. clarifies Nora's meaning. The expression first occurs in TS. 'H' which also gives it as two words.

6 Texas TS. reads 'It is, surely'.

7 TS. 'H' reads 'with two gardens with oats in them to be reaped above under the hill, and a power of sheep for the fair at Aughavanna'.

8 The tramp's speech and Nora's reply omitted in Texas TS.

9 Vigo edition alone reads 'he is not tidied'.

Cottage kitchen; turf fire on the right; a bed near it against the wall with a
body lying on it covered with a sheet. A door is at the other end of the
room, with a low table near it, and stools, or wooden chairs. There are a
couple of glasses on the table, and a bottle of whiskey, as if for a wake, with
two cups, a tea-pot, and a home-made cake. There is another small door
near the bed. NORA BURKE *is moving about the room, settling a few*
things and lighting candles on the table, looking now and then at the
bed with an uneasy look.[1] *Someone knocks softly at the door ⟨on the*
left⟩.[2] *She takes up a stocking with money from the table and puts it in*
her pocket. Then she opens the door.

TRAMP [*outside*]. Good evening to you, lady of the house.

NORA. Good evening kindly, stranger,[3] it's a wild night, God help you,
to be out in the rain falling.

TRAMP. It is surely, and I walking to Brittas from the Aughrim fair.

NORA. Is it walking on your feet, stranger?

TRAMP. On my two feet, lady of the house, and when I saw the light
below I thought maybe if you'd a sup of new milk and a quiet decent
corner where a man could sleep . . . . [*He looks in past her and sees the
body on the bed.*[4]] The Lord have mercy on us all!

NORA. It doesn't matter any way,[5] stranger, come in out of the rain.

TRAMP [*coming in slowly and going towards the bed*]. Is it departed he is?

NORA. It is, stranger.[6] He's after dying on me, God forgive him, and
there I am now with a hundred sheep beyond on the hills,[7] and no
turf drawn for the winter.

TRAMP [*looking closely at the body*]. It's a queer look is on him for a
man that's dead.

NORA [*half-humorously*]. He was always queer, stranger, and I suppose
them that's queer and they living men will be queer bodies after.[8]

TRAMP. Isn't it a great wonder you're letting him lie there, and he not
tidied,[9] or laid out itself?

¹ Vigo edition and Box File E TS. retain throughout Synge's early habit of adding the *l* in such abbreviations as 'I'ld', 'he'ld', 'she'ld', etc. In his later plays Synge scrupulously altered this form for the final TS.; in order to be consistent similar alterations are made throughout the text of this edition.

² Texas TS. adds *more*.

³ Texas TS. reads 'lady of the house'.

⁴ TS. 'H' adds 'the way the trouts with the big heads on them would be lepping out on the bank'.

⁵ Although Box File E TS. reads thus, Texas TS. differs as follows:

NORA [*covering the face again*].—Well he was always cold, every day since I knew him, and every night, stranger, and maybe cold would be no sign of death with the like of him. [*She comes away from the bed.*] I'm thinking it's dead he is surely. . . .

⁶ *Samhain* and Texas TS. include 'lady of the house' after 'reward you'.

⁷ Direction *from the table* is taken from Texas TS. TS. 'H' stage directions read [*She pushes a pipe and tobacco towards him, and goes on folding the clothes.*]

⁸ Texas TS. alone differs from this exchange:

NORA [*getting a pipe and tobacco from the table*]. I've no pipes saving his own, stranger, but they're sweet pipes to smoke, and let you sit down now and be taking your rest.

TRAMP. And thanking you kindly, lady of the house. [*He sits down on a stool at the fire, filling a pipe.*] I've walked. . . .

Vigo version appears to be Synge's final decision as to staging.

NORA [*coming to the bed*]. I was afeard, stranger, for he put a black curse on me this morning if I'd touch his body the time he'd¹ die sudden, or let anyone touch it except his sister only, and it's ten miles away she lives, in the big glen over the hill.

TRAMP [*looking at her and nodding slowly*]. It's a queer story he wouldn't let his own wife touch him, and he dying quiet in his bed.

NORA. He was an old man, and an odd man, stranger, and it's always up on the hills he was, thinking thoughts in the dark mist. [*She pulls back a bit ⟨more⟩² of the sheet.*] Lay your hand on him now, and tell me if it's cold he is surely.

TRAMP. Is it getting the curse on me you'd be, woman of the house?³ I wouldn't lay my hand on him for the Lough Nahanagan and it filled with gold.⁴

NORA [*looking uneasily at the body*]. Maybe cold would be no sign of death with the like of him, for he was always cold, every day since I knew him,—and every night, stranger—[*she covers up his face and comes away from the bed*];⁵ but I'm thinking it's dead he is surely, for he's complaining a while back of a pain in his heart, and this morning, the time he was going off to Brittas for three days or four, he was taken with a sharp turn. Then he went into his bed and he was saying it was destroyed he was, the time the shadow was going up through the glen, and when the sun set on the bog beyond he made a great lep, and let a great cry out of him, and stiffened himself out the like of a dead sheep.

TRAMP [*crosses himself*]. God rest his soul.

NORA [*pouring him out a glass of whiskey*]. Maybe that would do you better than the milk of the sweetest cow in County Wicklow.

TRAMP. The Almighty God reward you,⁶ and may it be to your good health. [*He drinks.*]

NORA [*giving him a pipe and tobacco ⟨from the table⟩*].⁷ I've no pipes saving his own, stranger, but they're sweet pipes to smoke.

TRAMP. Thank you kindly, lady of the house.

NORA. Sit down now, stranger, and be taking your rest.⁸

¹ TS. 'H' adds stage direction [*putting the clothes into the cupboard*].

² Texas TS. reads 'through that door'.

³ *Samhain* includes 'lady of the house' after 'place', but it is struck out of Texas TS. and omitted from Vigo edition.

⁴ Texas TS. adds stage direction *sitting at the table*.
⁵ Texas TS. and *Samhain* both add 'stranger' after 'afeard' and do not include it in Nora's next sentence.

⁶ Texas TS. reads 'It is surely, the Lord have mercy on us all.' TS. 'H' adds stage direction [*N. rakes up the fire and puts turf on it.*]

⁷ TS. 'H' adds stage direction *trying to be indifferent but getting serious as he talks, putting her off.*]

TRAMP [*filling a pipe and looking about the room*]. I've walked a great way through the world, lady of the house, and seen great wonders, but I never seen a wake till this day with fine spirits, and good tobacco, and the best of pipes, and no one to taste them but a woman only.

NORA.[1] Didn't you hear me say it was only after dying on me he was when the sun went down, and how would I go out into the glen and tell the neighbours and I a lone woman with no house near me?

TRAMP [*drinking*]. There's no offence, lady of the house?

NORA. No offence in life, stranger. How would the like of you passing in the dark night know the lonesome way I was with no house near me at all?

TRAMP [*sitting down*]. I knew rightly. [*He lights his pipe so that there is a sharp light beneath his haggard face.*] And I was thinking, and I coming in through the door,[2] that it's many a lone woman would be afeard of the like of me in the dark night, in a place wouldn't be as lonesome as this place,[3] where there aren't two living souls would see the little light you have shining from the glass.

NORA [*slowly*].[4] I'm thinking many would be afeard,[5] but I never knew what way I'd be afeard of beggar or bishop or any man of you at all. [*She looks towards the window and lowers her voice.*] It's other things than the like of you, stranger, would make a person afeard.

TRAMP [*looking round with a half-shudder*]. It is surely, God help us all![6]

NORA [*looking at him for a moment with curiosity*]. You're saying that, stranger, as if you were easy afeard.

TRAMP [*speaking mournfully*].[7] Is it myself, lady of the house, that does be walking round in the long nights, and crossing the hills when the fog is on them, the time a little stick would seem as big as your arm, and a rabbit as big as a bay horse, and a stack of turf as big as a towering church in the city of Dublin? If myself was easily afeard, I'm telling you, it's long ago I'd have been locked into the Richmond Asylum, or maybe have run up into the back hills with nothing on me but an old shirt, and been eaten with crows the like of Patch Darcy—the Lord have mercy on him—in the year that's gone.

¹ Texas TS. has direction [*with surprise*].

² *Samhain* and Texas TS. add 'lady of the house' after 'queer talk'.

³ Texas TS. has direction [*sighing, after an instant's pause*].

⁴ Texas TS. adds direction *and looks at a clock hanging on the wall*; *Samhain* reads *looks at the clock again*.

NORA [*with interest*].¹ You knew Darcy?

TRAMP. Wasn't I the last one heard his living voice in the whole world?

NORA. There were great stories of what was heard at that time, but would anyone believe the things they do be saying in the glen?

TRAMP. It was no lie, lady of the house . . . I was passing below on a dark night the like of this night, and the sheep were lying under the ditch and every one of them coughing, and choking, like an old man, with the great rain and the fog . . . Then I heard a thing talking —queer talk,² you wouldn't believe at all, and you out of your dreams,—and 'Merciful God,' says I, 'if I begin hearing the like of that voice out of the thick mist, I'm destroyed surely.' Then I run, and I run, and I run, till I was below in Rathvanna. I got drunk that night, I got drunk in the morning, and drunk the day after,—I was coming from the races beyond—and the third day they found Darcy . . . Then I knew it was himself I was after hearing, and I wasn't afeard any more.

NORA [*speaking sorrowfully and slowly*].³ God spare Darcy, he'd always look in here and he passing up or passing down, and it's very lonesome I was after him a long while [*she looks over at the bed and lowers her voice, speaking very clearly*], and then I got happy again—if it's ever happy we are, stranger—for I got used to being lonesome. [*A short pause; then she stands up.*⁴] Was there anyone on the last bit of the road, stranger, and you coming from Aughrim?

TRAMP. There was a young man with a drift of mountain ewes, and he running after them this way and that.

NORA [*with a half-smile*]. Far down, stranger?

TRAMP. A piece only.

[*She fills the kettle and puts it on the fire.*]

NORA. Maybe, if you're not easy afeard, you'd stay here a short while alone with himself?

TRAMP. I would surely. A man that's dead can do no hurt.

NORA [*speaking with a sort of constraint*]. I'm going a little back to the west, stranger, for himself would go there one night and another, and whistle at that place, and then the young man you're after seeing

1 Texas TS. reads 'and tell the priest and people when the sun goes up'.

2 Texas TS. adds direction *and then stands up*.

3 Texas TS. adds 'now' after 'easy'.

4 *Samhain* reads 'Maybe if you'd find a' etc.

5 *Samhain* adds 'lady of the house' after 'It's true, surely,'. It is struck out in Box File E TS. Texas TS. reads 'It is maybe, God have mercy on us all!'

6 The word *listening* is taken from Texas TS.

—a kind of a farmer has come up from the sea to live in a cottage beyond—would walk round to see if there was a thing we'd have to be done, and I'm wanting him this night, the way he can go down into the glen when the sun goes up and tell the people that himself is dead.[1]

TRAMP [*looking at the body in the sheet[2]*]. It's myself will go for him, lady of the house, and let you not be destroying yourself with the great rain.

NORA. You wouldn't find your way, stranger, for there's a small path only, and it running up between two sluigs where an ass and cart would be drowned. [*She puts a shawl over her head.*] Let you be making yourself easy,[3] and saying a prayer for his soul, and it's not long I'll be coming again.

TRAMP [*moving uneasily*]. Maybe if you'd a[4] piece of a grey thread and a sharp needle—there's great safety in a needle, lady of the house— I'd be putting a little stitch here and there in my old coat, the time I'll be praying for his soul, and it going up naked to the saints of God.

NORA [*takes a needle and thread from the front of her dress and gives it to him*]. There's the needle, stranger, and I'm thinking you won't be lonesome, and you used to the back hills, for isn't a dead man itself more company than to be sitting alone, and hearing the winds crying, and you not knowing on what thing your mind would stay?

TRAMP [*slowly*]. It's true, surely,[5] and the Lord have mercy on us all!

[NORA *goes out.* THE TRAMP *begins stitching one of the tags in his coat, saying the 'De Profundis' under his breath. In an instant the sheet is drawn slowly down, and* DAN BURKE *looks out.* THE TRAMP *moves uneasily, then looks up, and springs to his feet with a movement of terror.*]

DAN [*with a hoarse voice*]. Don't be afeard, stranger; a man that's dead can do no hurt.

TRAMP [*trembling*]. I meant no harm, your honour; and won't you leave me easy to be saying a little prayer for your soul?

[*A long whistle is heard outside.*]

DAN [⟨*listening,*⟩[6] *sitting up in his bed and speaking fiercely*]. Ah, the devil mend her . . . Do you hear that, stranger? Did ever you hear another

¹ In place of this sentence Texas TS. reads 'Bring me a drop of whiskey quick before she'll come back.'

² Texas TS. reads 'drop of it at all?'

³ *Samhain* adds 'stranger' after 'cupboard'. It is struck out of Box File E TS. TS. 'H' originally had the following exchange, which Synge struck out before submitting the draft:

DAN [*after drinking*]. Go over now to that cupboard, stranger, and open the door.

TRAMP. Is it your old clothes that you want?

DAN. What is it you see in the west corner by the wall?

TRAMP. A bit of a black stick, master of the house.

DAN. Bring that stick, stranger.

⁴ *Samhain* adds 'your honour?' after 'that'; Texas TS. adds 'one your wanting?'; Box File E TS. strikes out both 'master of the house' and 'your honour'.

⁵ *Samhain* substitutes 'stranger' for 'surely'. Texas TS. reads 'It is, surely'.

⁶ *Samhain* adds 'stranger' after 'while'.

⁷ *Samhain* reads 'Is there somebody above?'

⁸ Texas TS. adds direction *at the door*.

⁹ *Samhain* adds 'stranger' after 'anything'. Texas TS. reads 'And then let you seem to be falling to sleep, and don't be letting on you know anything'.

woman could whistle the like of that with two fingers in her mouth? [*He looks at the table hurriedly.*] I'm destroyed with the drouth, and let you bring me a drop quickly before herself will come back.[1]

TRAMP [*doubtfully*]. Is it not dead you are?

DAN. How would I be dead, and I as dry as a baked bone, stranger?

TRAMP [*pouring out the whiskey*]. What will herself say if she smells the stuff on you, for I'm thinking it's not for nothing you're letting on to be dead?

DAN. It is not, stranger, but she won't be coming near me at all, and it's not long now I'll be letting on, for I've a cramp in my back, and my hip's asleep on me, and there's been the devil's own fly itching my nose. . . . It's near dead I was wanting to sneeze, and you blathering about the rain, and Darcy [*bitterly*]—the devil choke him—and the towering church. [*Crying out impatiently.*] Give me that whiskey. Would you have herself come back before I taste a drop at all?[2] [TRAMP *gives him the glass and he drinks.*] . . . Go over now to that cupboard,[3] and bring me a black stick you'll see in the west corner by the wall.

TRAMP [*taking a stick from the cupboard*]. Is it that?[4]

DAN. It is, stranger; it's a long time I'm keeping that stick, for I've a bad wife in the house.

TRAMP [*with a queer look*]. Is it herself, master of the house, and she a grand woman to talk?

DAN. It's herself, surely,[5] it's a bad wife she is—a bad wife for an old man, and I'm getting old, God help me, though I've an arm to me still. [*He takes the stick in his hand.*] Let you wait now a short while,[6] and it's a great sight you'll see in this room in two hours or three. [*He stops to listen.*] Is that[7] somebody above?

TRAMP [*listening*[8]]. There's a voice speaking on the path.

DAN. Put that stick here in the bed, and smooth the sheet the way it was lying. [*He covers himself up hastily.*] Be falling to sleep now and don't let on you know anything,[9] or I'll be having your life. I wouldn't have told you at all but it's destroyed with the drouth I was.

1 Texas TS. reads [*covering him up*].

2 Texas TS. reads [*in an imploring voice under the sheet*].

3 Texas TS. indicates *left of table*.

4 *Samhain* and Texas TS. have [NORA *goes to the table and puts tea in tea-pot.*]

TRAMP [*covering his head*].[1] Have no fear, master of the house. What is it I know of the like of you that I'd be saying a word or putting out my hand to stay you at all? [*He goes back to the fire, sits down on a stool with his back to the bed and goes on stitching his coat.*]

DAN [*under the sheet, querulously*].[2] Stranger.

TRAMP [*quickly*]. Whisht, whisht. Be quiet I'm telling you, they're coming now at the door.

[NORA *comes in with* MICHAEL DARA, *a tall, innocent young man, behind her.*]

NORA. I wasn't long at all, stranger, for I met himself on the path.

TRAMP. You were middling long, lady of the house.

NORA. There was no sign from himself?

TRAMP. No sign at all, lady of the house.

NORA [*to* MICHAEL]. Go over now and pull down the sheet, and look on himself, Michael Dara, and you'll see it's the truth I'm telling you.

MICHAEL. I will not, Nora, I do be afeard of the dead.

[*He sits down on a stool next*[3] *the table facing* THE TRAMP. NORA *puts the kettle on a lower hook of the pot-hooks, and piles turf under it.*]

NORA [*turning to* TRAMP]. Will you drink a sup of tea with myself and the young man, stranger, or [*speaking more persuasively*] will you go into the little room and stretch yourself a short while on the bed. I'm thinking it's destroyed you are walking the length of that way in the great rain.

TRAMP. Is it go away and leave you, and you having a wake, lady of the house? I will not surely. [*He takes a drink from his glass which he has beside him.*] And it's none of your tea I'm asking either. [*He goes on stitching.*]

[NORA *makes the tea.*][4]

MICHAEL [*after looking at the tramp rather scornfully for a moment*]. That's a poor coat you have, God help you, and I'm thinking it's a poor tailor you are with it.

¹ Stage direction from Texas TS., following TS. 'H'.

² TS. 'H' strikes out direction [MICHEAL *turns round on the form with his face to the table.* NORA *sits down beside him.*]

³ *Samhain* reads [*making the tea*]; Texas TS. reads [*pouring out tea*].

⁴ *Samhain* reads 'and not miss one of them'.

⁵ *Samhain* adds directions [*She comes to the table with tea-pot.* MICHEAL *turns round on the stool with his back to the fire.*] Texas TS. reads [*cuts bread for* MICHEAL].

⁶ TS. 'H' strikes out 'and if you gave him a plate of stirabout'.

⁷ *Samhain* adds direction *and pours out tea.*

⁸ Texas TS. adds direction *as he takes the tea and bread she gives him.*

⁹ *Samhain* reads 'in the night' for 'it night'.

TRAMP ⟨[*looks up at him for a moment*]⟩.[1] If it's a poor tailor I am, I'm thinking it's a poor herd does be running back and forward after a little handful of ewes the way I seen yourself running this day, young fellow, and you coming from the fair.

NORA [*comes back to the table. To* MICHAEL *in a low voice*]. Let you not mind him at all, Michael Dara. He has a drop taken, and it's soon he'll be falling asleep.[2]

MICHAEL. It's no lie he's telling, I was destroyed surely . . . They were that wilful they were running off into one man's bit of oats, and another man's bit of hay, and tumbling into the red bogs till it's more like a pack of old goats than sheep they were . . . Mountain ewes is a queer breed, Nora Burke, and I'm not used to them at all.

NORA [*settling the tea things*].[3] There's no one can drive a mountain ewe but the men do be reared in the Glen Malure, I've heard them say, and above by Rathvanna, and the Glen Imaal, men the like of Patch Darcy, God spare his soul, who would walk through five hundred sheep and miss one of them,[4] and he not reckoning them at all.

MICHAEL [*uneasily*]. Is it the man went queer in his head the year that's gone?

NORA It is surely.[5]

TRAMP [*plaintively*]. That was a great man, young fellow, a great man I'm telling you. There was never a lamb from his own ewes he wouldn't know before it was marked, and[6] he'd run from this to the city.of Dublin, and never catch for his breath.

NORA [*turning round quickly*]. He was a great man surely, stranger, and isn't it a grand thing when you hear a living man saying a good word of a dead man, and he mad dying?

TRAMP. It's the truth I'm saying, God spare his soul.

[*He puts the needle under the collar of his coat, and settles himself to sleep in the chimney-corner.* NORA *sits down at the table:*[7] *their backs are turned to the bed.*]

MICHAEL [*looking at her with a queer look*[8]]. I heard tell this day, Nora Burke, that it was on the path below Patch Darcy would be passing up and passing down, and I heard them say he'd never pass it night[9] or morning without speaking with yourself

¹ Stage direction from *Samhain*.

² *Samhain* and Texas TS. add 'Nora Burke' after 'knowing'.

³ Additional stage direction from *Samhain* and Texas TS.

⁴ TS. 'H' adds direction [*lowering his voice and drawing a little nearer to her*].

⁵ *Samhain* and Texas TS. add final 'him'.

⁶ Texas TS. adds, *glances round again at* THE TRAMP.

⁷ TS. 'H' places the action with the stocking later and has Nora speaking *with her tea cup in her hand*. At the end of this speech [*She puts down her cup without drinking, and sways herself on her stool.*]

⁸ *Samhain* reads 'sitting at the foot'; Texas TS. reads 'sitting here at the foot'.

⁹ *Samhain* reads 'while I've been sitting here'; Texas TS. reads 'while I've been here I'm saying'.

¹⁰ *Samhain* omits entire line 'with the young growing behind me and the old passing'.

NORA [*in a low voice*]. It was no lie you heard, Michael Dara.

MICHAEL [*as before*].[1] I'm thinking it's a power of men you're after knowing[2] if it's in a lonesome place you live itself.

NORA [*slowly*,[3] *giving him his tea*]. It's in a lonesome place you do have to be talking with someone, and looking for someone, in the evening of the day, and if it's a power of men I'm after knowing they were fine men, for I was a hard child to please, and a hard girl to please [*she looks at him a little sternly*], and it's a hard woman I am to please this day, Michael Dara, and it's no lie, I'm telling you.

MICHAEL [*looking over to see that* THE TRAMP *is asleep and then*, *pointing to the dead man*[4]]. Was it a hard woman to please you were when you took himself for your man?

NORA. What way would I live and I an old woman if I didn't marry a man with a bit of a farm, and cows on it, and sheep on the back hills?

MICHAEL [*considering*]. That's true, Nora, and maybe it's no fool you were, for there's good grazing on it, if it is a lonesome place, and I'm thinking it's a good sum he's left behind.[5]

NORA [*taking the stocking with money from her pocket, and putting it on the table*[6]]. I do be thinking in the long nights it was a big fool I was that time, Michael Dara, for what good is a bit of a farm with cows on it, and sheep on the back hills, when you do be sitting, looking out from a door the like of that door, and seeing nothing but the mists rolling down the bog, and the mists again, and they rolling up the bog, and hearing nothing but the wind crying out in the bits of broken trees were left from the great storm, and the streams roaring with the rain?[7]

MICHAEL [*looking at her uneasily*]. What is it ails you this night, Nora Burke? I've heard tell it's the like of that talk you do hear from men, and they after being a great while on the back hills.

NORA [*putting out the money on the table*]. It's a bad night, and a wild night, Michael Dara, and isn't it a great while I am at the foot[8] of the back hills, sitting up here boiling food for himself, and food for the brood sow, and baking a cake when the night falls? [*She puts up the money, listlessly, in little piles on the table.*] Isn't it a long while I am sitting here[9] in the winter, and the summer, and the fine spring, with the young growing behind me and the old passing,[10] saying to myself

1 *Samhain* reads 'be as easy as turning a cake'.

2 *Samhain* reads 'walking the roads or'.

3 Stage directions taken from Texas TS.

4 *Samhain* reads 'five pounds and ten notes. It's a good sum, surely'. Texas TS. reads 'five pounds, and three notes, a good sum surely'.

5 Vigo edition reads 'taking' for 'talking'.

6 Texas TS. adds 'below' before 'in the fair'.

7 Texas TS. adds stage direction [*He looks furtively at the bed, then draws closer to her at the end of the table so that his back is turned towards it.*] TS. 'H' strikes out the following exchange:

MIKE. Tell me one thing, Nora, will I have a right to come to his burying beyond at the seven Churches? Or would I do right to stay off from himself that day?

NORA. Why would you stay off, Micheal Dara?

MIKE [*uneasily*]. They do be telling queer things of the dead, and in the spring of the year I'll be having a power of sheep to herd on the mountains beyond Aughavanna, and I wouldn't like that there'ld be anything at all could take a hold on the thoughts passing in my head.

NORA [*looking at him half-humorously*]. And do the like of you have thoughts passing, Micheal Dara,

MIKE. We do surely. . . . We'ld do right to wait till he'ld be quiet a while. . . .

8 Texas TS. and *Samhain* read 'pounds'.

9 Texas TS. and *Samhain* read 'right now to wait'.

10 *Samhain* omits 'back'.

11 Texas TS. adds the direction *and then sitting down close to him.*

12 TS. 'H' begins with [*There are movements under the sheet. Then the old man sits up.* . . .

13 Texas TS. strikes out and *Samhain* omits 'there'.

one time, to look on Mary Brien who wasn't that height [*holding out her hand*], and I a fine girl growing up, and there she is now with two children, and another coming on her in three months or four [*she pauses*].

MICHAEL [*moving over three of the piles*]. That's three pounds we have now, Nora Burke.

NORA [*continuing in the same voice*]. And saying to myself another time, to look on Peggy Cavanagh, who had the lightest hand at milking a cow that wouldn't be easy, or turning a cake,[1] and there she is now walking round on the roads,[2] or sitting in a dirty old house, with no teeth in her mouth, and no sense, and no more hair than you'd see on a bit of a hill and they after burning the furze from it. ⟨[*She pauses again.*][3]⟩

MICHAEL. That's five pounds and ten notes, a good sum, surely! . . .[4] It's not that way you'll be talking[5] when you marry a young man, Nora Burke, and they were saying[6] in the fair my lambs were the best lambs, and I got a grand price, for I'm no fool now at making a bargain when my lambs are good.[7]

NORA. What was it you got?

MICHAEL. Twenty pound[8] for the lot, Nora Burke . . . We'd do right to wait now[9] till himself will be quiet a while in the Seven Churches, and then you'll marry me in the chapel of Rathvanna, and I'll bring the sheep up on the bit of a hill you have on the back[10] mountain, and we won't have anything we'd be afeard to let our minds on when the mist is down.

NORA [*pouring him out some whiskey[11]*]. Why would I marry you, Mike Dara? You'll be getting old, and I'll be getting old, and in a little while, I'm telling you, you'll be sitting up in your bed—the way himself was sitting—with a shake in your face, and your teeth falling, and the white hair sticking out round you like an old bush where sheep do be leaping a gap.

[[12]DAN BURKE *sits up noiselessly from under the sheet, with his hand to his face. His white hair is sticking out round his head.*]

NORA [*goes on slowly without hearing him*]. It's a pitiful thing to be getting old, but it's a queer thing surely . . . It's a queer thing to see an old man sitting up there[13] in his bed, with no teeth in him, and a

[1] Texas TS. reads: 'the way you do hear the herds talking and they after being a long while above, walking in the mists'. *Samhain* is similar to Vigo edition except for the omission of the word 'that'.

[2] Vigo edition alone omits the first word 'The'.

[3] *Samhain* reads: 'Is he dead or is he living?' Texas TS. corresponds to Vigo edition.

[4] *Samhain*, Texas TS., and TS. 'H' add the following sentence: '[*To* THE TRAMP.] I'd have waited a while longer if it hadn't been for the itch of my nose, but I've heard enough, surely.'

[5] *Samhain* reads 'put your foot through it again.' Texas TS. corresponds to Vigo edition.

[6] Vigo edition alone reads 'cross road'.

[7] *Samhain* and Texas TS. read: 'And it's soon with that life you'll be getting old, Nora Burke'.

rough word in his mouth, and his chin the way it would take the bark from the edge of an oak board you'd have building a door . . . God forgive me, Michael Dara, we'll all be getting old, but it's a queer thing surely.

MICHAEL. It's too lonesome you are from living a long time with an old man, Nora, and you're talking again like a herd that would be coming down from the thick mist[1] [*he puts his arm round her*], but it's a fine life you'll have now with a young man, a fine life surely . . .

> [DAN *sneezes violently.* MICHAEL *tries to get to the door, but before he can do so,* DAN *jumps out of the bed in queer white clothes, with the stick in his hand, and goes over and puts his back against it.*]

MICHAEL. The[2] Son of God deliver us . . . [*Crosses himself, and goes backward across the room.*]

DAN [*holding up his hand at him*]. Now you'll not marry her the time I'm rotting below in the Seven Churches, and you'll see the thing I'll give you will follow you on the back mountains when the wind is high.

MICHAEL [*to* NORA]. Get me out of it, Nora, for the love of God. He always did what you bid him, and I'm thinking he would do it now.

NORA [*looking at* THE TRAMP]. Is it dead he is or living?[3]

DAN [*turning towards her*]. It's little you care if it's dead or living I am, but there'll be an end now of your fine times, and all the talk you have of young men and old men, and of the mist coming up or going down. [*He opens the door.*][4] You'll walk out now from that door, Nora Burke, and it's not to-morrow, or the next day, or any day of your life, that you'll put in your foot through it again.[5]

TRAMP [*standing up*]. It's a hard thing you're saying, for an old man, master of the house, and what would the like of her do if you put her out on the roads?

DAN. Let her walk round the like of Peggy Cavanagh below, and be begging money at the cross roads,[6] or selling songs to the men. [*To* NORA.] Walk out now, Nora Burke, and it's soon you'll be getting old with that life, I'm telling you;[7] it's soon your teeth'll be falling

1 The phrase 'your teeth'll be falling' does not appear in *Samhain* or the Texas TS. TS. 'H' strikes out a continuation of Dan's speech: 'or the like of an old post where they do be scratching with the fly and then they'll find you some day I'm telling you, and you stretched like a dead dog with the frost on you at the butt of a ditch [*he pauses to drink*].'

2 *Samhain* reads 'if it's bad you are itself, Daniel Burke' etc. Texas TS. reads 'If it's a bad way you are itself,' etc.

3 Texas TS. reads 'walk out now through that door'.

4 Texas TS. adds the final clause, 'he'd have a right surely.'

5 Texas TS. reads 'What would the like of him do with me now?'

6 Texas TS. reads 'walk out now from that door I'm saying' etc. TS. 'H' reads 'walk out through the door I'm telling you' etc. Early version of TS. 'H' adds 'and let you not be passing this way if it's hungry you are or wanting a bed.'

7 Texas TS. gives stage direction [*going past* NORA *to the door*].

8 Texas TS. reads 'a grand morning, God help me, when I'm going', etc. *Samhain* reads 'a grand morning when I'm going out, God help me', etc. In the final phrase, *Samhain* differs by adding 'on': 'walking on the roads'. Texas TS. adds stage direction [*passing behind the table*].

and your head'll be the like of a bush where sheep do be leaping a gap.[1]

[*He pauses; she looks round at* MICHAEL.]

MICHAEL [*timidly*]. There's a fine Union below in Rathdrum.

DAN. The like of her would never go there . . . It's lonesome roads she'll be going, and hiding herself away till the end will come, and they find her stretched like a dead sheep with the frost on her, or the big spiders, maybe, and they putting their webs on her, in the butt of a ditch.

NORA [*angrily*]. What way will yourself be that day, Daniel Burke? What way will you be that day and you lying down a long while in your grave? For it's bad you are living, and it's bad you'll be when you're dead. [*She looks at him a moment fiercely, then half turns away and speaks plaintively again.*] Yet, if it is itself, Daniel Burke,[2] who can help it at all, and let you be getting up into your bed, and not be taking your death with the wind blowing on you, and the rain with it, and you half in your skin.

DAN. It's proud and happy you'd be if I was getting my death the day I was shut of yourself. [*Pointing to the door.*] Let you walk out through[3] that door, I'm telling you, and let you not be passing this way if it's hungry you are, or wanting a bed.

TRAMP [*pointing to* MICHAEL]. Maybe himself would take her.[4]

NORA. What would he do with me now?[5]

TRAMP. Give you the half of a dry bed, and good food in your mouth.

DAN. Is it a fool you think him, stranger, or is it a fool you were born yourself? Let her walk out of that door,[6] and let you go along with her stranger—if it's raining itself—for it's too much talk you have surely.

TRAMP [*going over to* NORA].[7] We'll be going now, lady of the house—the rain is falling but the air is kind, and maybe it'll be a grand morning by the grace of God.

NORA. What good is a grand morning when I'm destroyed surely, and I going out to get my death walking the roads?[8]

1 Texas TS. adds stage direction [*turning towards her*].

2 Vigo edition reads 'in the place'. The present reading is taken from Texas TS. and *Samhain*.

3 TS. 'H' strikes out the following continuation: 'You'll not be saying;—"It's soon I'll be sitting with no teeth in my head," but you ⟨'ll⟩ be saying, "What is it I'll put between them when the sun goes up" . . .'.

4 On the back of a page of one of the early drafts in TS. 'H' Synge has written the following speech: 'DAN. Take your shawl Nora Burke. Would you be going in your bare head in rain falling.'

5 The stage directions for the Tramp here vary considerably in the three versions. Texas TS. reads: [*looks at him defiantly, and continues to* NORA, *who puts a shawl over her head*]. *Samhain* reads: [*on the other side of her, pulling her eagerly by the sleeve*].

6 TS. 'H' strikes out 'when the stars do be moving on it with the little twish of the wind, and you'll hear the grouse' etc.

7 Texas TS. and *Samhain* read 'you'll hear them singing when' etc.

8 Texas TS. reads 'but it's a fine bit of talk you have, and' etc.

9 Texas TS. reads [*He goes out, and she turns to* DAN *as she is in the doorway*.]

10 Texas TS. and *Samhain* alter the form of this sentence to read 'You'll have a black life from this day, Daniel Burke' etc.

11 Texas TS. and *Samhain* again alter the wording to read 'and it's not long till you'll be lying again under that sheet, I'm telling you', etc.

TRAMP.[1] You'll not be getting your death with myself, lady of the house, and I knowing all the ways a man can put food in his mouth. . . . We'll be going now, I'm telling you, and the time you'll be feeling the cold and the frost, and the great rain, and the sun again, and the south wind blowing in the glens, you'll not be sitting up on a wet ditch the way you're after sitting in this[2] place, making yourself old with looking on each day and it passing you by. You'll be saying one time, 'It's a grand evening by the grace of God,' and another time, 'It's a wild night, God help us, but it'll pass surely.' You'll be saying—[3]

DAN [goes over to them crying out impatiently]. Go out of that door, I'm telling you, and do your blathering below in the glen.[4]

[NORA gathers a few things into her shawl.]

TRAMP [at the door].[5] Come along with me now, lady of the house, and it's not my blather you'll be hearing only, but you'll be hearing the herons crying out over the black lakes,[6] and you'll be hearing the grouse, and the owls with them, and the larks and the big thrushes when the days are warm, and it's not from the like of them you'll be hearing a talk of getting old like Peggy Cavanagh, and losing the hair off you, and the light of your eyes, but it's fine songs you'll be hearing when[7] the sun goes up, and there'll be no old fellow wheezing the like of a sick sheep close to your ear.

NORA. I'm thinking it's myself will be wheezing that time with lying down under the Heavens when the night is cold, but you've a fine bit of talk, stranger, and it's with yourself I'll go.[8] [She goes towards the door, then turns to DAN.][9] You think it's a grand thing you're after doing with your letting on to be dead, but what is it at all? What way would a woman live in a lonesome place the like of this place, and she not making a talk with the men passing? And what way will yourself live from this day, with none to care you? What is it you'll have now but a black life, Daniel Burke,[10] and it's not long, I'm telling you, till you'll be lying again under that sheet, and you dead surely.[11]

[She goes out with THE TRAMP. MICHAEL is slinking after them, but DAN stops him.]

DAN. Sit down now and take a little taste of the stuff, Michael Dara, there's a great drouth on me, and the night is young.

[1] Texas TS. reads 'turn of day'.

[2] Texas TS. and *Samhain* omit 'God help you'.

MICHAEL [*coming back to the table*]. And it's very dry I am surely, with the fear of death you put on me, and I after driving mountain ewes since the turn of the day.[1]

DAN [*throwing away his stick*]. I was thinking to strike you, Michael Dara, but you're a quiet man, God help you,[2] and I don't mind you at all. [*He pours out two glasses of whiskey, and gives one to* MICHAEL.]

DAN. Your good health, Michael Dara.

MICHAEL. God reward you, Daniel Burke, and may you have a long life and a quiet life, and good health with it. [*They drink.*]

CURTAIN

THE WELL OF THE SAINTS[1]

A PLAY IN THREE ACTS

[1] Box File E TS. questions the title *The Well of the Saints* and suggests 'or *The Cross-roads of Grianan*?' This title page, which appears to belong to the final draft, has on the reverse a rough pencil sketch of the scene, corresponding to the final description. An earlier draft of the title page gives the title *When the Blind See.*

PREFACE TO THE FIRST EDITION OF
THE WELL OF THE SAINTS
by W. B. YEATS

MR. SYNGE AND HIS PLAYS[1]

Six years ago I was staying in a students' hotel in the Latin Quarter, and somebody, whose name I cannot recollect, introduced me to an Irishman, who, even poorer than myself, had taken a room at the top of the house.[2] It was J. M. Synge, and I, who thought I knew the name of every Irishman who was working at literature, had never heard of him. He was a graduate of Trinity College, Dublin, too, and Trinity College does not, as a rule, produce artistic minds. He told me that he had been living in France and Germany, reading French and German literature, and that he wished to become a writer. He had, however, nothing to show but one or two poems and impressionistic essays, full of that kind of morbidity that has its root in too much brooding over methods of expression, and ways of looking upon life, which come, not out of life, but out of literature, images reflected from mirror to mirror. He had wandered among people whose life is as picturesque as the Middle Ages, playing his fiddle to Italian sailors, and listening to stories in Bavarian woods, but life had cast no light into his writings. He had learned Irish years ago, but had begun to forget it, for the only language that interested him was that conventional language of modern poetry which has begun to make us all weary. I was very weary of it, for I had finished *The Secret Rose*, and felt how it had separated my imagination from life, sending my Red Hanrahan, who should have trodden the same roads with myself, into some undiscoverable coun-try.[3] I said: 'Give up Paris. You will never create anything by reading Racine, and Arthur Symons will always be a better critic of French literature. Go to the Aran Islands. Live there as if you were one of the people themselves; express a life that has never found expression.' I had

---

[1] The 1905 edition alone included this title. The above text is taken from the corrected version printed in *Essays and Introductions* (Macmillan, 1961), pp. 298–305.

[2] In *The Bounty of Sweden* (1925) Yeats gives a more precise date, 1896, for this meeting.

[3] Since writing this I have, with Lady Gregory's help, put *Red Hanrahan* into the common speech.—W. B. Y.

just come from Aran, and my imagination was full of those grey islands where men must reap with knives because of the stones.

He went to Aran and became a part of its life, living upon salt fish and eggs, talking Irish for the most part, but listening also to the beautiful English which has grown up in Irish-speaking districts, and takes its vocabulary from the time of Malory and of the translators of the Bible, but its idiom and its vivid metaphor from Irish. When Mr. Synge began to write in this language, Lady Gregory had already used it finely in her translations of Dr. Hyde's lyrics and plays, or of old Irish literature, but she had listened with different ears. He made his own selection of word and phrase, choosing what would express his own personality. Above all, he made word and phrase dance to a very strange rhythm, which will always, till his plays have created their own tradition, be difficult to actors who have not learned it from his lips. It is essential, for it perfectly fits the drifting emotion, the dreaminess, the vague yet measureless desire, for which he would create a dramatic form. It blurs definition, clear edges, everything that comes from the will, it turns imagination from all that is of the present, like a gold background in a religious picture, and it strengthens in every emotion whatever comes to it from far off, from brooding memory and dangerous hope. When he brought *The Shadow of the Glen*, his first play, to the Irish National Theatre Society, the players were puzzled by the rhythm,[1] but gradually they became certain that his Woman of the Glen, as melancholy as a curlew, driven to distraction by her own sensitiveness, her own fineness, could not speak with any other tongue, that all his people would change their life if the rhythm changed. Perhaps no Irish countryman had ever that exact rhythm in his voice, but certainly if Mr. Synge had been born a countryman, he would have spoken like that. It makes the people of his imagination a little disembodied; it gives them a kind of innocence even in their anger and their cursing. It is part of its maker's attitude towards the world, for while it makes the clash of wills among his persons indirect and dreamy, it helps him to see the subject-matter of his art with wise, clear-seeing,

---

[1] 'At first I found Synge's lines almost impossible to learn and deliver. Like the wandering ballad-singer I had to "humour" them into a strange tune, changing the metre several times each minute. It was neither verse nor prose. The speeches had a musical lilt, absolutely different to anything I had heard before. Every passage brought some new difficulty and we would all stumble through the speeches until the tempo in which they were written was finally discovered. I found I had to break the sentences—which were uncommonly long—into sections, chanting them, slowly at first, then quickly as I became more familiar with the words.' Maire Nic Shiubhlaigh and Edward Kenny, *The Splendid Years* (Dublin, 1955), pp. 42–43.

unreflecting eyes; to preserve the integrity of art in an age of reasons and purposes.[1] Whether he write of old beggars by the roadside, lamenting over the misery and ugliness of life, or of an old Aran woman mourning her drowned sons, or of a young wife married to an old husband, he has no wish to change anything, to reform anything; all these people pass by as before an open window, murmuring strange, exciting words.[2]

If one has not fine construction, one has not drama, but if one has not beautiful or powerful and individual speech, one has not literature, or, at any rate, one has not great literature. Rabelais, Villon, Shakespeare, William Blake, would have known one another by their speech. Some of them knew how to construct a story, but all of them had abundant, resonant, beautiful, laughing, living speech. It is only the writers of our modern dramatic movement, our scientific dramatists, our naturalists of the stage, who have thought it possible to be like the greatest, and yet to cast aside even the poor persiflage of the comedians, and to write in the impersonal language that has come, not out of individual life, nor out of life at all, but out of necessities of commerce, of Parliament, of Board Schools, of hurried journeys by rail.

If there are such things as decaying art and decaying institutions, their decay must begin when the element they receive into their care from the life of every man in the world begins to rot. Literature decays when it no longer makes more beautiful, or more vivid, the language which unites it to all life, and when one finds the criticism of the student, and the purpose of the reformer, and the logic of the man of science, where there should have been the reveries of the common heart, ennobled into some raving Lear or unabashed Don Quixote. One must not forget that the death of language, the substitution of phrases as nearly impersonal as algebra for words and rhythms varying from man to man, is but a part of the tyranny of impersonal things. I have been reading through a bundle of German plays, and have found everywhere a desire, not to express hopes and alarms common to every

[1] 'In one thing he and Lady Gregory are the strongest souls I have ever known. He and she alike have never for an instant spoken to me the thoughts of their inferiors as their own thoughts. I have never known them to lose the self-possession of their intellects.' W. B. Yeats, *Estrangement: Extracts from a Diary kept in 1909* (1926), in *Autobiographies* (Macmillan, 1961), p. 473.

[2] 'Synge seemed by nature unfitted to think a political thought, and with the exception of one sentence, spoken when I first met him in Paris, that implied some sort of Nationalist conviction, I cannot remember that he spoke of politics or showed any interest in man in the mass, or in any subject that is studied through abstractions and statistics.' W. B. Yeats, *J. M. Synge and the Ireland of his Time* (1910), in *Essays and Introductions*, p. 319.

man that ever came into the world, but politics or social passion, a veiled or open propaganda. Now it is duelling that has need of reproof; now it is the ideas of an actress, returning from the free life of the stage, that must be contrasted with the prejudice of an old-fashioned town; now it is the hostility of Christianity and Paganism in our own day that is to find an obscure symbol in a bell thrown from its tower by spirits of the wood. I compare the work of these dramatists with the greater plays of their Scandinavian master, and remember that even he, who has made so many clear-drawn characters, has made us no abundant character, no man of genius in whom we could believe, and that in him also, even when it is Emperor and Galilean that are face to face, even the most momentous figures are subordinate to some tendency, to some movement, to some inanimate energy, or to some process of thought whose very logic has changed it into mechanism—always to 'something other than human life.'

We must not measure a young talent, whether we praise or blame, with that of men who are among the greatest of our time, but we may say of any talent, following out a definition, that it takes up the tradition of great drama as it came from the hands of the Masters who are acknowledged by all time, and turns away from a dramatic movement which, though it has been served by fine talent, has been imposed upon us by science, by artificial life, by a passing order.

When the individual life no longer delights in its own energy, when the body is not made strong and beautiful by the activities of daily life, when men have no delight in decorating the body, one may be certain that one lives in a passing order, amid the inventions of a fading vitality. If Homer were alive to-day, he would only resist, after a deliberate struggle, the temptation to find his subject not in Helen's beauty, that every man has desired, nor in the wisdom and endurance of Odysseus that has been the desire of every woman that has come into the world, but in what somebody would describe, perhaps, as 'the inevitable contest,' arising out of economic causes, between the country-places and small towns on the one hand, and, upon the other, the great city of Troy, representing one knows not what 'tendency to centralisation.'[1]

Mr. Synge has in common with the great theatre of the world, with that of Greece and that of India, with the creator of Falstaff, with Racine, a delight in language, a preoccupation with individual life.[2] He

[1] '. . . I did not see, until Synge began to write, that we must renounce the deliberate creation of a kind of Holy City in the imagination, and express the individual.' W. B. Yeats, *Estrangement*, *Autobiographies*, pp. 493–4.

[2] 'He loves all that has edge, all that is salt in the mouth, all that is rough to the hand,

resembles them also by a preoccupation with what is lasting and noble, that came to him, not, as I think, from books, but while he listened to old stories in the cottages, and contrasted what they remembered with reality. The only literature of the Irish country people is their songs, full often of extravagant love, and their stories of kings and of kings' children. 'I will cry my fill, but not for God, but because Finn and the Fianna are not living,' says Oisin in the story. Every writer, even every small writer, who has belonged to the great tradition, has had his dream of an impossibly noble life, and the greater he is, the more does it seem to plunge him into some beautiful or bitter reverie. Some, and of these are all the earliest poets of the world, gave it direct expression; others mingle it so subtly with reality that it is a day's work to disentangle it; others bring it near by showing us whatever is most its contrary. Mr. Synge, indeed, sets before us ugly, deformed or sinful people, but his people, moved by no practical ambition, are driven by a dream of that impossible life. That we may feel how intensely his Woman of the Glen dreams of days that shall be entirely alive, she that is 'a hard woman to please' must spend her days between a sour-faced old husband, a man who goes mad upon the hills, a craven lad and a drunken tramp; and those two blind people of *The Well of the Saints* are so transformed by the dream that they choose blindness rather than reality. He tells us of realities, but he knows that art has never taken more than its symbols from anything that the eye can see or the hand measure.

It is the preoccupation of his characters with their dream that gives his plays their drifting movement, their emotional subtlety. In most of the dramatic writing of our time, and this is one of the reasons why our dramatists do not find the need for a better speech, one finds a simple motive lifted, as it were, into the full light of the stage. The ordinary student of drama will not find anywhere in *The Well of the Saints* that excitement of the will in the presence of attainable advantages, which he is accustomed to think the natural stuff of drama, and if he see it played he will wonder why act is knitted to act so loosely, why it is all like a decoration on a flat surface, why there is so much leisure in the dialogue, even in the midst of passion.[1] If he see *The Shadow of the Glen,*

---

all that heightens the emotions by contest, all that stings into life the sense of tragedy. . .'
W. B. Yeats, *J. M. Synge and the Ireland of his Time, Essays and Introductions*, pp. 326–7.

[1] '. . . perhaps I was Synge's convert. It was certainly a day of triumph when the first act of *The Well of the Saints* held its audience, though the two chief persons sat side by side under a stone cross from start to finish.' W. B. Yeats, 'An Introduction for my Plays' (1937), in *Essays and Introductions*, p. 528. Yeats mentions the 'long quiet periods' in a letter to Frank Fay in August 1904, *The Letters of W. B. Yeats*, ed. Allan Wade (1955).

he will ask, Why does this woman go out of her house? Is it because she cannot help herself, or is she content to go? Why is it not all made clearer? And yet, like everybody when caught up into great events, she does many things without being quite certain why she does them. She hardly understands at moments why her action has a certain form, more clearly than why her body is tall or short, fair or brown. She feels an emotion that she does not understand. She is driven by desires that need for their expression, not 'I admire this man,' or 'I must go, whether I will or no,' but words full of suggestion, rhythms of voice, movements that escape analysis. In addition to all this, she has something that she shares with none but the children of one man's imagination. She is intoxicated by a dream which is hardly understood by herself, but possesses her like something half remembered on a sudden wakening.

While I write, we are rehearsing *The Well of the Saints*, and are painting for it decorative scenery, mountains in one or two flat colours and without detail, ash-trees and red salleys with something of recurring pattern in their woven boughs. For though the people of the play use no phrase they could not use in daily life, we know that we are seeking to express what no eye has ever seen.

W. B. YEATS

ABBEY THEATRE
January 27, 1905

PERSONS[1]

MARTIN DOUL, a weather-beaten, blind beggar
MARY DOUL, his wife, a weather-beaten, ugly
woman, blind also, nearly fifty
TIMMY, a middle-aged, almost elderly, but vigorous
smith
MOLLY BYRNE, a fine-looking girl with fair hair
BRIDE, another handsome girl
MAT SIMON
THE SAINT, a wandering Friar
OTHER GIRLS AND MEN

SCENE

*Some lonely mountainous district in the east of Ireland,
one or more centuries ago. The first act is in the autumn;
the second towards the end of winter; and the third at the
beginning of spring.*

[1] *When the Blind See* TS. includes another character, 'Patch Ruadh'.

[1] Early drafts, including *When the Blind See* TS., set the scene at a cross-roads, with rushes by the roadside, centre stage.

[2] Earliest TS. draft adds direction *Some one is heard singing, then dark Martin and his wife, both blind, grope their way in, the wife with a bundle of rushes under her arm.* The next draft drops Martin's singing but retains the rushes. *When the Blind See* TS. concludes the description with *The first scene is to be played quietly with slight genial humour.* Not until the 'rough final' draft did Synge decide to bring the Douls in from the left, although the alteration may simply have been a transfer to stage perspective.

[3] It was not until the final TS. 'C' that Synge added the first exchange of dialogue. All earlier drafts begin with Martin's speech, 'The sun's a long way from the east this day, Mary Doul, you were that length' etc. Earlier stage directions have Martin *putting his hands on the stone cross and turning his face to the sun.*

[4] In succeeding drafts the fair is situated 'west', of 'Aughrim', 'Rathvanna', and finally 'Clash', the common diminutive form of Ballinaclash. One early draft has Martin complaining, 'and they'll be spending their money without thinking on us. You're a hard woman to get moving you think that much of your hair.'

[5] The earliest draft adds 'and maybe I'll get used to it before I die.'

[6] *When the Blind See* TS. adds explanation *for rush-lights.*

[7] Not until the final draft 'C' does Synge strike out the word 'here' after 'sitting out'.

[8] *When the Blind See* TS. expands 'ones' to 'little light girls', but it is then altered back to the one word.

[9] The early drafts add 'and I heard Molly Byrne saying last night it's little more than a fright you are'.

ACT ONE

Roadside with big stones, etc. on the right; low loose wall at back with
gap near centre; at left, ruined doorway of church with bushes beside it.[1]
MARTIN DOUL *and* MARY DOUL *grope in on left and pass over to*
stones on right, where they sit.[2]

MARY DOUL. What place are we now, Martin Doul?

MARTIN DOUL. Passing the gap.

MARY DOUL [*raising her head*]. The length of that! Well, the sun's
coming warm this day if it's late autumn itself.

MARTIN DOUL [*putting out his hands in sun*]. What way wouldn't it be
warm and it getting high up in the south?[3] You were that length
plaiting your yellow hair you have the morning lost on us, and the
people are after passing to the fair of Clash.[4]

MARY DOUL. It isn't going to the fair, the time they do be driving their
cattle and they with a litter of pigs maybe squealing in their carts,
they'd give us a thing at all. [*She sits down.*] It's well you know that,
but you must be talking.[5]

MARTIN DOUL [*sitting down beside her and beginning to shred rushes*[6] *she*
gives him]. If I didn't talk I'd be destroyed in a short while listening to
the clack you do be making, for you've a queer cracked voice, the
Lord have mercy on you, if it's fine to look on you are itself.

MARY DOUL. Who wouldn't have a cracked voice sitting out[7] all the
year in the rain falling? It's a bad life for the voice, Martin Doul,
though I've heard tell there isn't anything like the wet south wind
does be blowing upon us, for keeping a white beautiful skin—the
like of my skin—on your neck and on your brows, and there isn't
anything at all like a fine skin for putting splendour on a woman.

MARTIN DOUL [*teasingly, but with good-humour*]. I do be thinking odd
times we don't know rightly what way you have your splendour,
or asking myself, maybe, if you have it at all, for the time I was a
young lad, and had fine sight, it was the ones[8] with sweet voices
were the best in face.[9]

MARY DOUL. Let you not be making the like of that talk when you've
heard Timmy the smith, and Mat Simon, and Patch Ruadh, and a

¹ Again Synge gradually becomes more specific, from 'below in the west' to 'in the west' to 'Ballinahinch' to 'Ballinaclash' to 'Ballinacree', which is struck out in the final TS. and altered to 'Ballinatone'.

² An early draft expands Martin's speech: 'It was the beautiful dark woman they did call you surely and I'm thinking they wouldn't tell you a lie, but it was the like of that Molly Byrne was saying at the fall of night.' The later *When the Blind See* TS. originally read, 'It was the beautiful dark woman they did call you surely, but why would any person believe the lies of the world, and I heard' etc. A fragment marked 'Slip A' includes the following exchange:

Byrne saying it's little more than a fright you are.

MARY. You heard her say the like of that?

MARTIN. I did surely, at the fall of night, and I was thinking it round in my head the time you were snoring in your sleep.

MARY. It's a queer thing you'd be heeding the like of that talk when . . .

³ The earliest version does not name Molly Byrne and refers to 'red Jack was after praising my hair'. Later versions name both Molly and Timmy the smith, adding 'and she seeking marriage with himself'.

⁴ The TS. marked 'rough final' is the first to include Martin's interjection, adding the question 'of a woman of your age?'

⁵ Second direction added from Quinn edition and final TS.

⁶ Until the final draft Martin begins his speech with 'There's a power of deceit and villainy walking the world and it's no lie, and I do' etc.

⁷ A later correction to the final draft cuts this speech considerably: '. . . their sight, I'm telling you, and it's great joy they have to be telling fools' lies, the like of what Molly Byrne was telling to yourself.' The singular form of 'fool's' in the Quinn and 1905 editions appears to be a typographical error.

On the back of the preceding page in the *When the Blind See* TS. Synge has written an additional exchange to follow Mary's speech:

MARTIN. It's lies she was telling surely for I've a great ear, God help me, for feeling the truth in a voice.

MARY. It's little ear you need to know the like of her would be telling you lies.

MARTIN. If it's lies she does be telling etc.

⁸ In an early draft Synge includes the following interjection:

MARY. You've a great wish God forgive you to be hearing her voice.

MARTIN. It should be etc.

Pause is indicated in earlier drafts.

power besides saying fine things of my face, and you know rightly it was 'the beautiful dark woman', they did call me in Ballinatone.[1]

MARTIN DOUL [*as before*]. If it was itself I heard Molly Byrne saying at the fall of night it was little more than a fright you were.[2]

MARY DOUL [*sharply*]. She was jealous, God forgive her, because Timmy the smith[3] was after praising my hair—

MARTIN DOUL [*with mock irony*]. Jealous![4]

MARY DOUL. Ay, jealous, Martin Doul, and if she wasn't itself, the young and silly do be always making game of them that's dark, and they'd think it a fine thing if they had us deceived, the way we wouldn't know we were so fine-looking at all. [*She puts her hand to her face with a complacent gesture and smoothes her hair back with her hands.*[5]]

MARTIN DOUL [*a little plaintively*].[6] I do be thinking in the long nights it'd be a grand thing if we could see ourselves for one hour, or a minute itself, the way we'd know surely we were the finest man, and the finest woman, of the seven counties of the east. . . [*bitterly*] and then the seeing rabble below might be destroying their souls telling bad lies, and we'd never heed a thing they'd say.

MARY DOUL. If you weren't a big fool you wouldn't heed them this hour Martin Doul, for they're a bad lot those that have their sight, and they do have great joy, the time they do be seeing a grand thing, to let on they don't see it at all, and to be telling fools' lies, the like of what Molly Byrne was telling to yourself.[7]

MARTIN DOUL. If it's lies she does be telling she's a sweet beautiful voice you'd never tire to be hearing, if it was only the pig she'd be calling, or crying out in the long grass, maybe, after her hens. . . .[8] [*Speaking pensively.*] It should be a fine soft, rounded woman, I'm thinking, would have a voice the like of that.

MARY DOUL [*sharply again, scandalized*]. Let you not be minding if it's flat or rounded she is, for she's a flighty, foolish woman you'll hear when you're off a long way, and she making a great noise and laughing at the well.

MARTIN DOUL. Isn't laughing a nice thing the time a woman's young?

MARY DOUL [*bitterly*]. A nice thing is it? A nice thing to hear a woman making a loud braying laugh the like of that? Ah, she's a great one

¹ Early drafts expand Mary's comments to add 'It's a queer woman would never stir a short way without having Mat Simon close by on the one side, or Patch Ruadh, maybe close by on the other, while there's Timmy the smith, God help him, would make her his wife sitting up in his forge, getting mighty fussy the times she'll come walking the road, the way' etc.

² In the draft marked 'rough final' Synge questions the introductory clause 'I do be always sitting quiet, God help me, and I'm not' etc., finally removing it in the final TS.

³ In the 'rough final' draft Synge substitutes 'bad ones' for 'villainy'.

⁴ One of the earliest drafts reads 'them that do be gaping around, with their goggildy eyes'.

⁵ Earlier drafts read 'MARTIN [*thoughtfully*]. I'm thinking if the men seen you walking free they'd say more of you surely for I'm told' etc. and 'MARTIN [*pensively*]. It's a foolish talking lot they are surely, and yet I'm told' etc.

⁶ In one of the early drafts Synge has written in the margin of this speech 'Insert Phil the fine one'.

⁷ The two earliest drafts include the following exchange:

MARTIN [*counting the pith*]. There's the worth of two pence we have done already. The pith is tight and springy this day with the grand warmth of the sun, and it's fine to be working when the things are right under your hand and you can feel how well you're doing.

MARY [*listening*]. There's someone coming up the road now. Let you be singing your song, they think well to find the like of us making merry and we not seeing them at all.

[MARTIN *sings*. TIMMY THE SMITH *comes up the road.*]

Synge 'translated' these first pages for Max Meyerfeld (see Appendix C).

⁸ All but the final draft have Timmy coming in on the right. The Houghton TS. of Timmy's part also has him entering from the right.

⁹ The final TS. and Quinn edition read 'know', but all the earlier drafts and the 1905 edition read 'knew'. In his notes to Max Meyerfeld, his German translator, Synge explains the line, 'pretending a little while ago that you knew my step'.

¹⁰ In the first draft Timmy the smith's wife is still alive, as the following speech indicates:

I know it when your wife's after breaking your head. But it's few times only I've heard you walking up the like of that. . . . Is herself ailing again? If I'd an old speckled looking female the like of that

TIM. She is not God forgive her, but I'm after seeing a great sight this day. [*He begins to go by.*]

MARY. A great sight is it? Let you sit down then and tell us, it's in a mighty haste you are this day, and you with your back to the still.

TIM [*turning towards them*]. I was going up to tell them above at the houses . . . there'll be great doings in this place in a short while.

Later drafts eliminate the wife but suggest other reasons for Timmy's haste: 'Maybe you've a thorn in your heel?', or 'when you're after shoeing the red horse and paring his heels'. In his notes to Meyerfeld Synge defines 'a thing wasn't right' as 'a thing that is uncanny, mysterious, supernatural'.

for drawing the men, and you'll hear Timmy himself, the time he does be sitting in his forge, getting mighty fussy if she'll come walking from Grianan, the way you'll hear his breath going, and he wringing his hands.[1]

MARTIN DOUL [*slightly piqued*]. I've heard him say a power of times, it's nothing at all she is when you see her at the side of you, and yet I never heard any man's breath getting uneasy the time he'd be looking on yourself.

MARY DOUL.[2] I'm not the like of the girls do be running round on the roads, swinging their legs, and they with their necks out looking on the men . . . Ah, there's a power of villainy[3] walking the world, Martin Doul, among them that do be gadding around, with their gaping[4] eyes, and their sweet words, and they with no sense in them at all.

MARTIN DOUL [*sadly*]. It's the truth, maybe,[5] and yet I'm told it's a grand thing to see a young girl walking the road.

MARY DOUL. You'd be as bad as the rest of them if you had your sight, and I did well surely, not to marry a seeing man[6]—it's scores would have had me and welcome—for the seeing is a queer lot, and you'd never know the thing they'd do.

[*A moment's pause.*][7]

MARTIN DOUL [*listening*]. There's someone coming on the road.

MARY DOUL. Let you put the pith away out of their sight, or they'll be picking it out with the spying eyes they have, and saying it's rich we are, and not sparing us a thing at all.

[*They bundle away the rushes.* TIMMY THE SMITH *comes in on left.*[8]]

MARTIN DOUL [*with a begging voice*]. Leave a bit of silver for blind Martin, your honour. Leave a bit of silver, or a penny copper itself, and we'll be praying the Lord to bless you and you going the way.

TIMMY [*stopping before them*]. And you letting on a while back you knew[9] my step! [*He sits down.*]

MARTIN DOUL [*with his natural voice*]. I know it when Molly Byrne's walking in front, or when she's two perches, maybe, lagging behind, but it's few times I've heard you walking up the like of that, as if you'd met a thing wasn't right and you coming on the road.[10]

¹ 'Rough final' TS. adds direction *annoyed at his mistake.*

² In his notes to Meyerfeld Synge defined 'playing shows' as 'playing little plays, or performing in circuses such as are seen in country fairs', and 'lepping' as 'leaping, jumping'.

³ To Meyerfeld Synge explains Timmy's last words as meaning 'too clever to take notice of me'.

⁴ An early draft gives the direction [*dubiously*].

⁵ In his notes to Meyerfeld Synge explains 'it's wonder enough we are ourselves' as 'we are such fine-looking wonderful blind people that we are wonder enough for this place, and we don't wish you to do anything here that people would think of instead of us'.

⁶ The first draft of this speech adds the direction *in a whisper.*
⁷ The word 'there' after 'behind' is not struck out until the 'rough final' TS. To Meyerfeld Synge explains 'still' as 'a pot-still for distilling illicit whiskey, or poteen'.
⁸ *When the Blind See* TS. experiments with the wording 'I'd a good sup near at hand' etc., but this is not followed through in any other draft.

⁹ In a fragment from draft 'A' Mary asks, 'Are they hanging a blustering thief the like of Martin Doul, above at the bit of a tree?' which is then altered in MS. to 'Let you ⟨tell⟩ us now Timmy, and not be heeding himself. Maybe they're hanging a thief above at the bit of a tree?'

TIMMY [*hot and breathless, wiping his face*]. You've good ears, God bless you, if you're a liar itself, for I'm after walking up in great haste from hearing wonders in the fair.

MARTIN [*rather contemptuously[1]*]. You're always hearing queer wonderful things, and the lot of them nothing at all, but I'm thinking, this time, it's a strange thing surely, you'd be walking up before the turn of day, and not waiting below to look on them lepping, or dancing, or playing shows[2] on the green of Clash.

TIMMY [*huffed*]. I was coming to tell you it's in this place there'd be a bigger wonder done in a short while [MARTIN DOUL *stops working and looks at him*], than was ever done on the green of Clash, or the width of Leinster itself, but you're thinking, maybe, you're too cute a little fellow to be minding me at all.[3]

MARTIN DOUL [*amused but incredulous*]. There'll be wonders in this place is it?

TIMMY. Here at the crossing of the roads.

MARTIN DOUL.[4] I never heard tell of anything to happen in this place since the night they killed the old fellow going home with his gold, the Lord have mercy on him, and threw down his corpse into the bog. Let them not be doing the like of that this night, for it's ourselves have a right to the crossing roads, and we don't want any of your bad tricks, or your wonders either, for it's wonder enough we are ourselves.[5]

TIMMY. If I'd a mind I'd be telling you of a real wonder this day, and the way you'll be having a great joy, maybe, you're not thinking on at all.

MARTIN DOUL [*interested[6]*]. Are they putting up a still behind[7] in the rocks? It'd be a grand thing if I'd a sup handy[8] the way I wouldn't be destroying myself groping up across the bogs in the rain falling.

TIMMY [*still moodily*]. It's not a still they're bringing or the like of it either.

MARY DOUL [*persuasively, to* TIMMY]. Maybe they're hanging a thief, above at the bit of a tree?[9] I'm told it's a great sight to see a man hanging by his neck, but what joy would that be to ourselves, and we not seeing it at all?

¹ Timmy's introductory sentence, 'It's that is the wonder, Mary Doul . . . Did ever' etc., is not struck out until the 'rough final' draft.

² In an early draft Mary replies, 'I have great talk of them many places and I walking the world'.

³ Although Synge retains this speech, in an early draft he suggests his doubts by writing a series of question marks after it.

⁴ In his notes to Max Meyerfeld Synge writes '*naggin* is a small measure of quantity, half a pint, I think. . . .' Actually a naggin or noggin is a gill, ¼ pt.

⁵ The early drafts read 'and I'm thinking one of the Brians would go for it—they've a great wish to look on the wonders of the earth,—if we gave him' etc.

⁶ The first two drafts include the following speech by Martin: 'Would a naggin be enough, Timmy? Maybe you'ld want to put your whole head down into it and flap it round by your ears?' Timmy replies, 'Wait now, wait now, let you take your time God help you. There is no good at all to be sending' etc.

⁷ 'Rough final' draft reads *shouting at*.

TIMMY [*more pleasantly*]. They're hanging no one this day, Mary Doul, and yet with the help of God, you'll see a power hanged before you die.

MARY DOUL. Well you've queer humbugging talk. . . . What way would I see a power hanged, and I a dark woman since the seventh year of my age?

TIMMY.[1] Did ever you hear tell of a place across a bit of the sea, where there is an island, and the grave of the four beautiful saints?

MARY DOUL. I've heard people have walked round from the west and they speaking of that.[2]

TIMMY [*impressively*]. There's a green ferny well, I'm told, behind of that place, and if you put a drop of the water out of it, on the eyes of a blind man, you'll make him see as well as any person is walking the world.

MARTIN DOUL [*with excitement*]. Is that the truth, Timmy? I'm thinking you're telling a lie.

TIMMY [*gruffly*]. That's the truth, Martin Doul, and you may believe it now, for you're after believing a power of things weren't as likely at all.[3]

MARY DOUL. Maybe we could send a young lad to bring us the water. I could wash a naggin[4] bottle in the morning, and I'm thinking Patch Ruadh would go for it,[5] if we gave him a good drink, and the bit of money we have hid in the thatch.[6]

TIMMY. It'd be no good to be sending a sinful man the like of ourselves, for I'm told the holiness of the water does be getting soiled with the villainy of your heart, the time you'd be carrying it, and you looking round on the girls, maybe, or drinking a small sup at a still.

MARTIN DOUL [*with disappointment*]. It'd be a long terrible way to be walking ourselves, and I'm thinking that's a wonder will bring small joy to us at all.

TIMMY [*turning on*[7] *him impatiently*]. What is it you want with your walking? It's as deaf as blind you're growing if you're not after hearing me say it's in this place the wonder would be done.

¹ A fragment of draft 'A' questions these entire two speeches by Timmy and Martin, but they are altered only slightly in succeeding drafts. Synge explains 'blather' to Meyerfeld as 'foolish talk, nonsense'.

² 'Rough final' draft reads [*standing up angrily*].

³ 'Rough final' draft adds [*he goes a little to right*].

⁴ 'Rough final' draft reads *controlling her impatience with graciousness*. Quinn edition places Mary Doul R.C.

⁵ 'Rough final' draft adds dots to indicate pause and direction TIMMY *turns back again*.

⁶ 'Rough final' draft adds direction [*She pushes* TIMMY *down beside her and sits down*], which Synge then alters in MS. to *and stands in front of him*. In his notes to Meyerfeld Synge defines 'huffy' as 'offended'.

⁷ In Houghton TS. of Timmy's part the words 'a saint of the Almighty God' are struck out in pencil.

⁸ Until the final draft, Timmy's speech begins, 'There's a holy man below, a sort of a saint I think they call him, who's going round' etc. In the Houghton TS. 'saint' is struck out and 'holy man' is written above in pencil.

⁹ The earliest draft of this speech ends '. . . any little drop at all is enough to make the dumb screech and the deaf to hear as sharp as a cat and the blind to see as well as myself.'

¹⁰ One of the earliest drafts gives the direction [*stands up nervously*].

¹¹ The question mark occurs in all versions except the 1905 and Quinn editions.

¹² *When the Blind See* TS. adds the direction [*pushing him back*]. Another draft reads [MARTIN *hardly listens.*]

¹³ The delivery of the lines here calls for the dash which occurs in the later TS. versions. The earlier drafts alter the order of this speech: 'Sit down, God help you. We're after telling him the way you are, and he's coming up now to cure the two of you and to say his prayers beyond in the church, for it's fine prayers he does be saying, and fasting, God help him, till he's as thin as one of the empty rushes you have there on your knee.' After the last of these versions Synge has written 'Bring psy. to point'. The Houghton TS. of Timmy's part includes the phrase 'God help him' after 'fasting', but it is struck out and 'at your feet' added in pencil above the line.

¹⁴ Houghton TS. separates 'we're after telling him the way you are' from the rest of the sentence with dashes, but there is no evidence of this in the other TSS.

¹⁵ *When the Blind See* TS. reads [*looking eagerly at* MARY].

MARTIN DOUL [*with a flash of anger*]. If it is can't you open the big slobbering mouth you have and say what way it'll be done, and not be making blather till the fall of night.¹

TIMMY [*jumping up*].² I'll be going on now [MARY DOUL *rises*], and not wasting time talking civil talk with the like of you.³

MARY DOUL [*standing up, disguising her impatience*⁴]. Let you come here to me, Timmy, and not be minding him at all. [TIMMY *stops, and she gropes up to him and takes him by the coat.*] . . .⁵ You're not huffy with myself, and let you tell me the whole story and don't be fooling me more . . .⁶ Is it yourself has brought us the water?

TIMMY. It is not, surely.

MARY DOUL. Then tell us your wonder, Timmy . . . What person'll bring it at all?

TIMMY [*relenting*]. It's a fine holy man will bring it, a saint of the Almighty God.⁷

MARY DOUL [*overawed*]. A saint is it?

TIMMY. Ay, a fine saint,⁸ who's going round through the churches of Ireland, with a long cloak on him, and naked feet, for he's brought a sup of the water slung at his side, and, with the like of him, any little drop is enough to cure the dying, or to make the blind see as clear as the grey hawks do be high up, on a still day, sailing the sky.⁹

MARTIN DOUL [*feeling for his stick*].¹⁰ What place is he, Timmy?¹¹ I'll be walking to him now.

TIMMY.¹² Let you stay quiet, Martin. He's straying around saying prayers at the churches and high crosses, between this place and the hills, and he with a great crowd going behind—for it's fine prayers he does be saying, and fasting with it, till he's as thin as one of the empty rushes you have there on your knee—¹³ then he'll be coming after to this place to cure the two of you, we're after telling him the way you are,¹⁴ and to say his prayers in the church.

MARTIN DOUL [*turning suddenly to*¹⁵ MARY DOUL]. And we'll be seeing ourselves this day. Oh, glory be to God, is it true surely?

MARY DOUL [*very pleased, to* TIMMY]. Maybe I'd have time to walk down and get the big shawl I have below, for I do look my best, I've heard them say, when I'm dressed up with that thing on my head.

¹ This exchange between Mary Doul and Timmy does not appear until the final TS.

² This speech originally belonged to Mary in a slightly different form: 'I hear the words of a big crowd now coming up by the stream.'

³ One early draft reads 'as easy as if it was a dozen new laid eggs you'd be lifting in your hat'. Houghton TS. has Timmy looking right instead of left; the word 'saint' is struck out and 'holy man' added in pencil; there is no instruction for Timmy to go to the entrance; a comma is put after 'now'.

⁴ In *When the Blind See* TS. and earlier drafts the saint comes in and passes over to the church with people following him, stopping in groups across the stage. Synge explains the name 'Bride' to Meyerfeld as being 'simply an Irish Christian name, a shortened form of Bridget'. The final 'e' is pronounced. In Quinn edition Molly crosses to C.L. of Martin Doul.

⁵ The 1905 edition has a full point before 'God help you'. In Houghton TS. Timmy does not cross to Molly Byrne.

⁶ One early draft reads 'three' instead of 'two'.
⁷ Houghton TS. has no comma after 'wonder'.

⁸ Synge explained 'he'll be climbing above' to Meyerfeld as 'he will have to climb through ⟨the woods⟩ up in Grianan'.

⁹ A late draft gives the direction *half to herself.*

¹⁰ Several late drafts include the following exchange:
MARTIN [*to* MOLLY]. And are you fit to cure the two of us with the things in your hand?
MOLLY [*toying with can*]. We wouldn't try, Martin, when himself is coming in a short while and he's after telling us by our hope of grace not to lift up the lid from the tin can.

TIMMY. You'd have time surely—[1]

MARTIN DOUL [*listening*]. Whisht now . . . I hear people again coming by the stream.[2]

TIMMY [*looking out left, puzzled*]. It's the young girls I left walking after the saint. . . . They're coming now [*goes up to entrance*] carrying things in their hands, and they walking as easy as you'd see a child walk, who'd have a dozen eggs hid in her bib.[3]

MARTIN DOUL [*listening*]. That's Molly Byrne, I'm thinking.

> [MOLLY BYRNE *and* BRIDE *come on left and cross to* MARTIN DOUL, *carrying water-can,* SAINT'*s bell, and cloak.*][4]

MOLLY [*volubly*]. God bless you, Martin. I've holy water here from the grave of the four saints of the west, will have you cured in a short while and seeing like ourselves—

TIMMY [*crosses to* MOLLY, *interrupting her*]. He's heard that,[5] God help you. But where at all is the saint, and what way is he after trusting the holy water with the likes of you?

MOLLY BYRNE. He was afeard to go a far way with the clouds is coming beyond, so he's gone up now through the thick woods to say a prayer at the crosses of Grianan, and he's coming on this road to the church.

TIMMY [*still astonished*]. And he's after leaving the holy water with the two[6] of you? It's a wonder,[7] surely. [*Comes down left a little.*]

MOLLY BYRNE. The lads told him no person could carry them things through the briars, and steep, slippy-feeling rocks he'll be climbing above,[8] so he looked round then, and gave the water, and his big cloak, and his bell to the two of us, for young girls, says he, are the cleanest holy people you'd see walking the world.

> [MARY DOUL *goes near seat.*]

MARY DOUL [*sits down, laughing to herself*[9]]. Well, the saint's a simple fellow, and it's no lie.

MARTIN DOUL [*leaning forward, holding out his hands*].[10] Let you give me the water in my hand, Molly Byrne, the way I'll know you have it surely.

¹ To Meyerfeld Synge explained 'wonders is' as 'miracles are'.

² The 1905 and Quinn editions put a comma after 'us', thereby destroying the rhythm of the sentence.

³ Quinn edition adds L.C.

⁴ An early draft adds the following speech by Martin Doul: 'Wouldn't it be a fine thing for a blind man to have a bell the like of that the way he could be ringing it every place to bring the kindly Christian people to his side?'

⁵ Synge experimented with different actions here in intermediate drafts. He appears first to have tried the cloak on Molly:

MOLLY [*putting the cloak about her*]. Stand up now Martin till I put his old cloak about you and we see what way you'd look you a holy saint.

MARTIN. Let you not be troubling me, when I'm waiting and puzzling for my sight.

MOLLY [*putting it on herself, takes bell*]. I'd make a fine saint Timmy, and isn't that the truth?

TIMMY. Oh, God help us, there'd be queer doings if the like of you went in among the holy men of God. . . . Oh, you're a right one, Molly, and it's no lie.

BRIDE [*looking out R.*]. There's the saint coming now on the selvage of the hill.

A later draft gives the cloak to Martin but includes the following exchange:

TIMMY [*jealous of* MARTIN, *looking out right*]. Leave him alone now, Molly Byrne. . . . There's the saint with a crowd after him coming out through the selvage of the wood.

MARTIN [*stands up hastily*]. And he's coming to us now?

MOLLY [*looking out*]. He'll be a while still coming through the lane and he not seeing us with the great height of the thorns.

⁶ When returning proofs to his publisher, A. H. Bullen, on 14 January 1905, Synge explained, 'I have had to make a good many corrections in one scene of the first act, as the MS. was used by our company for rehearsing—since it has been in my hands,—and I find that the prompter has written in a certain number of technical stage directions which could not be left in the printed volume.' It seems likely that this is the scene referred to, and that the confusion of the directions in the 1905 and Quinn editions, [MARTIN DOUL *rises, comes forward, centre a little*] during Molly's speech, when the next speech has him [*standing up, a little diffidently*], is an oversight on Synge's part concerning some of the prompter's 'technical stage directions'.

⁷ 1905 and Quinn editions have comma after 'times'.

⁸ Houghton TS. has full point instead of question mark after 'cloak'. To Meyerfeld Synge explains 'making game' as 'playing with'.

⁹ Earlier drafts alter the stage directions slightly: [*She slips behind* MARTIN, *and throws the saint's cloak round him, then closes it in front and pulls him partly down the stage. He still holds bell.*]

MARTIN [*pleased with her attention*]. What is it you're doing Molly Byrne?

MOLLY [*spins him round and lets him go*]. Isn't that a grand holy-looking saint?

A draft of about the same time includes Molly's question, 'Tell me now Martin Doul, what thing is it in the width of the world you're wanting most to set your eyes on at the turn of day?'

¹⁰ To Meyerfeld Synge explains Molly's last words as referring to 'the archangels down in hell that quarrelled or fought with the A. God'.

MOLLY BYRNE [*giving it to him*]. Wonders is[1] queer things, and maybe it'd cure you, and you holding it alone.

MARTIN DOUL [*looking round*]. It does not, Molly. I'm not seeing at all. [*He shakes the can.*] There's a small sup only. Well, isn't it a great wonder the little trifling thing would bring seeing to the blind, and be showing us[2] the big women and the young girls, and all the fine things is walking the world. [*He feels for* MARY DOUL *and gives her the can.*]

MARY DOUL [*shaking it*]. Well, glory be to God—

MARTIN DOUL [*pointing to* BRIDE]. And what is it herself has, making sounds in her hand?

BRIDE [*crossing[3] to* MARTIN DOUL]. It's the saint's bell, you'll hear him ringing out the time he'll be going up some place, to be saying his prayers.

[MARTIN DOUL *holds out his hands; she gives it to him.*]

MARTIN DOUL [*ringing it*]. It's a sweet, beautiful sound.

MARY DOUL. You'd know I'm thinking by the little silvery voice of it, a fasting holy man was after carrying it a great way at his side.[4]

[BRIDE *crosses a little right behind* MARTIN DOUL.]

MOLLY BYRNE [*unfolding* SAINT's *cloak*]. Let you stand up now, Martin Doul, till I put his big cloak on you, the way we'd see how you'd look, and you a saint of the Almighty God.[5]

MARTIN DOUL [*rises, comes forward centre, a little diffidently*].[6] I've heard the priests a power of times[7] making great talk and praises of the beauty of the saints.

[MOLLY BYRNE *slips cloak round him.*]

TIMMY [*uneasily*]. You'd have a right to be leaving him alone, Molly. What would the saint say if he seen you making game with his cloak?[8]

MOLLY BYRNE [*recklessly*]. How would he see us, and he saying prayers in the wood? [*She turns* MARTIN DOUL *round.*][9] Isn't that a fine holy-looking saint, Timmy the smith? [*Laughing foolishly.*] There's a grand handsome fellow, Mary Doul, and if you seen him now, you'd be as proud, I'm thinking, as the archangels below, fell out with the Almighty God.[10]

¹ A late draft reads [MARTIN *rings his bell not knowing what to do.*]

² The 1905 and Quinn editions put a semicolon instead of a comma after 'God help you', thereby destroying the rhythm.

³ The horseplay with the saint's bell, cloak, and can does not appear in the early versions of this scene. The following transition occurs instead:

MOLLY. You'll be a great pair now and you with your sight.

MARTIN. It'll be a great change, a great change surely. I'm half thinking if it wasn't that I'm destroyed wanting to see herself is after being ten years beside me I'd do the way I am, for it isn't a bad way at all, Timmy the smith.

TIMMY. Well herself is worth seeing.

MARY. He's after tormenting himself since he heard Sally saying I wasn't much more than a fright. He's a bigger fool than you'ld think, Timmy the smith, if he's a fine handsome man itself.

TIMMY [*looking at them half pityingly*]. The two of you will have a great wonder to see this day, God help you.

⁴ *When the Blind See* TS. prefaces Timmy's comments with the words, 'You'd do right not to be minding too much the power of talk you've heard and I'm thinking you know rightly the way' etc.

⁵ It was not until after the *When the Blind See* TS. that Synge decided to strike out the following exchange at this point:

MARTIN. I've heard her yellow hair, and her white skin, and the big eyes she has are a wonder surely. . . . [*in a more humorous tone*] and isn't it well for her she has them, with her cracked voice, and her crinkledy hands, and her feet slouching under her and she going the road?

MOLLY. Here's the saint coming again, and let you be quiet now and not saying queer things or maybe he wouldn't cure you till he'd make you fast and pray, and grow as thin as himself.

To Meyerfeld Synge explained 'selvage' as 'edge'.

MARY DOUL [*with quiet confidence going to* MARTIN DOUL *and feeling his cloak*]. It's proud we'll be this day, surely.

[MARTIN DOUL *is still ringing bell.*][1]

MOLLY BYRNE [*to* MARTIN DOUL]. Would you think well to be all your life walking round the like of that Martin Doul, and you bell-ringing with the saints of God?

MARY DOUL [*turning on her, fiercely*]. How would he be bell-ringing with the saints of God and he wedded with myself?

MARTIN DOUL. It's the truth she's saying, and if bell-ringing is a fine life, yet I'm thinking, maybe, it's better I am wedded with the beautiful dark woman of Ballinatone.

MOLLY BYRNE [*scornfully*]. You're thinking that, God help you,[2] but it's little you know of her at all.

MARTIN DOUL. It's little surely, and I'm destroyed this day waiting to look upon her face.[3]

TIMMY [*awkwardly*]. It's well you know the way she is, for the like of you do have great knowledge in the feeling of your hands.[4]

MARTIN DOUL [*still feeling the cloak*]. We do maybe. Yet it's little I know of faces, or of fine beautiful cloaks, for it's few cloaks I've had my hand to, and few faces [*plaintively*], for the young girls is mighty shy, Timmy the smith, and it isn't much they heed me, though they do be saying I'm a handsome man.

MARY DOUL [*mockingly, with good-humour*]. Isn't it a queer thing the voice he puts on him, when you hear him talking of the skinny young-looking girls, and he married with a woman he's heard called the wonder of the western world?

TIMMY [*pityingly*]. The two of you will see a great wonder this day, and it's no lie.

MARTIN DOUL. I've heard tell her yellow hair, and her white skin, and her big eyes are a wonder, surely—

BRIDE [*who has looked out left*]. Here's the saint coming from the selvage of the wood . . . Strip the cloak from him, Molly, or he'll be seeing it now.[5]

[1] It seems evident from Synge's notes to Meyerfeld that 'we' was inadvertently omitted in the final text. One draft gives Martin the following speech instead at this point:

MARTIN [*breathless and exasperated*]. You have me all pulled and destroyed Molly [*settling himself*], and no breath left for me prayers—

[2] Several drafts include the following dialogue:

MOLLY. He'll not see what way you are for he'd walk by the finest woman in Ireland I'm thinking and not notice her at all, for when he set them things in my hands he never lifted the eyes of him for one look on my face.

BRIDE [*arranging* MARTIN'S *clothes*]. It's yourself will have a great time now Martin looking on the girls, and you working every day, and taking a farm maybe and growing rich beyond the lot of us.

The first TS. draft adds a further question from Martin: 'He won't want me to give a thing at all for doing the job?' and later the remark, 'It'll be a queer thing to see the sun shining and it a score of years and beyond it since my eyes were shut.'

[3] Houghton TS. reads 'holy father. They do' etc.

[4] To Meyerfeld's query about 'stripping rushes for lights' Synge replied, 'the people used to make "rush lights" by taking the outside skin off rushes, and then soaking them, the rushes, in grease'. 'A bit of copper' he explained as 'a few pence'.

[5] The Texas TS. includes the following paraphrase in MS., evidently intended for Meyerfeld: 'The grave of the "four beauties of God" is on a bare starved rock, so it is little wonder, perhaps, that it is with bare starving people that the water should be used, and I go to those that are just like yourselves, who are wrinkled and poor, people that rich men would hardly look at, but would throw a coin to or a crust of bread.'

[6] The earliest drafts of this scene expand Martin's reaction to the Saint's words:

MARTIN [*uneasily*]. When they look at herself, who is a fine woman, they do often throw two coins or a trifle of meat.

SAINT [*severely*]. What do we know of women who are fine or foul? What is any woman at all but a thing of weakness and sin?

MARTIN [*under his breath*]. Oh, fasting is a great thing, fasting and praying is a great thing surely.

[7] An early draft suggests a slightly different reaction: [*puzzled for a moment*].

MOLLY BYRNE [*hastily to* BRIDE]. Take the bell and put herself by the stones. [*To* MARTIN DOUL.] Will you hold your head up till I loosen the cloak. [*She pulls off the cloak and throws it over her arm. Then she pushes* MARTIN DOUL *over and stands him beside* MARY DOUL.] Stand there now, quiet, and let you not be saying a word.

[*She and* BRIDE *stand a little on their left, demurely, with bell, etc., in their hands.*]

MARTIN DOUL [*nervously arranging his clothes*]. Will he mind the way we are, and we not tidied or washed cleanly at all?[1]

MOLLY BYRNE. He'll not see what way you are. . . . He'd walk by the finest woman in Ireland, I'm thinking, and not trouble to raise his two eyes to look upon her face.[2] . . . Whisht!

[SAINT *comes on left, with crowd.*]

SAINT. Are these the two poor people?

TIMMY [*officiously*]. They are, holy father,[3] they do be always sitting here at the crossing of the roads, asking a bit of copper from them that do pass, or stripping rushes for lights,[4] and they not mournful at all, but talking out straight with a full voice, and making game with them that likes it.

SAINT [*to* MARTIN DOUL *and* MARY DOUL]. It's a hard life you've had not seeing sun or moon, or the holy priests itself praying to the Lord, but it's the like of you who are brave in a bad time will make a fine use of the gift of sight the Almighty God will bring to you to-day. [*He takes his cloak and puts it about him.*] It's on a bare starving rock that there's the grave of the four beauties of God, the way it's little wonder, I'm thinking, if it's with bare starving people the water should be used. [*He takes the water and bell and slings them round his shoulders.*] So it's to the like of yourselves I do be going, who are wrinkled and poor, a thing rich men would hardly look at at all, but would throw a coin to or a crust of bread.[5]

MARTIN DOUL [*moving uneasily*]. When they look on herself who is a fine woman—[6]

TIMMY [*shaking him*]. Whisht now, and be listening to the saint.

SAINT [*looks at them a moment,[7] continues*]. If it's raggy and dirty you are itself, I'm saying, the Almighty God isn't at all like the rich men of

¹ The 1905 and Quinn editions place a comma after 'water', thereby altering the rhythm.

² The 'rough final' TS. offers two different geographical versions of the saint's journey: 'in a little curagh into Casilagh Bay, and beyond the Corrib into Athenry, and by Alwin of Leinster to the place we are' and later, 'in a little curagh into Cashla Bay, and across by Roscommon and the Allen plain'. See Introduction (p. xxiii) for Synge's production notes of this scene.

³ All of the drafts call for a pause here.

⁴ To Meyerfeld Synge explained this speech as meaning 'come now so that we can watch, or come now and let us watch'.

⁵ To Meyerfeld Synge commented about 'the words of women and smiths', 'this phrase is almost a quotation from an old hymn of Saint Patrick. In Irish folklore smiths were thought to be magicians, and more or less in league with the powers of darkness. Perhaps the phrase cannot be translated?' The lines in 'St. Patrick's Breastplate', translated from the Irish by Whitley Stokes, John Strachan, and Kuno Meyer, are:

> I summon to-day all these powers between me and those evils,
> Against every cruel merciless power that may oppose my body and soul,
> Against incantations of false prophets,
> Against black laws of pagandom,
> Against false laws of heretics,
> Against craft of idolatry,
> Against spells of women and smiths and wizards,
> Against every knowledge that corrupts man's body and soul.

⁶ Apparently Synge had first contemplated making the cure take place on stage: [*He goes up the stage a little with* MARTIN *who kneels down as the* SAINT *prays over him.* MARY *goes a little back and prays also in such a position that she is out of* MARTIN's *view as he stands up again.* . . . ⟨*The crowd watches as the* SAINT⟩ *takes water from a vessel and puts* ⟨*it*⟩ *on* MARTIN's *eyes.*]

⁷ Houghton TS. reads 'big brave man'. The word 'big' is struck out and 'fine' written above with a different pencil from the other alterations in this TS. An alternative, 'body of a man', is written in pencil above the speech.

⁸ To Meyerfeld Synge explains 'the water would do rightly' as 'the water would have the same effect—would do very well'.

Ireland; and, with the power of the water[1] I'm after bringing in a little curagh into Cashla Bay, he'll have pity on you, and put sight into your eyes.[2]

MARTIN DOUL [*taking off his hat*]. I'm ready now, holy father—

SAINT [*taking him by the hand*]. I'll cure you first, and then I'll come for your wife. We'll go up now into the church, for I must say a prayer to the Lord . . .[3] [*To* MARY DOUL *as he moves off*.] And let you be making your mind still and saying praises in your heart, for it's a great wonderful thing when the power of the Lord of the world is brought down upon your like.

PEOPLE [*pressing after him*]. Come now till we watch.[4]

BRIDE. Come, Timmy.

SAINT [*waving them back*]. Stay back where you are, for I'm not wanting a big crowd making whispers in the church. Stay back there, I'm saying, and you'd do well to be thinking on the way sin has brought blindness to the world, and to be saying a prayer for your own sakes against false prophets and heathens, and the words of women and smiths,[5] and all knowledge that would soil the soul or the body of a man.

> [PEOPLE *shrink back. He goes into church.* MARY DOUL *gropes half way towards the door and kneels near path.* PEOPLE *form a group at right.*][6]

TIMMY. Isn't it a fine, beautiful voice he has, and he a fine, brave man[7] if it wasn't for the fasting?

BRIDE. Did you watch him moving his hands?

MOLLY BYRNE. It'd be a fine thing if some one in this place could pray the like of him, for I'm thinking the water from our own blessed well would do rightly[8] if a man knew the way to be saying prayers, and then there'd be no call to be bringing water from that wild place, where, I'm told, there are no decent houses, or fine-looking people at all.

BRIDE [*who is looking in at door from right*]. Look at the great trembling Martin has shaking him, and he on his knees.

TIMMY [*anxiously*]. God help him. . . . What will he be doing when he sees his wife this day? I'm thinking it was bad work we did when

¹ During successive drafts Synge expanded this discussion, gradually drawing in more characters. In the first draft there is simply Molly's reply to Timmy's question about Martin's reaction to the truth, 'He'll have other things now to look at along with his wife.' The next draft includes Bride, who takes over this reply, adding 'When he sees her now he'll be having our lives', and in her speeches Molly justifies the pleasure their lies have given him. The *When the Blind See* TS. includes Mat Simon's mocking comment to Molly about her own man, to which Molly replies, 'It's not yourself will be my man, Mat Simon, though you'd sell heaven and earth, I'm thinking, in spite of the talk you have, if you'd get me for the two.' Mat Simon replies 'You'd do right to get the old saint to wed you with Timmy beyond. Himself would give you a fine house, and have a strong arm to beat if you were growing flighty again.' A further intermediary draft develops this approach:

TIMMY. Hold your tongue, Mat Simon. Don't you know well when the saint comes out I'm going to ask him would he wed Molly with myself.

MOLLY. He'll ⟨be⟩ passing back I heard him say at the spring of the year and that would be a better time when you'll have ⟨a⟩ house thatched for me, and good bars on the door.

TIMMY. The spring would do surely, and that way you won't be eating your head off the whole of the winter, when it's little there is to do and there's a great price on the meal.

The final form arrives with Timmy, parting Molly and Mat Simon, [*uneasily*]: 'Let you not be raising your voice, Molly, while the saint's standing above, he'ld not think it a seemly sounding thing maybe in a woman of your age.'

² The saint's Latin appears to be a very late addition. According to Synge's letter to Meyerfeld, 19 November 1905, Martin's cry and the saint's prayer were cut in rehearsals; this Synge 'did not think necessary but the stage manager thought they retarded the climax'.

³ According to Synge's own copy of *The Well of the Saints*, he considered cutting the phrase 'and the green bits of ferns in them'. This may have been one of the phrases he was thinking of when he wrote to Meyerfeld in the same letter, 'Some of the cuts are very unimportant and I made them because I thought the speeches *spoke* more lightly without the words I cut out. In your translation it is hard to say whether the same cuts are advisable or others. I seemed to feel that in the German the first scene of Act II was a little inclined to drag but really these are points on which you and the stage manager who directs the rehearsals will be able to judge much better than I can. Till one gets into the actual rehearsal it is I think better to do as little cutting as possible. Then if a speech drags on the stage it must of course be amended.'

⁴ Earlier drafts give further stage directions: *They all turn towards the door, the men standing between the church and* MOLLY. The earliest draft has Mary Doul hidden from Martin's view by 'ivy or something'.

⁵ Houghton TS. has exclamation mark after 'at all'.

we let on she was fine-looking, and not a wrinkled wizened hag the way she is.

MAT SIMON. Why would he be vexed, and we after giving him great joy and pride, the time he was dark?

MOLLY BYRNE [*sitting down in* MARY DOUL'*s seat and tidying her hair*]. If it's vexed he is itself, he'll have other things now to think on as well as his wife, and what does any man care for a wife, when it's two weeks, or three, he is looking on her face?

MAT SIMON. That's the truth now, Molly, and it's more joy dark Martin got from the lies we told of that hag is kneeling by the path, than your own man will get from you, day or night, and he living at your side.

MOLLY BYRNE [*defiantly*]. Let you not be talking, Mat Simon, for it's not yourself will be my man, though you'd be crowing and singing fine songs if you'd that hope in you at all.

TIMMY [*shocked, to* MOLLY BYRNE]. Let you not be raising your voice when the saint's above at his prayers.[1]

BRIDE [*crying out*]. Whisht. . . . Whisht. . . . I'm thinking he's cured.

MARTIN DOUL [*crying out in the church*]. Oh, glory be to God—

SAINT [*solemnly*]. Laus patri sit et filio cum spiritu paraclito
                    Qui suae dono gratiae miseratus est Hiberniae—[2]

MARTIN DOUL [*ecstatically*]. Oh, glory be to God, I see now surely. . . . I see the walls of the church, and the green bits of ferns in them,[3] and yourself, holy father, and the great width of the sky.

[*He runs out half foolish with joy, and comes past* MARY DOUL *as she scrambles to her feet, drawing a little away from her as he goes by.*[4]]

TIMMY [*to the others*]. He doesn't know her at all.[5]

[SAINT *comes out behind* MARTIN DOUL *and leads* MARY DOUL *into the church.* MARTIN DOUL *comes on to the* PEOPLE. *The Men are between him and the Girls. He verifies his position with his stick.*]

MARTIN DOUL [*crying out joyfully*]. That's Timmy, I know Timmy by the black of his head. . . . That's Mat Simon, I know Mat by the

[1] The early drafts read, 'That's Timmy. I know Timmy by the dirt of his head. . . . That's Mat Simon, I know Mat by the twist in his nose. That should be Patch Ruadh with the squinty eye and the carroty hair . . .' etc.

To Meyerfeld Synge explained 'gamey eyes' as 'tricky, merry eyes' and 'Patch Ruadh' as 'red Patch'.

[2] In his own copy of the 1905 edition, Synge has put round brackets around the words 'The blessing of God on this day, and them that brought me the saint'.

[3] An early version reads '. . . and I'm not a bad one at all, at least I'm not thinking I am . . . [*he presses close to her*]'. The entire speech varies little from its first appearance in the earliest drafts. To Meyerfeld Synge explained 'a bad one' as 'an ugly man'.

[4] The earliest version reads 'Go away out of it you old goat, and don't be soiling my dress. . . .'

[5] All the drafts except the 1905 and Quinn editions indicate a pause after Martin Doul's words.

length of his legs. . . . That should be Patch Ruadh, with the gamey eyes in him, and the fiery hair.[1] [*He sees* MOLLY BYRNE *on* MARY DOUL's *seat, and his voice changes completely.*] Oh, it was no lie they told me, Mary Doul. Oh, glory to God and the seven saints I didn't die and not see you at all. The blessing of God on the water, and the feet carried it round through the land. The blessing of God on this day, and them that brought me the saint,[2] for it's grand hair you have [*she lowers her head, a little confused*], and soft skin, and eyes would make the saints, if they were dark awhile and seeing again, fall down out of the sky. [*He goes nearer to her.*] Hold up your head, Mary, the way I'll see it's richer I am than the great kings of the east. Hold up your head, I'm saying, for it's soon you'll be seeing me, and I not a bad one at all. [*He touches her and she starts up.*][3]

MOLLY BYRNE. Let you keep away from me, and not be soiling my chin.[4]

[PEOPLE *laugh loudly.*]

MARTIN DOUL [*bewildered*]. It's Molly's voice you have. . . .[5]

MOLLY BYRNE. Why wouldn't I have my own voice? Do you think I'm a ghost?

MARTIN DOUL. Which of you all is herself? [*He goes up to* BRIDE.] Is it you is Mary Doul? I'm thinking you're more the like of what they said. [*Peering at her.*] For you've yellow hair, and white skin, and it's the smell of my own turf is rising from your shawl. [*He catches her shawl.*]

BRIDE [*pulling away her shawl*]. I'm not your wife, and let you get out of my way.

[PEOPLE *laugh again.*]

MARTIN DOUL [*with misgiving, to another girl*]. Is it yourself it is? You're not so fine looking, but I'm thinking you'd do, with the grand nose you have, and your nice hands and your feet.

GIRL [*scornfully*]. I never seen any person that took me for blind, and a seeing woman, I'm thinking, would never wed the like of you.

[*She turns away, and the* PEOPLE *laugh once more, drawing back a little and leaving him on their left.*]

¹ The 1905 and Quinn editions read 'Try again, Martin, try again, and you'll be finding her yet.' The version given in the text follows the alterations Synge made in his own copy of the 1905 edition. Houghton TS. has written in in pencil: 'ALL—Try again Martin, you'll find her yet.' This alteration appears to be one of those made by Synge in rehearsal, so that the words 'spoke more lightly', as he put it in his letter to Meyerfield.

² The earliest drafts read [*looking round with suspicion*], instead of [*passionately*].

³ The 1905 and Quinn editions read mistakenly 'you're'.

⁴ Early drafts offer variations on Martin's diatribe: 'Ah, you're a fine lot the pack of you for a man to see with giggling weeping eyes, and your rotten teeth, and the whole of you scratching your hair . . . When I find herself I'll be walking off to the south and not be looking on the like of you more. . . .' and 'It's jealous you are maybe, a drift of giggling sluts the like of you, of a fine woman was called every place the wonder of the western world.'

⁵ One late draft reads instead: [*he pauses without hearing her*].

⁶ All versions but the 1905 edition place a question mark here.

⁷ One late version is more explicit in directions [MARTIN *wheels round so that they are face to face.*]

⁸ The various drafts indicate pauses at the end of Molly Byrne's and Martin Doul's speeches. To Meyerfeld Synge explains that 'the two of you' are Molly and Mary.

Synge tried different encounters between Martin and Mary Doul. In the first draft the saint leads Mary down to the people:

SAINT. The Lord is merciful to the smallest, and he has given back their clear sight to these two. [*The truth begins to dawn on* MARTIN *he staggers back among the crowd.*]

SAINT [*letting go her hand*]. Go down now to your husband, and let you be thanking God day & night saying prayers, and keeping your fasts and your feasts and your saying of your sins, and all the things are right before the Lord.

[MARY *draws a little near* TIMMY *the smith doubtfully but the people point her out* MARTIN *and the two of them meet face to face.*]

MARTIN. Oh you crew of cursed liars, you loafing tattling drunken swine. . . . etc.

The second draft uses Timmy as the intermediary:

TIMMY. Don't think bad of them laughing Martin Doul, your wife's in with the saint in the blessed church getting her sight. [MARTIN *turns round towards the door of the church just as* MARY *appears on the threshold, & comes down towards them with a silly simpering smile.*] Come down here to himself, Mary. He's been crying out for you and running round for & thinking to find hid with the girls. . . .

MARY. Himself's not Phil the fine one, let you not be telling me lies.

TIMMY. It's himself surely by the cross within the holy house of God. [MARTIN & MARY *stare at each other for an instant with horror.*]

⁹ All versions except the 1905 and Quinn editions place a comma after 'sight'.

¹⁰ The 1905 and Quinn editions place a comma after 'Lord God', thereby altering the rhythm. The second draft offers a slightly different version of Martin's speech: 'Let you never look down a deep pool Mary or you'll be drowning when you see the sight you'd see.'

¹¹ The second draft reads [MARY *is looking at her hair and the skin of her arms.*] Synge's own copy of the 1905 edition adds the word 'my' before 'big eyes'.

¹² An early version adds *by degrees*.

¹³ All TS. drafts place a comma after 'eyes'.

¹⁴ Of 'a wisp on any grey mare' Synge explained to Meyerfeld: 'a tangle of dirty hair on any grey horse—he is thinking of the dirty grey mountain ponies of Ireland and their knotted shaggy manes'.

PEOPLE [*jeeringly*]. Try again, Martin, try again, you'll find her yet.[1]

MARTIN DOUL [*passionately*].[2] Where is it you have her hidden away? Isn't it a black shame for a drove of pitiful beasts the like of you to be making game of me, and putting a fool's head on me the grand day of my life? Ah, you're thinking you're a fine lot, with your[3] giggling, weeping eyes, a fine lot to be making game of myself, and the woman I've heard called the great wonder of the west. . . .[4]

[*During this speech, which he gives with his back towards the church,* MARY DOUL *has come out with her sight cured, and come down towards the right with a silly simpering smile, till she is a little behind* MARTIN DOUL.]

MARY DOUL [*when he pauses*].[5] Which of you is Martin Doul?[6]

MARTIN DOUL [*wheeling round*].[7] It's her voice surely. . . . [*They stare at each other blankly.*]

MOLLY BYRNE [*to* MARTIN DOUL]. Go up now and take her under the chin and be speaking the way you spoke to myself. . . .

MARTIN DOUL [*in a low voice, with intensity*]. If I speak now, I'll speak hard to the two of you. . . .[8]

MOLLY BYRNE [*to* MARY DOUL]. You're not saying a word, Mary. What is it you think of himself, with the fat legs on him, and the little neck like a ram?

MARY DOUL. I'm thinking it's a poor thing when the Lord God gives you sight,[9] and puts the like of that man in your way.

MARTIN DOUL. It's on your two knees you should be thanking the Lord God you're not looking on yourself, for if it was yourself you seen, you'd be running round in a short while like the old screeching madwoman is running round in the glen.[10]

MARY DOUL [*beginning to realize herself*]. If I'm not so fine as some of them said, I have my hair, and my big eyes, and my white skin—[11]

MARTIN DOUL [*breaking out into a passionate cry*].[12] Your hair, and your big eyes,[13] is it? . . . I'm telling you there isn't a wisp on any grey mare[14] on the ridge of the world isn't finer than the dirty twist on your head. There isn't two eyes in any starving sow, isn't finer than the eyes you were calling blue like the sea.

¹ Several early drafts extend Martin's speech: 'the sea, and your skin, God help me, there isn't anything in the wide earth is the like of it at all. [*He turns away*.]'

The second draft varies the quarrel further:

MARTIN. And your skin ... My own hand God help me has a softer skin than your brow.

MARY. If an old woman seen the like of that hand and she picking sticks for the night she'd put it down under her pot and I'm thinking it's fast it would burn. [*To the people*.] We'd have a right to be going now for his lies are as limp as his back.

Again, the earliest draft implies a delight in the quarrel: 'Let you find a better lie than that or I won't stand hearing you at all.'

In Synge's own copy of the 1905 edition he has put round brackets around the words 'It's the devil ... of sows' and 'I'm saying', indicating a possible cut during rehearsal.

² The early drafts read 'that didn't ever rear a child for me itself'. In his notes to Meyerfeld Synge explained, '"rear" as used by Irish peasants includes the idea of "bringing forth" as well as "bringing up" and as is shown in Mary's next speech the first idea is really what is in their minds. Could you get a popular word with the two meanings? If not it would perhaps be best to make Martin say that she was never even fit to *have* a child.'

³ In Synge's own copy of the 1905 edition he has put round brackets around the words 'the larks, and the crows, and', indicating a possible cut.

⁴ A late draft gives the direction [*ending in a half-sob of passion*].

One TS. fragment gives Martin the following reply: 'Hell itself will be lonesome, Mary Doul, when you're put there sleeping at last, for a short sight of you would drive off the devils and the damned souls east and west through the world.'

⁵ To Meyerfeld Synge explains 'liefer' as 'rather'.

The early drafts, including *When the Blind See* TS., extend the quarrel; Synge then struck out the speeches, writing in the margin 'contrast':

MARTIN. If you'd ever reared a child wasn't a blind child it's a bad destroying fit it'd have got some day when it waked up sudden and seen you looking down on its head, a fit I'm thinking would have left it small sense for its life.

MARY. Maybe your own mother was the like of you and it's for that you've no sense in you this day, go on now don't be making a stir and calling the people to look on you, and you a speckled looking fright I'm saying should be hiding yourself away in a lonesome place and not putting up the old head you have till night would be coming in the hills. It'd be a better thing to be blind your whole life than looking on the like of you.

⁶ Earlier drafts reverse the speakers here, with Martin raising his stick first, and Mary retaliating by picking up a stone.

⁷ To Meyerfeld Synge explains 'row and the' as 'noise when the' etc.

⁸ It is not until a late draft marked 'D' that Timmy's speeches are introduced here. In all the early drafts Martin's plea occurs after Timmy's explanation to the saint.

MARY DOUL [*interrupting him*]. It's the devil cured you this day with your talking of sows; it's the devil cured you this day, I'm saying, and drove you crazy with lies.[1]

MARTIN DOUL. Isn't it yourself is after playing lies on me, ten years, in the day, and in the night, but what is that to you now the Lord God·has given eyes to me, the way I see you an old, wizendy hag, was never fit to rear a child to me itself.[2]

MARY DOUL. I wouldn't rear a crumpled whelp the like of you. It's many a woman is married with finer than yourself should be praising God if she's no child, and isn't loading the earth with things would make the heavens lonesome above, and they scaring the larks, and the crows, and[3] the angels passing in the sky.[4]

MARTIN DOUL. Go on now to be seeking a lonesome place where the earth can hide you away, go on now, I'm saying, or you'll be having men and women with their knees bled, and they screaming to God for a holy water would darken their sight, for there's no man but would liefer be blind a hundred years, or a thousand itself, than to be looking on your like.[5]

MARY DOUL [*raising her stick*]. Maybe if I hit you a strong blow you'd be blind again, and having what you want—

[SAINT *is seen in church-door with his head bent in prayer.*]

MARTIN DOUL [*raising his stick and driving* MARY DOUL *back towards left*]. Let you keep off from me now if you wouldn't have me strike out the little handful of brains you have about on the road.[6]

[*He is going to strike her, but* TIMMY *catches him by the arm.*]

TIMMY. Have you no shame to be making a great row and the[7] saint above saying his prayers?

MARTIN DOUL. What is it I care for the like of him? [*Struggling to free himself.*] Let me hit her one good one for the love of the Almighty God, and I'll be quiet after till I die.[8]

TIMMY [*shaking him*]. Will you whisht, I'm saying.

SAINT [*coming forward, centre*]. Are their minds troubled with joy, or is their sight uncertain the way it does often be the day a person is restored?

1 The earliest drafts emphasize the sermon more than the hymn to nature in the saint's remarks: 'May the Lord who has given you sight send a little sense into your heads. You'll be strange maybe, a short while, and queer in your thoughts, and you looking on the world, and then you'll get used to seeing, and begin doing your work, and thanking God, and being happy in the light, and the hope of the day when your inner eyes will be opened as these eyes were opened to see the great glory of the Lord. What are we at all but blind men going forward to wake up—the way I do be waking men with the holy water— when the time comes in the end? [*He frees* MARTIN *and* MARY.]'

2 In a letter to Synge, Yeats pointed out the similarity of the saint's phrasing to Shakespear's *King Lear*; the earlier drafts read 'an evil thing in a woman'.

3 The Quinn edition reads 'it's a great pity' etc.

4 All the TS. drafts read 'Annamoe' for 'Annagolan'.

TIMMY. It's too certain their sight is, holy father, and they're after making a great fight, because they're a pair of pitiful shows.

SAINT [*coming between them*]. May the Lord who has given you sight send a little sense into your heads, the way it won't be on your two selves you'll be looking—on two pitiful sinners of the earth—but on the splendour of the Spirit of God, you'll see an odd time shining out through the big hills, and steep streams falling to the sea. For if it's on the like of that you do be thinking, you'll not be minding the faces of men, but you'll be saying prayers and great praises, till you'll be living the way the great saints do be living, with little but old sacks, and skin covering their bones.[1] [*To* TIMMY.] Leave him go now, you're seeing he's quiet again. [TIMMY *frees* MARTIN DOUL.] And let you [SAINT *turns to* MARY DOUL] not be raising your voice, a bad thing[2] in a woman, but let the lot of you, who have seen the power of the Lord, be thinking on it in the dark night, and be saying to yourselves it's great[3] pity, and love he has, for the poor, starving people of Ireland. [*He gathers his cloak about him.*] And now the Lord send blessing to you all, for I am going on to Annagolan,[4] where there is a deaf woman, and to Laragh where there are two men without sense, and to Glenassil where there are children, blind from their birth, and then I'm going to sleep this night in the bed of the holy Kevin, and to be praising God, and asking great blessing on you all. [*He bends his head.*]

CURTAIN

¹ Earlier drafts read [*putting his head out of the door*].

² The earliest draft reads [*complainingly*].

³ Synge explains 'whacking your thorns' to Meyerfeld as 'hacking, chopping, or cutting your sticks (of hawthorn)'.

⁴ Synge strikes out of the first draft the expression 'or robbing your till'.

⁵ The first draft reads 'a lazy gorging drinking basking hog the like of you'. Later drafts add the direction [*He picks up a stick and breaks it across his knee.*]

⁶ On the back of an early draft Synge has scribbled the following exchange:

TIMMY. There were two of you that time begging scheming at the cross-roads of Grianan.

MARTIN. Herself is getting great wealth I'm told working for the widow O'Flinn, but it's never a smell of coppers I get from her at all.

⁷ To Meyerfeld Synge explains 'rake ashes from' as 'rake out ashes *from under* the forge'.

ACT II

Village roadside, on left the door of a forge, with broken wheels, etc., lying about. A well near centre, with board above it, and room to pass behind it. MARTIN DOUL *is sitting near forge, cutting sticks.*

TIMMY [*heard hammering inside forge, then calls*].[1] Let you make haste out there. . . . I'll be putting up new fires at the turn of day, and you haven't the half of them cut yet.

MARTIN DOUL [*gloomily*].[2] It's destroyed I'll be whacking your old thorns[3] till the turn of day, and I with no food in my stomach would keep the life in a pig. [*He turns towards the door.*] Let you come out here and cut them yourself if you want them cut, for there's an hour every day when a man has a right to his rest.

TIMMY [*coming out, with a hammer, impatiently*]. Do you want me to be driving you off again to be walking the roads? There you are now, and I giving you your food, and a corner to sleep, and money with it, and to hear the talk of you, you'd think I was after beating you, or stealing your gold.[4]

MARTIN DOUL. You'd do it handy, maybe, if I'd gold to steal.

TIMMY [*throws down hammer; picks up some of the sticks already cut, and throws them into door*]. There's no fear of your having gold, a lazy, basking fool the like of you.[5]

MARTIN DOUL. No fear, maybe, and I here with yourself, for it's more I got a while since, and I sitting blinded in Grianan, than I get in this place, working hard, and destroying myself, the length of the day.[6]

TIMMY [*stopping with amazement*]. Working hard? [*He goes over to him.*] I'll teach you to work hard, Martin Doul. Strip off your coat now, and put a tuck in your sleeves, and cut the lot of them, while I'd rake the ashes from the forge,[7] or I'll not put up with you another hour itself.

MARTIN DOUL [*horrified*]. Would you have me getting my death sitting out in the black wintery air with no coat on me at all?

¹ In one of the later drafts Synge questions and finally removes the following exchange:

TIMMY. Work hard I'm saying and it's soon you'll be warm.

MARTIN. I'm not a hot sweaty fellow the like of yourself, thanks be unto God, and if I am working as hard as ten men itself I'm froze to the bone.

² To Meyerfeld Synge explained 'a power of queer things' as 'a great many bad things'.

³ The early drafts omit the preceding speeches about Martin stripping off his coat and include variations on the following exchange instead:

TIMMY. There's no fear of your having gold, Martin Doul, a lazy growling hog the like of you. . . . I'm thinking it was right your wife did to leave you on the road, and not be breaking her heart trying to keep you in the decency of clothes and food.

MARTIN [*crying out with disgust*]. Oh the Lord of Heaven have mercy on us all is there nothing any person can say without dragging in a word of Mary Doul? . . . . You know rightly Timmy the smith, it was I drove her away, for it's little use a wife the like of her is the day a man can see.

TIMMY [*giving him another stick*]. What is it I care which one of you was driving the other, but let you cut that now and make haste Martin, and not be breaking my head with your talk.

MARTIN. That's a terrible hard stick, Timmy and it with knots in it as big as the red ones of your cheek. If I cut strong timber the like of that you'd have a right to give me a sight more than you're giving me now.

TIMMY. If you don't cease troubling me I'll make you cut the double and not pay you at all. You're eating alone I'm thinking ten times more than you're worth.

⁴ The 1905 and Quinn editions put a question mark here, but there is no justification for it from any of the TS. drafts.

⁵ Synge explains 'a poor thing' to Meyerfeld as 'a miserable thing'.

⁶ The 1905 and Quinn editions put commas after 'beastly day' and 'the blind', but the punctuation of the majority of the drafts indicates a different rhythm.

⁷ In his notes to Meyerfeld Synge explains this passage, 'until I begin to think it is a good fortune blind people have, for they do not see those grey clouds blowing over the hills, and they do not see people with their noses red, like your nose, and their eyes weeping and watering like your eyes, God help you, T. the Smith'.

⁸ An earlier draft reads [*who is working with some metal*].

⁹ The 'rough final' TS. reads [*marking spaces in his speech with savage blows of his chopper*].

¹⁰ The 1905 and Quinn editions place a comma after 'world', thereby halting the rhythm.

¹¹ To Meyerfeld Synge explains 'a hard thing' as 'a wretched thing', 'it should be' as 'it must be', and 'slipping each way' as 'slipping every way, in every direction'.

¹² To Meyerfeld Synge explains 'you'd have a right to be minding' as 'you ought to take care'.

¹³ The 1905 and Quinn editions read 'after a while. Mary Doul's dimming again I've heard them say—and I'm thinking' etc. The alteration adopted in the text is taken from Synge's MS. alterations in his own copy of the 1905 edition. In the draft Synge sent to Meyerfeld he has altered it slightly differently: 'You know very well that Mary Doul is getting dim again—and I think that if' etc., but this may be a 'translation' in line with his other explanations to his German translator.

TIMMY [*with authority*].[1] Strip it off now, or walk down upon the road.

MARTIN DOUL [*bitterly*]. Oh, God help me! [*He begins taking off his coat.*] I've heard tell you stripped the sheet from your wife and you putting her down into the grave, and that there isn't the like of you for plucking your living ducks, the short days, and leaving them running round in their skins, in the great rains and the cold. [*He tucks up his sleeves.*] Ah, I've heard a power of queer things[2] of yourself, and there isn't one of them I'll not believe from this day, and be telling to the boys.[3]

TIMMY [*pulling over a big stick*]. Let you cut that now, and give me a rest from your talk, for I'm not heeding you at all.[4]

MARTIN DOUL [*taking stick*]. That's a hard terrible stick, Timmy, and isn't it a poor thing[5] to be cutting strong timber the like of that, when it's cold the bark is, and slippy with the frost of the air?

TIMMY [*gathering up another armful of sticks*]. What way wouldn't it be cold, and it freezing since the moon was changed? [*He goes into forge.*]

MARTIN DOUL [*querulously, as he cuts slowly*]. What way, indeed, Timmy? For it's a raw, beastly day we do have each day, till I do be thinking it's well for the blind[6] don't be seeing the like of them grey clouds driving on the hill, and don't be looking on people with their noses red, the like of your nose, and their eyes weeping, and watering, the like of your eyes, God help you, Timmy the smith.[7]

TIMMY [*seen blinking in doorway*].[8] Is it turning now you are against your sight?

MARTIN DOUL [*very miserably*].[9] It's a hard thing for a man to have his sight, and he living near to the like of you [*he cuts a stick, and throws it away*], or wed with a wife [*cuts a stick*], and I do be thinking it should be a hard thing for the Almighty God to be looking on the world[10] bad days, and on men the like of yourself walking around on it, and they slipping each way in the muck.[11]

TIMMY [*with pot-hooks which he taps on anvil*]. You'd have a right to be minding,[12] Martin Doul, for it's a power the saint cured lose their sight after a while—it's well you know Mary Doul's dimming again—[13] and I'm thinking the Lord if He hears you making that talk will have little pity left for you at all.

¹ The words 'Dark day is it?' are added from Synge's MS. notations in his own copy of the 1905 edition. In the Houghton TS. this is added in pencil as well as the word 'so' between 'not' and 'dark' in the next sentence. In his notes to Meyerfeld Synge explains, 'I made this addition when the play was performed to emphasize the situation.'

² To Meyerfeld Synge explains this first sentence as 'Don't be troubling yourself trying to frighten me!'

³ 'Rough final' TS. adds *singing a tune*.

⁴ Intermediate drafts have Mary ignoring both of them: [MARY *goes on slowly gathering sticks or something towards left.*]

⁵ To Meyerfeld Synge explains 'you'd have a right' as 'you ought to'. The Houghton TS. reads 'you're not' instead of 'you are not'.

⁶ Earlier drafts give Mary Doul an alternate reply: 'There's enough said between the two of us for this life surely.'

⁷ To Meyerfeld Synge explains 'and she after going by' as 'when she has just gone by'.
⁸ These lines are taken from the MS. amendments Synge made in his own copy of the 1905 edition, which reads '. . . the way you'd see a priest going where there'd be a drunken man in the side ditch talking with a girl'. (See Introduction pp. xxiii–iv.)

Intermediate drafts continue Timmy's speech somewhat differently:

. . . and hasn't she a good right to go east or west and not be minding you at all, when she's getting her living picking sticks and green things for the widow O'Flinn?

MARTIN. She'd make a fool of the Lord I'm thinking with the tongue in her head.

TIMMY. She's a plain seemly woman, Martin Doul, and it's well she did surely, to walk off and not be breaking her heart trying to keep you in the decency of clothes and food.

MARTIN DOUL. There's not a bit of fear of me losing my sight, and if it's a dark day itself it's too well I see every wicked wrinkle you have round by your eye.

TIMMY [*looking at him sharply*]. Dark day is it?[1] The day's not dark since the clouds broke in the east.

MARTIN DOUL. Let you not be tormenting yourself trying to make me afeard.[2] You told me a power of bad lies the time I was blind, and it's right now for you to stop, and be taking your rest [MARY DOUL *comes in unnoticed on right with a sack filled with green stuff on her arm*], for it's little ease or quiet any person would get if the big fools of Ireland weren't weary at times. [*He looks up and sees* MARY DOUL.] Oh, glory be to God, she's coming again. [*He begins to work busily with his back to her.*[3]]

TIMMY [*amused, to* MARY DOUL, *as she is going by without looking at them*]. Look on him now, Mary Doul. You'd be a great one for keeping him steady at his work, for he's after idling, and blathering, to this hour from the dawn of day.

MARY DOUL [*stiffly*]. Of what is it you're speaking, Timmy the smith?[4]

TIMMY [*laughing*]. Of himself, surely. Look on him there, and he with the shirt on him ripping from his back. You'd have a right to come round this night, I'm thinking, and put a stitch into his clothes, for it's long enough you are not speaking one to the other.[5]

MARY DOUL. Let the two of you not torment me at all. [*She goes out left, with her head in the air.*[6]]

MARTIN DOUL [*stops work and looks after her*]. Well, isn't it a queer thing she can't keep herself two days without looking on my face?

TIMMY [*jeeringly*]. Looking on your face is it? And she after going by[7] with her head turned the way you'd see a sainted lady going where there'd be drunken people in the side ditch singing to themselves.[8] [MARTIN DOUL *gets up and goes to corner of forge, and looks out left.*] Come back here and don't mind her at all. Come back here, I'm saying, you've no call to be spying behind her since she went off, and left you, in place of breaking her heart, trying to keep you in the decency of clothes and food.

¹ A slip fastened to the draft marked 'rough final' makes Timmy ask Martin Doul, 'Is there a sight of Molly on the road?' to which Martin replies, 'She's above with her can passing the turn.'

² In early drafts Synge experiments with this transition: 'Let ⟨you⟩ be quiet now I'm saying for I'm destroyed with the queer job they're after giving and I all the morning inside sweating and sneezing in the forge.'

³ A late draft adds the words 'taking me into the big fire you have flaming like the furnaces of hell'.

⁴ To Meyerfeld Synge explains 'sneezing' as 'he has been sweating and snuffling and sneezing with a cold in his head (spoken in derision)'.

⁵ An earlier draft reads *with suppressed satisfaction*.

⁶ Until the 'rough final' draft Timmy says, 'I'm making pot-hooks, and holds for a candle, and a sight of things you do have when' etc.

⁷ An early draft adds *speaks with constraint*.

⁸ An intermediate draft is even more specific in insult: '. . . for if you did the children you'd have maybe would be terrible to see, the devil himself wouldn't take them down into his hell. And what at all would the Almighty do with them then?'

⁹ The 'rough final' draft reads [*seriously offended for the first time*].

MARTIN DOUL [*crying out indignantly*]. You know rightly, Timmy, it was myself drove her away.

TIMMY. That's a lie you're telling, yet it's little I care which one of you was driving the other, and let you walk back here I'm saying to your work.

MARTIN DOUL [*turning round*]. I'm coming, surely. [*He stops and looks out right, going a step or two towards centre.*]

TIMMY. On what is it you're gaping, Martin Doul?

MARTIN DOUL. There's a person walking above . . . It's Molly Byrne I'm thinking, coming down with her can.[1]

TIMMY. If she is itself let you not be idling this day, or minding her at all, and let you hurry with them sticks, for I'll want you in a short while to be blowing in the forge.[2] [*He throws down pot-hooks.*]

MARTIN DOUL [*crying out*]. Is it roasting me now, you'd be?[3] [*He turns back and sees pot-hooks; he takes them up.*] Pot-hooks? Is it over them you've been inside sneezing[4] and sweating since the dawn of day?

TIMMY [*resting himself on anvil, with satisfaction*[5]] I'm making a power of things[6] you do have when you're settling with a wife, Martin Doul, for I heard tell last night the saint'll be passing again in a short while, and I'd have him wed Molly with myself. . . . He'd do it, I've heard them say, for not a penny at all.

MARTIN DOUL [*lays down hooks and looks at him steadily*[7]]. Molly'll be saying great praises now to the Almighty God and he giving her a fine stout hardy man the like of you.

TIMMY [*uneasily*]. And why wouldn't she, if she's a fine woman itself?

MARTIN DOUL [*looking up right*]. Why wouldn't she indeed, Timmy? . . . . The Almighty God's made a fine match in the two of you, for if you went marrying a woman was the like of yourself you'd be having the fearfullest little children, I'm thinking, was ever seen in the world.[8]

TIMMY [*seriously offended*].[9] God forgive you, if you're an ugly man to be looking at, I'm thinking your tongue's worse than your view.

MARTIN DOUL [*hurt also*]. Isn't it destroyed with the cold I am, and if I'm ugly itself I never seen any one the like of you for dreepiness this

¹ The 'rough final' draft adds the direction [*he points to the right*].

² To Meyerfeld's queries Synge explains 'dreepiness' as 'the red-nosed look people have when they have a cold in the head!', 'above' as 'çà-haut', and 'shanty' as a 'tumbled-down old house'.

³ An early draft adds 'and you without a decent, lively word you could speak with a girl'. A late draft questions Martin's introductory words to this speech, suggesting as an alternative, 'If it's strong you're itself I never' etc.

⁴ To Meyerfeld Synge explains 'no call' as 'no right'.

⁵ An earlier draft includes the words 'of fine looks the way you'll see all the girls below going washing their necks at the door, and maybe' etc.

⁶ The dots to indicate a pause are taken from an earlier version. Synge 'translated' this scene between Martin and Molly for Meyerfeld (see Appendix D).

⁷ The word 'of' is omitted in the 1905 and Quinn editions and in the final TS., but it occurs in all other drafts and was added to the revised 1932 edition.

⁸ Synge added this comma to his final TS. in ink, indicating the rhythm of the line.

⁹ The first draft of this scene gives Molly a different reply: 'You've got a great wag in your tongue, Martin, from being so long in the dark.'

day, Timmy the smith, and I'm thinking now herself's coming above[1] you'd have a right to step up into your old shanty,[2] and give a rub to your face, and not be sitting there with your bleary eyes, and your big nose, the like of an old scarecrow stuck down upon the road.[3]

TIMMY [*looking up the road uneasily*]. She's no call[4] to mind what way I look, and I after building a house with four rooms in it above on the hill. [*He stands up.*] But it's a queer thing the way yourself and Mary Doul are after setting every person in this place, and up beyond to Rathvanna, talking of nothing, and thinking of nothing, but the way they do be looking in the face. [*Going towards forge.*] It's the devil's work you're after doing with your talk of fine looks,[5] and I'd do right, maybe, to step in, and wash the blackness from my eyes.

[*He goes into forge.* MARTIN DOUL *rubs his face furtively with the tail of his coat.* MOLLY BYRNE *comes on right with a water-can, and begins to fill it at the well.*]

MARTIN DOUL. God save you, Molly Byrne.

MOLLY BYRNE [*indifferently*]. God save you.

MARTIN DOUL. That's a dark, gloomy day, and the Lord have mercy on us all.

MOLLY BYRNE. Middling dark. . . .[6]

MARTIN DOUL. It's a power of[7] dirty days, and dark mornings, and shabby-looking fellows [*he makes a gesture over his shoulder*] we do have to be looking on when we have our sight, God help us, but there's one fine thing we have, to be looking on a grand, white, handsome girl, the like of you . . . and every time I set my eyes on you,[8] I do be blessing the saints, and the holy water, and the power of the Lord Almighty in the heavens above.

MOLLY BYRNE. I've heard the priests say it isn't looking on a young girl would teach many to be saying their prayers.[9] [*Baling water into her can with a cup.*]

MARTIN DOUL. It isn't many have been the way I was, hearing your voice speaking, and not seeing you at all.

¹ To Meyerfeld Synge explains 'coaxing' as 'flattering, wheedling or the like'.

² In his final TS. Synge added commas after 'itself, 'had', and 'hear it'.

³ The first draft adds the direction [*with a giggle*].

⁴ An early draft includes the following exchange:

MARTIN. It's little I care what place she is, or if it's the truth you tell her itself.

MOLLY. Have you no shame at all, Martin Doul of the wicket cruel way you've turned again your wife?

⁵ Early drafts included the phrase 'with silken clothes on them, and' etc. The final TS. which Synge prepared for the printers reads 'when I was roused up and I the like of the little children' etc. Quinn edition omits 'found' and includes 'was'. To Meyerfeld Synge explains 'speckled' as 'varied, beautiful'.

⁶ The final TS. does not include a comma after 'dripping'.

⁷ The first draft gives a different direction: [*giggling*].

MOLLY BYRNE. That should have been a queer time for an old wicked, coaxing[1] fool to be sitting there with your eyes shut, and not seeing a sight of girl or woman passing the road.

MARTIN DOUL. If it was a queer time itself, it was great joy and pride I had, the time I'd hear your voice speaking and you passing to Grianan [*beginning to speak with plaintive intensity*], for it's of many a fine thing your voice would put a poor dark fellow in mind, and the day I'd hear it,[2] it's of little else at all I would be thinking.

MOLLY BYRNE.[3] I'll tell your wife if you talk to me the like of that. . . . You've heard, maybe, she's below picking nettles for the widow O'Flinn, who took great pity on her when she seen the two of you fighting, and yourself putting shame on her at the crossing of the roads.[4]

MARTIN DOUL [*impatiently*]. Is there no living person can speak a score of words to me, or say 'God speed you', itself, without putting me in mind of the old woman, or that day either at Grianan?

MOLLY BYRNE [*with malice*]. I was thinking it should be a fine thing to put you in mind of the day you called the grand day of your life.

MARTIN DOUL. Grand day, is it? [*Plaintively again, throwing aside his work, and leaning towards her.*] Or a bad black day when I was roused up and found I was the like of the little children do be listening to the stories of an old woman, and do be dreaming after in the dark night that it's in grand houses of gold they are,[5] with speckled horses to ride, and do be waking again, in a short while, and they destroyed with the cold, and the thatch dripping[6] maybe, and the starved ass braying in the yard?

MOLLY BYRNE [*working indifferently*].[7] You've great romancing this day, Martin Doul. Was it up at the still you were at the fall of night?

MARTIN DOUL [*stands up, comes towards her, but stands at far—right— side of well*]. It was not, Molly Byrne, but lying down in a little rickety shed. . . . Lying down across a sop of straw, and I thinking I was seeing you walk, and hearing the sound of your step on a dry road, and hearing you again, and you laughing and making great talk in a high room with dry timber lining the roof. For it's a fine sound your voice has that time, and it's better I am, I'm thinking,

¹ The final TS. adds a comma after 'stump' also, which might have been added deliberately to indicate where the emphasis should occur. In an intermediate draft Synge adds the line, 'Is it setting off you are to make love with myself?' and writes underneath, 'Introduce love scene better'.

² The punctuation of the final TS. differs slightly in this speech from that of the 1905 and Quinn editions, which have a comma before 'maybe' and not after 'feeling love'.

³ In his 'translation' for Meyerfeld Synge noted an alteration in his text (see Appendix D). In Notebook 28 (1903–4) Synge makes Martin reply, 'It is not Molly since I seen yourself with real eyes. I'm shut now of caring for lies/ it's little call I have to be caring for lies.'

⁴ This version is copied from Synge's alterations in his own copy to the 1905 edition, which reads, 'It is not, Molly, and the Lord forgive us all. [*He passes behind her and comes near her left.*] For I've heard tell' etc.

⁵ In his notes to Meyerfeld Synge explains that 'Cahir Iveraghig' means 'Cahir city of Iveragh' and adds that the town is Cahirciveen in Kerry. 'Reeks' he explains as 'mountains, the Macgillicuddy's *Reeks* in Kerry, near the Cork border, are well ⟨known⟩ mountains in Ireland'.

⁶ Synge tried several extensions of this speech in earlier drafts:

MOLLY [*looking up at him*]. What is it you're at, Martin Doul. Are you coming over to look on your own face in the well?

MARTIN. I'm not thinking on my own face but on your two feet and your shoes for I've been hearing great talk of towns beyond in Kerry and Cork that have sweet air and warm sun and light is a great wonder shining in the sky.

MOLLY [*stretching out her feet insolently*]. And is it my shoes you're begging to go searching for light?

MARTIN. It is not, Molly, but light's a grand thing for a man ever was blind, or a woman, the Lord forgive her, with a skin on her and a face the like of you [*pause she covers her feet; Martin takes courage*]—and we'd have a right to go off to them towns of the south . . . .

The TS. marked 'rough final' includes the following:

MARTIN. It is not Molly, and the Lord forgive us all. [*He passes behind her and draws near her left with shy uncertainty.*]—for I've heard tell there are lands beyond in Cahir Iveraghig and the Reeks of Cork with warm sun in them and fine light in the sky, and light's a fine thing for a man ever was blind or a woman God forgive her, with a fine neck maybe, and a skin on her the like of you. . . . [*He pauses shyly.*]

MOLLY. Let you not be stopping, Martin Doul, you're making fine talk surely.

MARTIN. It's making game of me you'd be.

MOLLY. What way would I make game of you, and you talking nice simple quality talk of Cahir Iveraghig and the Reeks of Cork?

MARTIN [*with bitter intensity*]. I was coming to say light's a grand thing for a man ever was blind or a woman, God forgive her, with a fine. . . .

⁷ The early drafts extend this speech: 'and getting our bread with telling stories and singing songs, or I'd let on again that I'm blind, and there won't be a sign at all of Timmy the smith with his cracked tongue or of the old woman walking after me with her black look and she not speaking at all. . . .'

⁸ An early draft reads instead [*pleased but indignant*].

⁹ The final TS. Synge prepared for the printers has no commas after 'Well' or 'show', although they appear in the 1905 and Quinn editions.

¹⁰ The final TS. has no commas around 'maybe', although the 1905 and Quinn editions have.

¹¹ All but the final drafts indicate a pause or dash at the end of Martin's speech.

lying down, the way a blind man does be lying, than to be sitting here in the grey light, taking hard words of Timmy the smith.

MOLLY BYRNE [*looking at him with interest*]. It's queer talk you have if it's a little, old, shabby stump of a man you are itself.[1]

MARTIN DOUL. I'm not so old as you do hear them say.

MOLLY BYRNE. You're old, I'm thinking, to be talking that talk with a girl.

MARTIN DOUL [*despondingly*]. It's not a lie you're telling maybe, for it's long years I'm after losing from the world, feeling love, and talking love,[2] with the old woman, and I fooled the whole while with the lies of Timmy the smith.

MOLLY BYRNE [*half invitingly*]. It's a fine way you're wanting to pay Timmy the smith. . . . And it's not his *lies* you're making love to this day, Martin Doul.

MARTIN DOUL. It is not, Molly, but with the good looks of yourself[3] [*passing behind her and coming near her left*], for if it's old I am maybe I've heard tell[4] there are lands beyond in Cahir Iveraghig and the Reeks of Cork[5] with warm sun in them, and fine light in the sky.[6] [*Bending towards her.*] And light's a grand thing for a man ever was blind, or a woman, with a fine neck, and a skin on her the like of you, the way we'd have a right to go off this day till we'd have a fine life passing abroad through them towns of the south, and we telling stories, maybe, or singing songs at the fairs.[7]

MOLLY BYRNE [*turning round half amused, and looking him over from head to foot*].[8] Well isn't it a queer thing when your own wife's after leaving you because you're a pitiful show[9] you'd talk the like of that to me?

MARTIN [*drawing back a little, hurt, but indignant*]. It's a queer thing maybe[10] for all things is queer in the world. [*In a low voice with peculiar emphasis.*] But there's one thing I'm telling you, if she walked off away from me, it wasn't because of seeing me, and I no more than I am, but because I was looking on her with my two eyes, and she getting up, and eating her food, and combing her hair, and lying down for her sleep.[11]

¹ Earlier drafts read [*with surprise*].

² A late draft adds the direction *and takes courage*.

³ The 1905 and Quinn editions and the 1932 revised edition read 'It's a few', but there is no indication of this in any of the drafts, and the additional article alters the rhythm of the speech.

⁴ The 1905 and Quinn editions and the 1932 revised edition begin a new sentence with 'Though it's' etc., but there is no indication of this in the TS. prepared for the printers, and the emphatic break affects the climax of the speech.

⁵ In his own copy Synge made this alteration to the 1905 edition, which read: '[*Quickly, with low, furious intensity.*] It's the truth I'm telling you. [*He puts his hand on her shoulder and shakes her.*] And you'd do right not to marry a man' etc.

⁶ Synge explained the words 'a man looking on bad days' etc. to Meyerfeld as meaning 'a man who has been for a long time looking at the bad weather and ugliness, which Martin now finds in the world, looking on = looking at, in this dialect.'

⁷ An earlier draft adds the words, 'and you like a south cloud would be turning red in the grey light till you'd see it flame with the dawn'.

⁸ The final TS. adds the phrase 'all days' after 'facing him' but this seems to destroy the parallelism and urgency of the speech.

⁹ All the drafts except the 1905 and Quinn editions add dots here to indicate a pause.

¹⁰ All the drafts except the 1905 and Quinn editions have dots here instead of an exclamation mark.

¹¹ This version follows the MS. alterations Synge made in his own copy to the 1905 edition, which reads: 'Let you not be fooling. Come along now the little path through the trees.'

MOLLY [*interested, off her guard*].[1] Wouldn't any married man you'd have be doing the like of that?

MARTIN DOUL [*seizing the moment that he has her attention*[2]]. I'm thinking by the mercy of God it's few sees anything but them is blind for a space. [*With excitement*.] It's[3] few sees the old women rotting for the grave, and it's few sees the like of yourself [*he bends over her*],[4] though it's shining you are, like a high lamp, would drag in the ships out of the sea.

MOLLY BYRNE [*shrinking away from him*]. Keep off from me, Martin Doul.

MARTIN DOUL [*quickly, with low, furious intensity*.[5] *He puts his hand on her shoulder and shakes her*]. You'd do right, I'm saying, not to marry a man is after looking out a long while on the bad days of the world,[6] for what way would the like of him have fit eyes to look on yourself, when you rise up in the morning and come out of the little door you have above in the lane,[7] the time it'd be a fine thing if a man would be seeing, and losing his sight, the way he'd have your two eyes facing him,[8] and he going the roads, and shining above him, and he looking in the sky, and springing up from the earth, the time he'd lower his head, in place of the muck that seeing men do meet all roads spread on the world.

MOLLY BYRNE [*who has listened half-mesmerized, starting away*]. It's the like of that talk you'd hear from a man would be losing his mind.

MARTIN DOUL [*going after her, passing to her right*]. It'd be little wonder if a man near the like of you would be losing his mind. Put down your can now, and come along with myself, for I'm seeing you this day, seeing you, maybe, the way no man has seen you in the world. [*He takes her by the arm and tries to pull her away softly to the right*.] Let you come on now, I'm saying, to the lands of Iveragh and the Reeks of Cork, where you won't set down the width of your two feet and not be crushing fine flowers, and making sweet smells in the air. . . .[9]

MOLLY BYRNE [*laying down can; trying to free herself*]. Leave me go, Martin Doul. . . .[10] Leave me go, I'm saying!

MARTIN DOUL. Come along now, let you come on the little path through the trees.[11]

¹ Intermediate drafts give versions of the following exchange here:

MOLLY [*putting up her hand to keep him off, calling out*]. Timmy the smith. . . . Timmy the smith. . . .

MARTIN. Are you going to make game of him, and his talk of having you wed?

TIMMY [*coming out of the forge*]. Is that where you are, Martin Doul, and you after leaving my sticks? [*He picks up an old coat and a bundle in a red handkerchief from the place where* MARTIN *had been sitting, and throws them out on the road.*]—I won't be destroying myself any more giving jobs to the like of you. . . . There's your old rubbish now, let you take it up for it's all you have, and walk off through the world. . . .

MARTIN [*to* MOLLY *in a whisper*]. Do you see that Molly it's long enough I am in this place and I'm ready now for the south, but it's more than my old rubbish I'm thinking will go along with me now.

MOLLY. Did ever you hear that them that loses their sight, loses their senses along with it, Timmy the smith?

² Earlier drafts have Mary Doul entering here, gathering nettles with gloved hands from the hedge at the bottom of the stage.

³ The final draft expands the directions here: [*He walks back left and picks up* MARTIN'S *coat and stick; some things fall out of pocket of coat; he stoops and gathers them up.* MARY *passes to right of* MARTIN *and* MOLLY, *with her head down but watching them intently.*]

⁴ The 1905 and Quinn editions place a comma after 'I', thereby destroying the rhythm.

⁵ The early drafts vary this speech somewhat: 'Let you not put shame on me before herself and the old smith. There's a cloud coming over me this moment, and let it not be that the like of that wicket grin I see in your ⟨eyes⟩ is the last thing I get my sight on in the mortal earth. Let you not be that cruel though I'm thinking fine women and foul women there isn't much choice from the lot of you—[*he looks across at his wife who is standing beside* TIMMY *the smith*].'

⁶ Earlier drafts add the words 'and there's no blackness but the blackness of your soul'. To Meyerfeld Synge explains 'a sight' as 'a great deal'.

⁷ To Meyerfeld Synge explains 'an old wretched road woman' as 'a wretched old beggar woman'.

MOLLY BYRNE [*crying out towards forge*]. Timmy. . . . Timmy the smith. . . . [TIMMY *comes out of forge, and* MARTIN DOUL *lets her go.* MOLLY BYRNE, *excited and breathless, pointing to* MARTIN DOUL.] Did ever you hear that them that loses their sight loses their sense along with it, Timmy the smith?[1]

TIMMY [*suspicious, but uncertain*]. He's no sense, surely, and he'll be having himself driven off this day from where he's good sleeping, and feeding, and wages for his work.

MOLLY BYRNE [*as before*]. He's a bigger fool than that, Timmy. Look on him now, and tell me if that isn't a grand fellow to think he's only to open his mouth to have a fine woman, the like of me, running along by his heels.

[MARTIN DOUL *recoils towards centre, with his hand to his eyes;* MARY DOUL *is seen on left coming forward softly.*][2]

TIMMY [*with blank amazement*]. Oh, the blind is wicked people, and it's no lie. But he'll walk off this day and not be troubling us more. [*He walks back left and picks up* MARTIN DOUL'*s coat and stick; some things fall out of coat pocket, which he gathers up again.*][3]

MARTIN DOUL [*turns round, sees* MARY DOUL, *whispers to* MOLLY BYRNE *with imploring agony*]. Let you not put shame on me, Molly, before herself and the smith. Let you not put shame on me and I[4] after saying fine words to you, and dreaming . . . dreams . . . in the night. [*He hesitates, and looks round the sky.*] Is it a storm of thunder is coming, or the last end of the world? [*He staggers towards* MARY DOUL, *tripping slightly over tin can.*] The heavens is closing, I'm thinking, with darkness and great trouble passing in the sky. [*He reaches* MARY DOUL, *and seizes her with both his hands—with a frantic cry.*] Is it the darkness of thunder is coming, Mary Doul? Do you see me clearly with your eyes?[5]

MARY DOUL [*snatches her arm away, and hits him with empty sack across the face*]. I see you a sight too clearly, and let you keep off from me now.[6]

MOLLY BYRNE [*clapping her hands*]. That's right, Mary. That's the way to treat the like of him is after standing there at my feet and asking me to go off with him, till I'd grow an old wretched road woman[7] the like of yourself.

¹ The earliest draft directs Mary Doul here, not Martin: [*She puts her hand up to her eyes and passes out down the stage. Sits down on a stone to watch.*]

² To Meyerfeld Synge explains 'does be soon turning the like of a handful of thin grass' as 'that soon turns the colour of a handful of thin grass etc'.

³ In his own copy Synge has written this version, differing considerably from the 1905 edition which reads: 'Ah, it's a better thing to have a simple, seemly face, the like of my face, for two score years, or fifty itself, than to be setting fools mad a short while, and then to be turning a thing would drive off the little children from your feet.'
The TS. marked 'rough final' prefaces this sentence with the direction [*threateningly*].

⁴ An intermediate draft adds the sentence, 'Was there ever the like of the two of them for making a man's thought dark and troubled in his head. . . .'

⁵ In his own copy of the 1905 edition Synge has altered the word 'for' to 'and'.
⁶ Houghton TS. has dashes instead of commas round 'if it's seeing or blind you are itself'.
⁷ To Meyerfeld Synge explains 'welt' as 'blow' and 'easy' as 'quiet'. During successive drafts the word 'clout' was changed to 'blow' and finally to 'welt'.

⁸ Intermediate drafts read 'The saint's coming again in a short while, and when he comes he'll be marrying Molly Byrne with myself, and it's well you know a girl is going to marry the like of me has no call to be standing out by the side of a ditch hearing bad talk from a raggy looking vagabond (thief) is setting off to be walking the world.'

⁹ To Meyerfeld Synge explains 'It's making game of you she is' as 'She is making a fool of you', and 'raise your voice' as 'speak out loudly, cry out'.

¹⁰ Earlier drafts add 'he's after soiling my shawl' or 'would you have him tearing my dress?'

MARY DOUL [*defiantly*]. When the skin shrinks on your chin, Molly Byrne, there won't be the like of you for a shrunk hag in the four quarters of Ireland. . . . It's a fine pair you'd be, surely!

[MARTIN DOUL *is standing at back right centre, with his back to the audience*].[1]

TIMMY [*coming over to* MARY DOUL]. Is it no shame you have to let on she'd ever be the like of you?

MARY DOUL. It's them that's fat and flabby do be wrinkled young, and that whitish yellowy hair she has does be soon turning the like of a handful of thin grass[2] you'd see rotting, where the wet lies, at the north of a sty. [*Turning to go out on right.*] Ah, isn't it a grand thing for the like of your make to be setting fools mad a short while, and then to be turning a thing will drive off the little children from your feet.[3]

[*She goes out.* MARTIN DOUL *has come forward again, mastering himself, but uncertain.*]

TIMMY. Oh, God protect us, Molly, from the words of the blind.[4] [*He throws down* MARTIN DOUL's *coat and stick.*] There's your old rubbish now, Martin Doul, and let you take it up, for it's all you have, and walk off through the world, and[5] if ever I meet you coming again, if it's seeing or blind you are itself,[6] I'll bring out the big hammer and hit you a welt with it will leave you easy[7] till the judgement day.

MARTIN DOUL [*rousing himself with an effort*]. What call have you to talk the like of that with myself?

TIMMY [*pointing to* MOLLY BYRNE]. It's well you know what call I have. It's well you know a decent girl, I'm thinking to wed, has no right to have her heart scalded with hearing talk—and queer, bad talk, I'm thinking—from a raggy-looking fool the like of you.[8]

MARTIN DOUL [*raising his voice*]. It's making game of you she is, for what seeing girl would marry with yourself? Look on him, Molly, look on him, I'm saying, for I'm seeing him still, and let you raise your voice,[9] for the time is come, and bid him go up into his forge and be sitting there by himself, sneezing, and sweating, and he beating pot-hooks till the judgement day. [*He seizes her arm again.*]

MOLLY BYRNE. Keep him off from me, Timmy![10]

¹ All the early drafts, including the TS. marked 'rough final', read 'and put the curse of Christ on his tongue?' Synge explains to Meyerfeld, '*Hell's long curse* can hardly be translated literally. It means a great curse, or the great curse of Hell. Any strong peasant curse would do.'

² Earlier drafts make Molly's speech even more vindictive: 'or down into the town where the people do be huddled like rats for it's with the like of them you'll get a true mate, and I'd have you learn the way' etc.

³ To Meyerfeld Synge explains 'it's destroyed I am with' as 'I am sick of the' etc., and 'it's near afeard I am' as 'I am almost afraid'.

⁴ Earlier drafts are even more explicit: 'with no strength in me to hurt a hair of their heads. They're sitting in there on the block I'm thinking with the fire lepping and the light in their eyes, herself talking sweet talk to Timmy and he sitting up scratching his leg maybe or biting his thumb and he not knowing rightly what kind of a word a man could speak to a girl. And I'm destroyed God help me with my sight gone from me and I not knowing itself what place my stick is or the old rags of my coat. . . .'

⁵ To Meyerfeld Synge explains 'the way I'll see them after' as 'so that I will see them afterwards'.

⁶ All earlier drafts add the direction [*raising his hand towards the door*].

⁷ To Meyerfeld Synge explains 'but the like of Heaven itself', etc. as 'but it will be Heaven, and I will take good care that the Lord Almighty does not know'. In a letter dated 1 September 1905 he adds the further comment, 'At the end of Act II you are right in supposing that Martin wishes to deceive God, his theology—folk-theology—is always vague and he fears that even in Hell God might plague him in some new way if he knew what an unholy joy Martin has found for himself.' An earlier letter, 21 August 1905, throws further light on the psychology of the play: 'I agree with you that the way I have treated their going blind again is open to criticism, but if I had taken the motive that their blindness was a punishment, I would have got out of the spirit of the play, or have fallen into needless complications or commonplaces so I passed lightly over the matter as it was not really essential to what is most important in the play.' Both these letters to Meyerfeld were reprinted in the *Yale Review*, July 1924 (see Appendix C).

TIMMY [*pushing* MARTIN DOUL *aside*]. Would you have me strike you, Martin Doul? Go along now after your wife, who's a fit match for you, and leave Molly with myself.

MARTIN DOUL [*despairingly*]. Won't you raise your voice, Molly, and lay hell's long curse on his tongue?¹

MOLLY BYRNE [*on* TIMMY's *left*]. I'll be telling him it's destroyed I am with the sight of you and the sound of your voice. Go off now after your wife, and if she beats you again, let you go after the tinker girls is above running the hills, or down among the sluts of the town, and you'll learn one day, maybe,² the way a man should speak with a well-reared civil girl the like of me. [*She takes* TIMMY *by the arm.*] Come up now into the forge till he'll be gone down a bit on the road, for it's near afeard I am³ of the wild look he has come in his eyes.

[*She goes into the forge.* TIMMY *stops in the doorway.*]

TIMMY. Let me not find you out here again, Martin Doul. [*He bares his arm.*] It's well you know Timmy the smith has great strength in his arm, and it's a power of things it has broken a sight harder than the old bone of your skull. [*He goes into the forge and pulls the door after him.*]

MARTIN DOUL [*stands a moment with his hand to his eyes*]. And that's the last thing I'm to set my sight on in the life of the world, the villainy of a woman and the bloody strength of a man. Oh, God, pity a poor blind fellow the way I am this day with no strength in me to do hurt to them at all.⁴ [*He begins groping about for a moment, then stops.*] Yet if I've no strength in me I've a voice left for my prayers, and may God blight them this day, and my own soul the same hour with them, the way I'll see them after,⁵ Molly Byrne and Timmy the smith, the two of them on a high bed, and they screeching in hell. . . .⁶ It'll be a grand thing that time to look on the two of them; and they twisting and roaring out, and twisting and roaring again, one day and the next day, and each day always and ever. It's not blind I'll be that time, and it won't be hell to me I'm thinking, but the like of Heaven itself, and it's fine care I'll be taking the Lord Almighty doesn't know.⁷ [*He turns to grope out.*]

CURTAIN

¹ To Meyerfeld Synge explains 'and hard set' as 'I'll find it hard' and 'himself' to mean 'the man of the house' or 'my husband' when it is used by a wife. The 1905 and Quinn editions omit the comma after 'I'll be now' and read 'pass me by' for 'passing me by', unlike all the drafts and the 1932 edition.

² It was not until after the fourth complete draft of the act that Synge thought of adding this speech and gesture about her hair.

³ To Meyerfeld Synge explains 'letting on' as 'pretending'.

⁴ The 1905 and Quinn editions break this speech with dashes after 'Molly Byrne' but the drafts do not indicate this intention, nor does it seem necessary at this point in Martin's speech. To Meyerfeld Synge explains that the spelling 'wicket' in the 1905 edition is simply a misprint for 'wicked'; it is corrected in the 1932 edition.

⁵ In the two earliest drafts of this opening scene Synge had Martin Doul groping in first, with variations on the following conversation:

MARTIN [*groaning*]. Well this time I'm destroyed surely. . . . I haven't a bit to eat and I haven't my handiness about me at all with cutting sticks and breaking stones and doing dirty jobs for all the rabble in the glen. . . . I'm an ugly dirty old divil I didn't know it at all but from this day I'll have no life in me to make the quality laugh and they passing the way, or stretch out their hands with a bit of silver to me and they passing the way. . . . What am I now but an old wretched whining crimpled hog . . . The divil mend Mary Doul, for putting lies on me, and letting on she was grand. The divil mend the old saint for making me see it was lies. The divil mend Timmy the smith for killing me with hard work and keeping me starving with an empty windy stomach in me in the day and in the night . . and ten thousand divils take the soul of Molly Byrne . . Ten thousand [*he lies back and shuts his eyes*] take her beautiful face, & her sweet voice, and her light step the time you'd see her passing the bog on the big stones and it raining a week. There's Timmy the dullest senseless dummy you'd mind in ten townlands of the world and it's him she went to talk to and wouldn't look at all upon the like of me. . . . Ah there's a time coming you'll not run from ⟨me⟩ Molly Byrne and herself was right that you'll be the foulest hag of all when you'll be old. . . . [*sleepily*] It's a sleepy thing when you've no hope left in you at all. [*He goes to sleep.*]

MARY [*comes in on the other side groping her way slowly*]. God help me . . . Ah God help me, the blackness wasn't so black at all the other time as it is this time, and it is hard set I'll be to make my living, working alone when it's few are passing and the days are short. [*She sits down and begins shredding rushes.*] It's long the days'll be now sitting up here by myself, and my hands are destroyed picking nettles for the Widow Brady and her turkeys God reward them all. [*She goes on working for a moment.*]

MARTIN [*moves half-wakening*]. You're an ugly dirty old divil Martin Doul but you didn't know it at all.

MARY [*starts violently*]. It's Martin's voice but did ever anyone hear him saying what wasn't a lie.

MARTIN [*sitting up*]. Mary Doul herself was a dirty wrinkled old beast but maybe she was better than no one at all. . . .

ACT III

Same as in first Act, but gap in centre has been filled with briars, or branches of some sort. MARY DOUL, *blind again, gropes her way in on left, and sits as before. She has a few rushes with her. It is an early spring day.*

MARY DOUL [*mournfully*]. Ah, God help me . . . God help me, the blackness wasn't so black at all the other time as it is this time, and it's destroyed I'll be now, and hard set to get my living working alone, when it's few are passing and the winds are cold. [*She begins shredding rushes.*] I'm thinking short days will be long days to me from this time, and I sitting here, not seeing a blink, or hearing a word, and no thought in my mind but long prayers that Martin Doul'll get his reward in a short while for the villainy of his heart. It's great jokes the people'll be making now, I'm thinking, and they passing me by, pointing their fingers, maybe, and asking what place is himself,[1] the way it's no quiet or decency I'll have from this day till I'm an old woman with long white hair and it twisting from my brow. [*She fumbles with her hair,[2] and then seems to hear something. Listens for a moment.*] There's a queer slouching step coming on the road. . . . God help me, he's coming surely.

[*She stays perfectly quiet.* MARTIN DOUL *gropes in on right, blind also.*]

MARTIN DOUL [*gloomily*]. The devil mend Mary Doul for putting lies on me, and letting on[3] she was grand. The devil mend the old saint for letting me see it was lies. [*He sits down near her.*] The devil mend Timmy the smith for killing me with hard work, and keeping me with an empty windy stomach in me, in the day and in the night. Ten thousand devils mend the soul of Molly Byrne [MARY DOUL *nods her head with approval*] and the bad wicked[4] souls is hidden in all the women of the world. [*He rocks himself, with his hand over his face.*] It's lonesome I'll be from this day, and if living people is a bad lot, yet Mary Doul herself, and she a dirty, wrinkled-looking hag, was better maybe to be sitting along with than no one at all.[5] I'll be getting my death now, I'm thinking, sitting alone in the cold air, hearing the night coming, and the blackbirds flying round in the

¹ All the TSS. read 'your dying oath on Jesus Christ'.

² In his own copy Synge has altered the 1905 edition from *face* to *hand*, and in his notes to Meyerfeld has also noted the alteration.

³ An intermediate draft has Martin stumbling *in among some branches of trees*.

⁴ Earlier drafts add the direction [*ironically*].
⁵ To Meyerfeld Synge explains 'There's a' as 'voilà in this passage' and 'a space' as 'a long time!'
⁶ An early draft adds the following discussion:

MARTIN [*sitting down*]. Maybe I'll be much the like of yourself, and that's a hard case surely, . . . You'll have no more talk from this day I'm thinking that you're the finest woman of the east.

MARY. If I don't I won't be hearing you talk either of your being a fine fellow with big arms on you and grand eyes. . . .

MARTIN. I won't surely. It's a power of joy we're after losing by the work of the saint and little gain we have from him at all.

MARY. There's no gain at all you're meaning. . . .

MARTIN. There's one thing I⟨'m⟩ after learning . . . I know the way in now to the back yard of the smith. . . . and where it is he has great heaps of turf piled up into the sky for keeping fires in the forge I know my way in there I⟨'m⟩ saying and on the dark windy nights I'll be finding that way I'm thinking and we won't be shivering at all from this day, and that's thanks to the saint. . . .

MARY. Fire is a grand thing. . . .

MARTIN. But it'll not make up for what we're after losing and it's no lie I'd liefer shiver every night out in the cold if I thought I had a grand woman the way I was thinking yourself sitting at my side than be in great comfort and warmth, with a thing beside me the like of what you are as I've seen you now. . . .

⁷ To Meyerfeld Synge explains 'bearing in mind' as 'remembering'.

briars crying to themselves, the time you'll hear one cart getting off a long way in the east, and another cart getting off a long way in the west, and a dog barking maybe, and a little wind turning the sticks. [*He listens and sighs heavily.*] I'll be destroyed sitting alone and losing my senses this time the way I'm after losing my sight, for it'd make any person afeard to be sitting up hearing the sound of his breath [*he moves his feet on the stones*], and the noise of his feet, when it's a power of queer things do be stirring, little sticks breaking, and the grass moving [MARY DOUL *half sighs, and he turns on her in horror*] till you'd take your dying oath on sun and moon[1] a thing was breathing on the stones. [*He listens towards her for a moment, then starts up nervously, and gropes about for his stick.*] I'll be going now, I'm thinking, but I'm not sure what place my stick's in, and I'm destroyed with terror and dread. [*He touches her hand as he is groping about and cries out.*] There's a thing with a cold living hand[2] on it sitting up at my side. [*He turns to run away, but misses his path and stumbles in against the wall.*[3]] My road is lost on me now! Oh, merciful God, set my foot on the path this day, and I'll be saying prayers morning and night, and not straining my ear after young girls, or doing any bad thing till I die—

MARY DOUL [*indignantly*]. Let you not be telling lies to the Almighty God.

MARTIN DOUL. Mary Doul is it? [*Recovering himself with immense relief.*] Is it Mary Doul, I'm saying?

MARY DOUL.[4] There's a sweet tone in your voice I've not heard for a space.[5] You're taking me for Molly Byrne, I'm thinking.

MARTIN DOUL [*coming towards her, wiping sweat from his face*]. Well, sight's a queer thing for upsetting a man. It's a queer thing to think I'd live to this day to be fearing the like of you, but if it's shaken I am for a short while, I'll soon be coming to myself.

MARY DOUL. You'll be grand then, and it's no lie.

MARTIN DOUL [*sitting down shyly, some way off*]. You've no call to be talking, for I've heard tell you're as blind as myself.[6]

MARY DOUL. If I am I'm bearing in mind[7] I'm married to a little dark stump of a fellow looks the fool of the world, and I'll be bearing in mind from this day the great hullabaloo he's after making from hearing a poor woman breathing quiet in her place.

¹ The 1905 and Quinn editions print this as one word, 'awhile'. A draft in Notebook 31 (April–May 1904) entitled Act III. B. 4. reads:

MARTIN. If yourself had a fright the like of that you'd have turned up your toes in the air, I'm thinking and begun screeching out the way you'd hear a pig screeching would have four men driving in a ring through the slit of its nose—

MARY. I wish to God four men would ⟨drive⟩ in a ring through the gritty bit of your tongue Martin Doul for every time I hear your voice speaking I do be bearing in mind I'm married with a little dark stumpy fellow looks the fool of the world.

MARTIN. You'd have a right to be bearing in mind that time what you seen some day when you looked down into a well or a pool maybe when there'd be no wind stirring and a clear light in the sky.

² To Meyerfeld Synge explains 'minding' as 'remember'.

³ The first draft has Mary looking into 'a bit of a bowl of tin', the second draft into 'a big glass was done in the town', and the third draft 'into the pond of Rathvanna'.

⁴ In his final draft Synge writes in an exclamation mark here and alters the direction to [*laughing sadly*].

⁵ To Meyerfeld Synge explains 'the length of that' as 'so far as that!' The 1932 edition places a comma after 'senses', but there is no comma in any of the drafts or in the 1905 and Quinn editions.

⁶ The 'rough final' draft has an exclamation mark added in ink by Synge. The 1905 and Quinn editions begin a new sentence after 'in a word', but this break is not justified in any of the drafts.

⁷ All the TS. drafts have a question mark at the end of Martin's speech. The drafts and the 1932 edition add a comma after 'telling'.

⁸ The 1905 and Quinn editions have no punctuation here; the 1932 edition places commas around 'maybe'; all the drafts, however, place the break after 'grey', thus making the next words one phrase. The third draft includes a further exchange:

MARY. Did ever you hear tell of Kitty Bawn?

MARTIN. Is it the woman with the white hair on her they were coming to look at the time she was four score years or beyond it, from France, and Spain, and the Islands of the north?

MARY. That's herself.

MARTIN. Was it her you seen in the pool of Rathvanna?

MARY [*complacently*]. I'll tell you what it is I seen. . . . I seen my hair will be grey, or white maybe. . . .

⁹ Synge explains 'the like of me' to Meyerfeld as 'anything to equal me, anything so fine as myself'.

¹⁰ To Meyerfeld Synge explains 'cute thinking' as 'clever'.

¹¹ The 'rough final' draft adds the direction [*He draws nearer to her.*]

¹² Synge explains 'the young men itself' to Meyerfeld as 'even the young men', and 'Kitty Bawn' as 'White Kitty'.

¹³ The 1932 edition alters this question mark to an exclamation mark, but there is no indication of this in any of the drafts. Quinn edition has a full point only.

¹⁴ To Meyerfeld Synge explains 'in a short while' as 'soon'.

MARTIN DOUL. And you'll be bearing in mind, I'm thinking, what you seen a while[1] back when you looked down into a well, or a clear pool, maybe, when there was no wind stirring and a good light in the sky.

MARY DOUL. I'm minding[2] that surely, for if I'm not the way the liars were saying below I seen a thing in them pools[3] put joy and blessing in my heart. [*She puts her hand to her hair again.*]

MARTIN DOUL [*laughing ironically*]. Well![4] They were saying below I was losing my senses but I never went any day the length of that[5]. . . . God help you, Mary Doul, if you're not a wonder for looks, you're the maddest female woman is walking the counties of the east.

MARY DOUL [*scornfully*]. You were saying all times you'd a great ear for hearing the lies in a word, a great ear, God help you, and you think you're using it now![6]

MARTIN DOUL. If it's not lies you're telling, would you have me think you're not a wrinkled poor woman is looking like three scores, maybe, or two scores and a half?[7]

MARY DOUL. I would not, Martin. [*She leans forward earnestly.*] For when I seen myself in them pools, I seen my hair would be grey,[8] or white maybe in a short while, and I seen with it that I'd a face would be a great wonder when it'll have soft white hair falling around it, the way when I'm an old woman there won't be the like of me[9] surely in the seven counties of the east.

MARTIN DOUL [*with real admiration*]. You're a cute thinking[10] woman, Mary Doul, and it's no lie.[11]

MARY DOUL [*triumphantly*]. I am surely, and I'm telling you a beautiful white-haired woman is a grand thing to see, for I'm told when Kitty Bawn was selling poteen below, the young men itself[12] would never tire to be looking in her face.

MARTIN DOUL [*taking off his hat and feeling his head, speaking with hesitation*]. Did you think to look, Mary Doul, would there be a whiteness the like of that coming upon me?

MARY DOUL [*with extreme contempt*]. On you, God help you?[13] . . . In a short while[14] you'll have a head on you as bald as an old turnip you'd see rolling round in the muck. You need never talk again of your fine looks, Martin Doul, for the day of that talk's gone for ever.

¹ To Meyerfeld Synge explains 'it's not far off we'd be from' as 'we should not be much worse off than in' etc., and 'a bit of comfort' as 'any consolation'. 'He means that if he had anything to comfort or console him for all their misery, as she has in her hope of beauty, he would be nearly as well off as before the curse.'

² The early drafts add the direction [*with malice*].

³ To Meyerfeld Synge explained 'griseldy' as 'grisly'. The 'rough final' draft adds a comma after 'made you'.

⁴ Exclamation mark is added from the TS. drafts. Earlier drafts expand the exchange between Martin and Mary Doul here:

MARTIN [*rubs his chin ruefully, then beams*]. My chin is it?. . . . I'll be finer than yourself yet, Mary Doul, and getting bags of half-pence on the road.

MARY. There isn't a bit of use in your lies.

⁵ The 'rough final' draft contemplates the alternative reply, 'I'm forgetting nothing but I wouldn't bother to go over your whole length from the sole of your foot to your skull.'

⁶ To Meyerfeld Synge explains 'There's talking' as '*voilà*'. 'He means that is grand talk (ironically) for a clever woman. Great talk indeed!' The drafts add exclamation marks at the end of both sentences, unlike the 1905, Quinn, and 1932 editions, which add one only after 'surely'. The 1905 and Quinn editions place a comma before 'surely'.

⁷ All the TS. drafts place a dash after 'while', thereby emphasizing Martin's description of the beard.

⁸ To Meyerfeld Synge explains, 'He does not mean here in the east of Ireland, but away in the "eastern world", a sort of wonderland very often spoken of in Irish folk-tales.'

⁹ Synge describes 'the quality' to Meyerfeld as 'the rich people'.

¹⁰ The 1932 edition follows the TS. drafts by adding a comma after 'have'. In an early draft Synge replaced 'tongue' with 'gob' but evidently thought better of it.

¹¹ To Meyerfeld Synge explains 'great talking' as 'great talking or chatting with each other'. 'She means that they will have a good time talking and quarrelling with each other as they were doing at the beginning of Act I.' An early draft adds the line, 'and it's a long while we have still for I've heard tell my great grandmother didn't die till she was past four score and ten'.

¹² To Meyerfeld Synge explained 'a priest itself' as 'even a priest' and 'would have' as 'who had'. The 1932 edition adds a comma after 'day', as does the 'rough final' draft.

¹³ Synge explains 'the way' to Meyerfeld as 'so that'.

MARTIN DOUL. That's a hard word to be saying, for I was thinking if I'd a bit of comfort, the like of yourself, it's not far off we'd be from[1] the good days went before, and that'd be a wonder surely. But I'll never rest easy, thinking you're a grey, beautiful woman, and myself a pitiful show.

MARY DOUL.[2] I can't help your looks, Martin Doul. It wasn't myself made you with your rat's eyes, and your big ears, and your griseldy[3] chin.

MARTIN DOUL [*rubs his chin ruefully, then beams with delight*]. There's one thing you've forgot, if you're a cute thinking woman itself![4]

MARY DOUL. Your slouching feet, is it? Or your hooky neck, or your two knees is black with knocking one on the other?[5]

MARTIN DOUL [*with delighted scorn*]. There's talking for a cute woman! There's talking surely![6]

MARY DOUL [*puzzled at the joy of his voice*]. If you'd anything but lies to say you'd be talking yourself.

MARTIN DOUL [*bursting with excitement*]. I've this to say, Mary Doul. I'll be letting my beard grow in a short while—[7] a beautiful, long, white, silken, streamy beard, you wouldn't see the like of in the eastern world.[8] . . . Ah, a white beard's a grand thing on an old man, a grand thing for making the quality[9] stop and be stretching out their hands with good silver or gold, and a beard's a thing you'll never have, so you may be holding your tongue.[10]

MARY DOUL [*laughing cheerfully*]. Well, we're a great pair, surely, and it's great times we'll have yet, maybe, and great talking before we die.[11]

MARTIN DOUL. Great times from this day, with the help of the Almighty God, for a priest itself would believe the lies of an old man would have a fine white beard growing on his chin.[12]

MARY DOUL. There's the sound of one of them twittering yellow birds do be coming in the spring-time from beyond the sea, and there'll be a fine warmth now in the sun, and a sweetness in the air, the way[13] it'll be a grand thing to be sitting here quiet and easy, smelling the things growing up, and budding from the earth.

¹ To Meyerfeld Synge explains 'the full river' as 'the flooded river'.

² An earlier draft added the direction *in a whisper*.

³ To Meyerfeld Synge explains 'Will we be running off' as 'Shall we run away'.

⁴ To Meyerfeld Synge explains 'sloughs' as 'bogs' and 'yeomen' as 'guards'.

⁵ An intermediate draft added the direction *speaking for the first time with frank affection in her voice*.

⁶ Synge made this alteration in his own copy to the 1905 edition, which reads, 'You're a grand man the world knows at finding your way winter or summer, if there was deep snow in it itself, or thick grass and leaves, maybe, growing from the earth.'

⁷ To Meyerfeld Synge explains 'would we have a right to be crawling' as 'should we crawl'.

⁸ To Meyerfeld Synge explains Martin's speech as 'I don't know what we should do! And isn't it a miserable thing to be blind so that you cannot even run away when you are afraid that your sight will be given to you?'

MARTIN DOUL. I'm smelling the furze a while back sprouting on the hill, and if you'd hold your tongue you'd hear the lambs of Grianan, though it's near drowned their crying is with the full river[1] making noises in the glen.

MARY DOUL [*listens*]. The lambs is bleating, surely, and there's cocks and laying hens making a fine stir a mile off on the face of the hill. [*She starts.*]

MARTIN DOUL. What's that is sounding in the west?

[*A faint sound of a bell is heard.*]

MARY DOUL. It's not the churches, for the wind's blowing from the sea.

MARTIN DOUL [*with dismay[2]*]. It's the old saint, I'm thinking, ringing his bell.

MARY DOUL. The Lord protect us from the saints of God! [*They listen.*] He's coming this road, surely.

MARTIN DOUL [*tentatively*]. Will we be running off,[3] Mary Doul?

MARY DOUL. What place would we run?

MARTIN DOUL. There's the little path going up through the sloughs. . . . If we reached the bank above, where the elders do be growing, no person would see a sight of us, if it was a hundred yeomen[4] were passing itself, but I'm afeard after the time we were with our sight we'll not find our way to it at all.

MARY DOUL [*standing up[5]*]. You'd find the way, surely. You're a grand man the world knows at finding your way if there was deep snow itself lying on the earth.[6]

MARTIN DOUL [*taking her hand*]. Come a bit this way, it's here it begins. [*They grope about gap.*] There's a tree pulled into the gap, or a strange thing happened since I was passing it before.

MARY DOUL. Would we have a right to be crawling[7] in below under the sticks?

MARTIN DOUL. It's hard set I am to know what would be right. And isn't it a poor thing to be blind when you can't run off itself, and you fearing to see?[8]

¹ Early drafts give Mary the speech, 'Whisht now there's a great crowd coming up from the street.' The saint and crowd come in immediately.

² The 1905 and Quinn editions place a semicolon, instead of a comma, after 'are', but there is no indication of this break in the drafts.

³ Included in the draft marked 'rough final' is the following additional exchange:

MARTIN [*groaning with dread*]. I'm thinking they can't but I'm hard set to know. That lot of them have sharp terrible eyes, the devil blind their souls.

[*A pause. MARTIN's foot is seen wagging with excitement.*]

MARY. Be quiet Martin. Do you not hear yourself wagging your toe?

This speech is then struck out and the following substituted after Martin's reply:

MARY. It's Molly Byrne we're hearing now.

MARTIN. The devil tear her soul.

MARY. Let you not be whispering sin, Martin Doul. . . .

⁴ The 1932 edition here corrects the spelling 'wicket' of the 1905 and Quinn editions.
⁵ The drafts end this comment with a dash instead of a question mark. Struck out of the 'rough final' draft is the following exchange:

MARTIN. Oh God help me I'm getting a sharp cramping pain in me Mary Doul, from the way I'm doubled up, and I in great terror of sight.

MARY. Isn't the saints wilful people, to be coming where they're not wanted, and when they're coming itself to be lagging and loitering when you're in great haste that they'd pass?

MARTIN. Oh Lord of Heaven, send him quickly this day or take him off unto yourself—

MARY [*interrupting him*]. You were always a fool Martin Doul. What good is it to be saying a prayer against a saint of God?

Notebook 31 (April–May 1904) contains a draft entitled 'Hiding! scene act III, 1' which is similar to this exchange, adding to Mary's reply the line, 'Would you go to the Kings of the world to keep you saved from the marching soldiers would put any woman in dread?' (See 'Bride and Kathleen: A Play of '98', 'Unpublished Material Part Two', pp. 215–17.)

MARY DOUL [*nearly in tears*]. It's a poor thing, God help us, and what good'll our grey hairs be itself, if we have our sight, the way we'll see them falling each day, and turning dirty in the rain?

[*The bell sounds near by.*]

MARTIN DOUL [*in despair*]. He's coming now, and we won't get off from him at all.

MARY DOUL. Could we hide in the bit of a briar is growing at the west butt of the church?

MARTIN DOUL. We'll try that, surely. [*He listens a moment.*] Let you make haste, I hear them trampling in the wood. [*They grope over to church.*][1]

MARY DOUL. It's the words of the young girls making a great stir in the trees. [*They find the bush.*] Here's the briar on my left, Martin; I'll go in first, I'm the big one, and I'm easy to see.

MARTIN DOUL [*turning his head anxiously*]. It's easy heard you are,[2] and will you be holding your tongue?

MARY DOUL [*partly behind bush*]. Come in now beside of me. [*They kneel down, still clearly visible.*] Do you think can they see us now, Martin Doul?

MARTIN DOUL. I'm thinking they can't, but I'm hard set to know, for the lot of them young girls, the devil save them, have sharp terrible eyes, would pick out a poor man I'm thinking, and he lying below hid in his grave.[3]

MARY DOUL. Let you not be whispering sin, Martin Doul, or maybe it's the finger of God they'd see pointing to ourselves.

MARTIN DOUL. It's yourself is speaking madness, Mary Doul, haven't you heard the saint say it's the wicked[4] do be blind?

MARY DOUL. If it is you'd have a right to speak a big terrible word would make the water not cure us at all.

MARTIN DOUL. What way would I find a big terrible word, and I shook with the fear, and if I did itself, who'd know rightly if it's good words or bad would save us this day from himself?[5]

¹ The 1905 and Quinn editions place a comma after 'tell'.

² Until the final draft Synge contemplated sending the saint directly into the church to marry Timmy and Molly Byrne, leaving Patch Ruadh and Mat Simon to find Martin and Mary Doul groping their way about the briars:

PATCH RUADH. Ah, Glory be to God, there's Martin Doul and his wife blind again and the two of them holding their hands. . . .

MAT SIMON. The saint would have a right now to blind Timmy and Molly when he's the two of them wed in the church. If they were blinded maybe you'd see them holding their hands the like of that in a score of years and that'd be a wonder surely.

PATCH [*going across to* MARTIN *and* MARY]. What is it you're doing Martin Doul groping round in the tree?

MARTIN [*dejectedly*]. We were looking for the little path Patch Ruadh but we've missed our way surely, for I'm no good now at finding my path.

MAT SIMON. Isn't it a queer thing when you were blind a score of years and not seeing for a half a one itself, you'd lose the little tricks you had for finding out your way. It's only a poor simple fellow you are I'm thinking with the lot of your talk.

MARTIN. Was it the saint we heard ringing his bell?

PATCH. Who else would it be? He's gone in now to the old church to make the wedding of Molly Byrne and Timmy the smith, you've heard tell I'm thinking they've been a great while making talk of being wed.

MARTIN [*gloomily letting go* MARY's *hand*]. The devil help the two of them.

PATCH. They're coming out now in a minute for he's saying a short prayer over them, and he with a long way to go before the fall of night. . . .

³ Synge explains 'the way he'll be curing you now' to Meyerfeld as 'so that he will cure you now'. The 1905 and Quinn editions add a comma after 'foolish man', unnecessarily causing a break in the rhythm.

MARY DOUL. They're coming. I hear their feet on the stones.

[SAINT *comes in on right with* TIMMY *and* MOLLY BYRNE *in holiday clothes, the others as before.*]

TIMMY. I've heard tell[1] Martin Doul and Mary Doul were seen this day about on the road, holy father, and we were thinking you'd have pity on them and cure them again.

SAINT. I would, maybe, but where are they at all? I'll have little time left when I have the two of you wed in the church.[2]

MAT SIMON [*at their seat*]. There are the rushes they do have lying round on the stones. It's not far off they'll be, surely.

MOLLY BYRNE [*pointing with astonishment*]. Look beyond, Timmy.

[*They all look over and see* MARTIN DOUL.]

TIMMY. Well, Martin's a lazy fellow to be lying in there at the height of the day. [*He goes over shouting.*] Let you get up out of that. You were near losing a great chance by your sleepiness this day, Martin Doul. . . . The two of them's in it, God help us all!

MARTIN DOUL [*scrambling up with* MARY DOUL]. What is it you want, Timmy, that you can't leave us in peace?

TIMMY. The saint's come to marry the two of us, and I'm after speaking a word for yourselves, the way he'll be curing you now, for if you're a foolish man[3] itself, I do be pitying you, for I've a kind heart, when I think of you sitting dark again, and you after seeing a while, and working for your bread.

[MARTIN DOUL *takes* MARY DOUL'*s hand and tries to grope his way off right, he has lost his hat, and they are both covered with dust, and grass seeds.*]

PEOPLE. You're going wrong. It's this way, Martin Doul.

[*They push him over in front of* SAINT *near centre.* MARTIN DOUL *and* MARY DOUL *stand with piteous hang-dog dejection.*]

SAINT. Let you not be afeard, for there's great pity with the Lord.

MARTIN DOUL. We aren't afeard, holy father.

¹ To Meyerfeld Synge explains 'It's many a time' as 'It often happened that'. The 1905 and Quinn editions add a comma after 'second time', again causing an unnecessary break in the rhythm.

² Earlier drafts read *standing up and taking* MARY *with his left hand, and his stick in his right*. The earliest draft adds the word *threatening*.

³ The 'rough final' draft adds the direction [*He turns to go again, but the people crowd round with astonishment, and he cannot pass through them.*]

⁴ The 'rough final' draft reads [*with surprise, and compassion*].

⁵ The 1905 and Quinn editions include after 'fasting itself' the words, 'for I'm thinking the Lord has brought you great teaching in the blinding of your eyes'. In his own copy of the 1905 edition Synge puts round brackets round these words, and also in his notes to Meyerfeld he indicates the cut. Question marks in the margin of his early drafts indicate that he debated the inclusion of this line for some time.

The earliest draft reads 'of penance, or pilgrimage, or Peter's pennies' etc.

⁶ The 1932 edition omits 'but'; however it is included in all other drafts including the 1905 and Quinn editions and the rhythm seems to require the extra syllable.

⁷ The 'rough final' draft reads [*querulously*]; the 1932 edition omits the stage direction altogether.

⁸ The next scene, from this speech to the rejection of Martin and Mary, was altered after the 1905 edition had been published. Three versions exist, the alterations by Synge to his own copy of the 1905 edition, four pages of emended typescript among Synge's papers, and the 1932 edition of the plays, which has taken alterations from the Abbey Theatre's copy of the play. In most cases these latter two versions coincide, although it seems likely from the variations that the four pages of TS. were Synge's final decision, altered only by the MS. changes in the 1905 edition. Unless otherwise stated the version printed is taken from these final TS. alterations and the further MS. alterations to his own text.

⁹ The 1932 edition adds the phrase 'holy father' after 'a short space'.

¹⁰ The additional speeches assigned to Timmy, Patch Ruadh, Mat Simon, and Molly Byrne in the 1932 edition are simply labelled 'P.' for 'People' in the TS. In the earliest draft of this scene the saint interjects, 'You're not worthy to have sight if you aren't praising the Lord for the things you saw from the moment I opened your eyes until the day they are shut.'

¹¹ There seems no justification for the 1932 alteration to [*puzzled*]. All other versions read [*severely*].

¹² The final TS. version places the comma after 'joy' instead of after 'earth'. To Meyerfeld Synge explains 'the image of the Lord is thrown upon men' as 'the image of God reflected by men, he is thinking of text, "God created man in his own image."' In an early draft the saint replies, 'I've seen many things in the world for I've walked to Rome through the countries of France, and England and Wales, but I never saw or heard tell' etc.

SAINT. It's many a time those that are cured with the well of the four beauties of God lose their sight when a time is gone, but those I cure a second time[1] go on seeing till the hour of death. [*He takes the cover from his can.*] I've a few drops only left of the water, but, with the help of God, it'll be enough for the two of you, and let you kneel down now upon the road.

[MARTIN DOUL *wheels round with* MARY DOUL *and tries to get away*][2].

SAINT. You can kneel down here, I'm saying, we'll not trouble this time going to the church.

TIMMY [*turning* MARTIN DOUL *round angrily*]. Are you going mad in your head, Martin Doul? It's here you're to kneel. Did you not hear his reverence, and he speaking to you now?

SAINT. Kneel down, I'm saying, the ground's dry at your feet.

MARTIN DOUL [*with distress*]. Let you go on your own way, holy father. We're not calling you at all.[3]

SAINT.[4] I'm not saying a word of penance, or fasting itself,[5] so you've no call now to be fearing me, but[6] let you kneel down till I give you your sight.

MARTIN DOUL [*more troubled*].[7] We're not asking our sight, holy father, and let you be walking on and leaving us in our peace at the crossing roads, for it's best we are this way, and we're not asking to see.[8]

SAINT [*to the* PEOPLE]. Is his mind gone that he's no wish to be cured this day, and looking out on the wonders of the world?

MARTIN DOUL. It's wonders enough I seen in a short space[9] for the life of one man only.

TIMMY.[10] Is it he see wonders?

PATCH RUADH. He's making game.

MAT SIMON. He's maybe drunk, holy father.

SAINT [*severely*].[11] I never heard tell of any person wouldn't have great joy to be looking on the earth, and the image of the Lord is thrown upon men.[12]

¹ The words *by degrees* added in 1932 edition.

² The 1932 edition has dots here to indicate a pause, although none is indicated in any of the other versions. The 1933 edition alone omits 'with' before 'Timmy the smith'.

³ Intermediate drafts read, 'And what was it I saw last but the villainy of hell looking out through the blinking beautiful eyes of the girl you're after wedding to Timmy the smith. And it was great sights I seen on the roads the time the cold wind would be driving, and your hands would be that cold you couldn't close up your small fingers touching your thumb.'

⁴ The 1932 edition transposes the words to an order uncommon in Synge, 'He's maybe right' etc.

⁵ To Meyerfeld Synge explains 'creels' as 'tall basket⟨s⟩ or hampers for fish or turf'.

⁶ The 1932 version reads 'What will you say now' etc.

⁷ The 1932 edition reads [*fiercely*]; the 'rough final' draft reads [*incredulously*].

⁸ This version follows Synge's MS. alterations to his copy of the 1905 edition. The 1932 edition roughly follows the frequently revised final TS. version: 'I'll say it's ourselves have finer sight than the lot of you, and we sitting abroad in the sweetness of the warmth of night hearing a late thrush, maybe, and the swift crying things do be racing in the air' etc. The 1932 edition alone reads 'crying' for 'flying'. Both later drafts cut Martin's first sentence in the 1905 and Quinn editions, 'Is it talking now you are of Knock and Balla-vore?' This cut is also noted by Synge in his comments to Meyerfeld.

⁹ The 1932 edition reads 'It's not, but lazy, holy father, and not wishing to work; for, awhile since, he' etc., with 'awhile' one word. The version printed here follows Synge's MS. alterations to his own copy of the 1905 edition.

MARTIN DOUL [*raising his voice, by degrees*[1]]. That's great sights, holy father. . . . What was it I seen my first day, but your own bleeding feet and they cut with the stones, and my last day, but the villainy of herself that you're wedding, God forgive you, with Timmy the smith.[2] That was great sights maybe. . . . And wasn't it great sights seeing the roads when north winds would be driving and the skies would be harsh, and you'd see the horses and the asses and the dogs itself maybe with their heads hanging and they closing their eyes—[3]

TIMMY. There's talking.

MAT SIMON. He's right maybe,[4] it's lonesome living when the days are dark.

MOLLY BYRNE. He's not right. Let you speak up, holy father, and confound him now.

SAINT [*coming close to* MARTIN DOUL *and putting his hand on his shoulder.*] Did you never set eyes on the summer and the fine spring in the places where the holy men of Ireland have built up churches to the Lord, that you'd wish to be closed up and seeing no sight of the glittering seas, and the furze is opening above, will soon have the hills shining as if it was fine creels[5] of gold they were, rising to the sky?

PATCH RUADH. That's it, holy father.

MAT SIMON. What have you now to say,[6] Martin Doul?

MARTIN DOUL [*fiercely*].[7] Isn't it finer sights ourselves had a while since and we sitting dark smelling the sweet beautiful smells do be rising in the warm nights and hearing the swift flying things racing in the air[8] [SAINT *draws back from him*], till we'd be looking up in our own minds into a grand sky, and seeing lakes, and broadening rivers, and hills are waiting for the spade and plough.

MAT SIMON [*roaring laughing*]. It's songs he's making now, holy father.

PATCH. It's mad he is.

MOLLY BYRNE. It's not, but lazy he is, holy father, and not wishing to work, for a while since[9] he was all times longing and screeching for the light of day.

¹ The 1932 edition reads instead [*with vehement bitterness*], but with reference to the stage direction the final TS. version reads 'text stet'.

² The 1932 edition reads 'my wife, and the look of your own wicked grin, the time you do be making game with a man.' The 1905 and Quinn editions and earlier drafts differ also: 'I was longing, surely, for sight, but I seen my fill in a short while with the look of my wife, and the look of yourself, Molly Byrne, and when you'd the queer wicket grin in your eyes you do have the time you're making game with a man.'

³ The 1932 edition reads 'There's talking. . . . Let you not' etc. However, manuscript alterations to the final TS. version suggest a briefer expression which is almost illegible.

⁴ The early drafts, including the 1905 and Quinn editions, give Molly a more explicit condemnation here: 'Let you not mind him, holy father, for it's bad things he was saying to me awhile back—bad things for a married man, your reverence—and you'd do right surely to leave him in darkness, if it's that is best fitting the villainy of his heart.'

⁵ Although there is no indication in Synge's own copy of the text, in his note to Meyerfeld Synge cuts the line as it appears in the 1905 edition: 'or with young girls would be making game of her below.' He explains 'making game of' as 'joking with'.

⁶ The 1932 edition gives this speech to Mat Simon: 'That's it. Cure Mary Doul, your reverence.' However, in the final TS. version Synge has written out 'People' in full.

⁷ The 1932 edition reads 'There's little use I'm thinking, talking to the like of him, but if you've any sense, Mary Doul, let you kneel down at my feet, and I'll bring sight into your eyes.'

⁸ The stage direction indicates retention of the exclamation mark as in the 1905 and Quinn editions. The 1932 edition puts dots to indicate a pause, with no exclamation mark.

⁹ An earlier draft reads 'saying hard words to me the time I'll be growing my beard.'

¹⁰ The 1932 edition follows the 1905 and Quinn editions here: 'If she's wanting her sight, I wouldn't have the like of you stop her at all.'

¹¹ The 1905 and Quinn editions and all the drafts read [*doubtfully*]; the 1932 edition alone alters it to [*confused*].

¹² The 1932 edition reads 'things you do need to keep you living in the world at all.'

¹³ The 1905 and Quinn editions and earlier drafts are more explicit here: 'If you had your sight, Mary, you could be walking up for him and down with him, and be stitching his clothes, and keeping a watch on him day and night the way no other woman would come near him at all.' The 1932 edition differs also: 'If you had your sight you could be keeping a watch on him that no other woman came near him in the night or day.'

¹⁴ The 1932 edition adds commas after 'down' and 'marriage'. The 1905 and Quinn editions read 'Kneel down now, I'm saying, for it's in haste I am to be going on with the marriage and be walking my own way before the fall of night.'

MARTIN DOUL [*turning on her*][1]. If I was, I seen my fill in a short while with the look of my wife, and of your own wicked grin, Molly Byrne, the time you're making game with a man.[2]

MOLLY BYRNE. ⟨My⟩ grin, is it?[3] Let you not mind him more, holy father, but leave him in darkness, if it's that is best fitting to the blackness of his heart.[4]

TIMMY. Cure Mary Doul, your reverence, who is a quiet poor woman never said a hard word but when she'd be vexed with himself, or with the young girls do be making game of her below.[5]

PEOPLE.[6] That's it, cure Mary Doul your reverence.

SAINT. There is little use, maybe, talking to the like of him, but if you have any sense, Mary Doul, kneel down at my feet, and I'll bring the sight into your eyes.[7]

MARTIN DOUL [*more defiantly*]. You will not, holy father![8] Would you have her looking on me, and saying hard words to me, till the hour of death?[9]

SAINT [*severely*]. If she's wishing her sight it isn't the like of you'll stop her.[10] [*To* MARY.] Kneel down, I'm saying.

MARY DOUL [*doubtfully*].[11] Let us be as we are, holy father, and then we'll be known again as the people is happy and blind, and we'll be having an easy time with no trouble to live, and we getting half-pence on the road.

MOLLY BYRNE. Let you not be raving. Kneel down and get your sight, and let himself be taking half-pence if he likes it best.

TIMMY. If it's choosing a wilful blindness you are, there isn't any one will give you a hap'worth of meal or be doing the little things you need to keep you at all living in the world.[12]

MAT SIMON. If you had your sight you could be keeping a watch that no other woman came near to him at all.[13]

MARY DOUL [*half persuaded*]. That's true, maybe. . . .

SAINT. Kneel down for I must be hastening with the marriage[14] and going my own way before the fall of night.

¹ The final TS. version indicates a pause here.

² The 1932 edition differs from other drafts by beginning a new sentence at 'We're not'.

³ Stage direction from 1932 edition. An early draft adds the line, 'It's a great wonder I'm thinking that people do be married at all or peaceful at all the time they do be getting up and lying down and they looking on each other from morning to the night.'

⁴ The final TS. version differs here from the 1932 edition, which reads 'Well, there's bitter hardness in the pity of your like, and what is it you want coming for to break our happiness and hour of ease. Let you rise up, Mary, and not heed them more.' The 1905 and Quinn editions read, 'Come along now, and don't mind him at all.'

⁵ Both these speeches are simply given as one speech by 'P' (People) in the final TS version.

⁶ This speech from the 1932 edition does not occur in the final TS. version which from now on indicates only those speeches which have been altered.

PEOPLE [*all together*]. Kneel down, Mary! Kneel down when you're bid by the saint!

MARY DOUL [*looking uneasily towards* MARTIN DOUL]. Maybe it's right they are, and I will if you wish it, holy father. . . .¹

[*She kneels down.* SAINT *takes off his hat and gives it to someone near him. All the men take off their hats. He goes forward a step to take* MARTIN DOUL's *hand away from* MARY DOUL.]

SAINT [*to* MARTIN DOUL]. Go aside now,² we're not wanting you here.

MARTIN DOUL [*pushes him away roughly, and stands with his left hand on* MARY DOUL's *shoulder*]. Keep off yourself, holy father, and let you not be taking my rest from me in the darkness of my wife. . . . What call have the like of you to be coming in where you're not wanted at all, and making a great mess with the holy water you have and the length of your prayers? [*Defiantly.*]³ Go on, I'm saying, and leave us this place on the road.

SAINT. If it was a seeing man I heard talking to me the like of that I'd put a black curse on him would weigh down his soul till it'd be falling to hell; but you're a poor blind sinner, God forgive you, and I don't mind you at all. [*He raises his can.*] Go aside now till I give the blessing to your wife, and if you won't go with your own will, there are those standing by will make you surely.

MARTIN DOUL [*pulling* MARY DOUL]. Make me, is it? Well, there's cruel hardship in the pity of your like, and what is it you want coming for to break our happiness and hour of rest. Let you rise up, Mary, against them and not heed them more.⁴

SAINT [*imperiously to* PEOPLE]. Let you take that man and drive him down upon the road.

MAT SIMON. Come now, Martin, come on.

PATCH RUADH. Come off now from talking badness to the holy saint.⁵

MARTIN DOUL [*throwing himself down on the ground clinging to* MARY DOUL]. I'll not come, I'm saying, and let you take his holy water to cure the blackness of your souls today.⁶

¹ The 1932 edition reads 'than be getting eyesight and new torments now.' The speech does not occur in the 1905 or Quinn editions.

² The 1932 edition reads, 'You have taken your choice. Drag him off from her, I'm saying.' The speech does not occur in the 1905 or Quinn editions.

³ The 1932 edition reads, 'That's it. That's it. Come forward till we drop him in the pool beyond.' Instead of this speech, the 1905 and Quinn editions give the direction [*Some men seize* MARTIN DOUL.]

⁴ The 1905 and Quinn editions give the direction [*struggling and shouting*]. This sentence in the 1932 edition corresponds roughly to the earlier versions, 'Make them leave me go, I'm saying, and let you not think badly of my heathen talk, but cure her this day, or do anything you will.'

⁵ The 1932 edition corresponds to the 1905 and Quinn editions, 'Let him be . . . Let him be, if his sense has come to him at all.'

⁶ To Meyerfeld Synge explains 'and be looking out on the holy men' as 'he will be looking himself at the holy men of God. (He is merely wheedling or flattering the saint, to hide his intention.)'

⁷ The 1932 edition corresponds to the 1905 and Quinn editions here: '. . . like ourselves; so if he has found a right mind at the last minute itself, I'll cure him, if the Lord will, and not be thinking of the hard, foolish words he's after saying this day to us all.'

⁸ The last sentence of the murmuring occurs only in the final TS. version.

MARY DOUL [*putting her arm round him*]. Leave him easy, holy father, when I'd liefer live dark all times beside him, than be seeing in new troubles now.[1]

SAINT. You've taken your choice. Drag him away.[2]

PEOPLE. That's it. Lift his head. [*They carry him to right.*][3]

MARTIN DOUL [*screaming*]. Make them leave me go, holy father. Make them leave me go, and let you have pity and forgive me for my heathen words, and you may cure her this day, holy father, and do anything that you will.[4]

SAINT [*to* PEOPLE]. Let him be if his sense is come to him at all.[5]

[*They put him down.*]

MARTIN DOUL [*shakes himself loose, feels for* MARY DOUL, *sinking his voice to a plausible whine*]. You may cure herself, surely, holy father, I wouldn't stop you at all—and it's great joy she'll have looking on your face—but let you cure myself along with her, the way I'll see when it's lies she's telling, and be looking out day and night upon the holy men of God.[6] [*He kneels down a little before* MARY DOUL.]

SAINT [*speaking half to the* PEOPLE]. Men who are dark a long while and thinking over queer thoughts in their heads, aren't the like of simple men, who do be working every day, and praying, and living like ourselves, and with that it's my part to be showing a love to you would take pity on the worst that live. So if you've found a right mind at the last minute itself, I'll cure you, if the Lord will, and not be thinking of the hard, foolish words you're after saying this day to us all.[7]

MARTIN DOUL [*listening eagerly*]. I'm waiting now, holy father.

SAINT [*with can in his hand, close to* MARTIN DOUL]. With the power of the water from the grave of the four beauties of God, with the power of this water, I'm saying, that I put upon your eyes— —

[*He raises can.* MARTIN DOUL *with a sudden movement strikes the can from* SAINT's *hand and sends it rocketing across stage.*]

PEOPLE [*with a terrified murmur*]. Will you look what he's done. Oh, glory be to God. There's a villain surely.[8]

¹ To Meyerfeld Synge explains 'the little splash' as 'gurgling sound of the water in vessel'.

In the earliest drafts Martin does not use the ruse of pretending to change his mind; instead [*He moves forward quickly and snatches the water from the* SAINT *and empties it on the ground.*]

² From now on the 1932 edition corresponds to the 1905 and Quinn editions except for the occasional difference in punctuation and the omission of the directions here. The interjection by the People in Martin's speech is recorded in the final TS. alterations to the scene.

³ In his own copy of the 1905 edition Synge strikes out the phrase 'at all in the townland of Grianan' which occurs after 'living near us' in the printed texts.

⁴ In the draft he sent to Meyerfeld Synge added the direction [*all together*].

⁵ In the margin of his own copy of the 1905 edition Synge alters 'with the pitch of my stone' to 'from the welt of my stick', thereby requiring a similar alteration in the stage direction which originally read [*picking up a stone*].

⁶ The 1932 edition adds the semicolon; 1905 and Quinn editions have no punctuation.

MARTIN DOUL [*stands up triumphantly, and pulls* MARY DOUL *up*]. If I'm a poor dark sinner I've sharp ears, God help me, and it's well I heard the little splash¹ of the water you had there in the can. Go on now, holy father, for if you're a fine saint itself, it's more sense is in a blind man, and more power maybe than you're thinking at all. Let you walk on now with your worn feet, and your welted knees, and your fasting, holy ways have left you with a big head on you and a thin pitiful arm.

PEOPLE. Go on from this.

[SAINT *looks at* MARTIN DOUL *for a moment severely, then turns away and picks up his can.*]

MARTIN DOUL. We're going surely, for if it's a right² some of you have to be working and sweating the like of Timmy the smith, and a right some of you have to be fasting and praying and talking holy talk the like of yourself, I'm thinking it's a good right ourselves have to be sitting blind, hearing a soft wind turning round the little leaves of the spring and feeling the sun, and we not tormenting our souls with the sight of the grey days, and the holy men, and the dirty feet is trampling the world. [*He gropes towards his stone with* MARY DOUL.]

MAT SIMON. It'd be an unlucky fearful thing, I'm thinking, to have the like of that man living near us at all.³ Wouldn't he bring down a curse upon us, holy father, from the heavens of God?

SAINT [*tying his girdle*]. God has great mercy, but great wrath for them that sin.

PEOPLE [*all together*].⁴ Go on now, Martin Doul. Go on from this place. Let you not be bringing great storms or droughts on us maybe from the power of the Lord. [*Some of them throw things at him.*]

MARTIN DOUL [*turning round defiantly and picking up his stick*]. Keep off now the yelping lot of you, or it's more than one maybe will get a bloody head on him from the welt of my stick.⁵ Keep off now, and let you not be afeard;⁶ for we're going on the two of us to the towns of the south, where the people will have kind voices maybe, and we won't know their bad looks or their villainy at all.

MARY DOUL [*despondingly*]. That's the truth, surely, and we'd have a right to be gone, if it's a long way itself, where you do have to be

¹ In his own copy of the 1905 edition Synge cuts the phrase 'as I've heard them say' which occurs after 'it's a long way itself'. To Meyerfeld Synge explains 'a slough of wet' as 'a wet quagmire or bog. Do you remember the "Slough of Despond" in Pilgrim's Progress of Bunyan. The word is used in same sense in Ireland now.'

² In his own copy of the 1905 edition Synge reverses the final exchange between Martin and Mary Doul. Originally Mary does not say her final speech until Martin has finished speaking. The comments by the Men are also added to his copy of the play.

³ The original ending in the early drafts has Timmy inviting all the people 'to the green below for the piper has come and we'll have dancing till the fall of night.'

walking with a slough of wet on the one side and a slough of wet on the other, and you going a stony path with a north wind blowing behind.[1]

MEN. Go on now. Go on from this place.

MARTIN DOUL. Keep off I'm saying. [*He takes* MARY DOUL'*s hand again.*] Come along now and we'll be walking to the south, for we've seen too much of everyone in this place, and it's small joy we'd have living near them, or hearing the lies they do be telling from the grey of dawn till the night. [*They go.*][2]

TIMMY. There's a power of deep rivers with floods in them where you do have to be lepping the stones and you going to the south, so I'm thinking the two of them will be drowned together in a short while, surely.

SAINT. They have chosen their lot, and the Lord have mercy on their souls. [*He rings his bell.*] And let the two of you come up now into the church, Molly Byrne and Timmy the smith, till I make your marriage and put my blessing on you all.[3]

[*He turns to the church, procession forms, and the curtain comes down, as they go slowly into the church.*]

CURTAIN

UNPUBLISHED MATERIAL

PART ONE

WHEN THE MOON HAS SET

A PLAY IN ONE ACT

(1900–1903)

WHEN THE MOON HAS SET

A PLAY IN ONE ACT[1]

⟨PERSONS

COLM SWEENY, a young man, heir to his uncle's estate

BRIDE, a young maid

SISTER EILEEN, a young nun in a nursing order, a distant cousin to Colm

MARY COSTELLO, a madwoman

SCENE

A country house in the east of Ireland, late spring or early summer at the turn of the century⟩[2]

---

[1] 'I wrote one play—which I have never published—in Paris, dealing with Ireland of course, but not a peasant play, before I wrote *Riders to the Sea*,' Synge wrote to Leon Brodzky on 12 December 1907.

'I wish to be emphatic about this play. It is just the kind of work which some theatrical experimenter with no literary judgment or indifferent to literature would be glad to get. It is quite complete. It might have a slight stage success with a certain kind of very modern audience. It was Synge's first play, he read it to Lady Gregory and myself in either two or three acts. He has since then, at what date I cannot now remember, though certainly not very recently, reduced it to one act. It is morbid and conventional though with an air of originality. The only thing interesting about it is that it shows his preoccupation with the thought of death. He knew my opinion about it at the time. It was after its rejection by us he took to peasant work.' W. B. Yeats, from a Memorandum to Synge's executors, 1909.

[2] No title-page or list of characters exists for this play, but it is evident from his diaries that Synge had chosen this title for the one-act version of the play he completed in May 1903. The following text is a conflation of two one-act versions marked 'J' and 'K'. 'K', although incomplete, appears to be later, and is used as the basic text, with additions from 'J' indicated in bold type. Editorial emendations are indicated by angled brackets.

Different versions spell Colm's name *Colum, Columb*, etc. The final form is used here throughout.

¹ The typescript in Item 51, a complete two-act version of the play, contains additional details of stage setting: *in the corner, a gun, dog-whips, etc. are lying as if thrown carelessly together⟨. . . .⟩ on the table⟨. . .⟩ there are several old books and a pile of manuscript⟨. . . .⟩ A harp stands in the corner.* Up until the final draft of the play Sister Eileen tunes the harp and sings the Cuilfhionn, which is then sung again by Mary Costello. In the two-act version of the play, the manuscript was used as a framework to the play, Sister Eileen reading from it at the rise of the curtain, Colm quoting from it at the end of the play. (See p. 174 note 3)

Until the final draft (52 'K'), the play opens with Sister Eileen standing near the table fashioning the crepe bow, then calling Bride to bring up some turf. In all the two-act versions but one, the uncle is dead before Colm returns with the doctor, who is sent away again without appearing on stage.

² The typescript in Item 51 describes Bride as [*talking with plaintive uncertain intonation*].

³ In an earlier draft (Item 50) this action called forth the following exchange:

s.e. [*standing up*]. Had we not better keep the blinds down at least for this evening.

c. This rain is more mournful than they are.

s.e. The people will think it strange.

c. They will not think much about it. We cannot sit ⟨in⟩ darkness, and it is too soon for the lights.

s.e. Let me pull down the blind next the lane.

c. The light is coming at that side. What does it matter. My uncle was not a man who would care about shows.

⁴ This sentence occurs unchanged in all drafts of the play

Old family library in country house; many books are in shelves round the walls. A turf fire has burnt low in the fireplace, which is on one side, with a large portrait above it. The principal door is on the right, but there is another in the back wall partly covered with a curtain and opening with two battants into the open air. Small window near the fireplace; another to the right of the end-door; both have the blinds down. A large lamp heavily shaded is burning near the table. A large bow of black crepe is resting on one of the chairs near the fire. BRIDE, *a young maid, is kneeling down settling the turf fire.* COLM *comes in on the left,* **wearing a big coat buttoned up to his chin.**[1]

COLM [*looking round the room*]. Sister Eileen has gone to bed?

BRIDE.[2] She has not, your honour. She's been in a great state fearing you were lost in the hills, and now she's after going down the hollow field to see would there be any sound of the wheels coming.

COLM. I came in the other way so she could not have heard me. [*Goes to* **large** *window*] Is she long gone?

BRIDE. A while only.

COLM. I wonder if I could find her. . . .

BRIDE. You could not, your honour, and you'd have a right to be sitting here and warming your feet, the way it's proud and happy she'll be to see you when she turns in from the shower is coming in the trees.

COLM [*pulling up the blind*].[3] I hope she will not miss her way. Perhaps if she sees the door open she will turn back. [*He stands looking out.*]

BRIDE [*a little impatiently*]. She'll be coming in a minute I'm telling you, and let you be taking your own rest. You're wanting it surely, for we were thinking it's destroyed you'd be driving alone in the night and the great rain, and you not used to anything but the big towns of the world.[4] [*She pulls a chair to the fire.*]

[COLM *comes over to the fire, wearily.* **He begins taking off his coat and heavy boots.** BRIDE *lifts up the bow of crepe from his chair.*]

¹ The typescript in Item 51 gives this comment and many similar ones to an old servant, Mrs. Byrne, who does not appear in later drafts.

BRIDE [*showing it to him*]. Isn't it a fine bow she's made with bits of rags that we found? I was watching her do it, and I'm telling you she's a wonder surely.

COLM [*with reserve*]. She is clever with her fingers.

BRIDE. Wait till your honour sees the way she has the room beyond, with fine flowers in it, and white candles, and grand clothes on the bed, and your poor uncle lying so easy with his eyes shut you'd be thinking it was an old man in his sleep. [*Turning to the fire with a sigh.*] Ah, it's a long way any person would go seeking the like of Sister Eileen, and it's very lonesome your honour'll be tomorrow or the next day when she is gone away to the town.[1]

COLM. She will stay for the funeral.

BRIDE. And what day, if myself may ask, will the funeral be?

COLM. I have settled it for Friday, but it was not easy, there were so many things to arrange.

BRIDE. It's great trouble the rich do have when there is even an old man to be buried, and it was that, I'm thinking, kept you the whole evening in the town.

COLM. It kept me a good while, but I went wrong coming home, and took the road through the bogs to the graveyard of Glan-na-nee.

BRIDE. The Lord have mercy on us! There does be no **one** at all passing that way but a few men do be carting turf, and isn't it a great wonder your honour got home safe, and wasn't lost in the hills?

COLM. I hardly knew where I was, but I found a woman there who told me my way.

BRIDE. It was a lonesome place for a woman, God help her, and the night coming.

COLM. She was nearly crazy I think, but she must have known the trap for she called out to me by my name and asked about my uncle.

BRIDE [*greatly interested*]. And was it much she said to your honour?

COLM. At first she spoke sensibly and told me how I was to go, but when she tried to say something else she had on her mind she got so confused I could not follow her. Then the mare got frightened at a sort of cry she gave, and I had to come away.

¹ In all but the final draft Bride's indignation is roused because of her relationship to Mary Costello . . . 'and it's fine people we were at one time. . . '.

² Until the final draft Colm prefaced his reply with 'I very seldom met my uncle.' In earlier drafts his recollection of his uncle's attending a relative's funeral gave rise to the passage from the *Autobiography* (see Appendix D, p. 279).

³ Earlier versions emphasize this element of madness.

In the typescript in Item 51 Colm describes a friend in Paris, a 'cellist, who has sent him a letter:

> He is interesting. He lives in a low room draped in black from the floor to the ceiling. He has a black quilt on his bed and two skulls on his chimney-piece with girls' hats on them. His matches are in a coffin, and his clock is a gallows. He sits there whenever he is not at work and drinks absinthe and vermouth.

S. EILEEN. You should make him live more wisely or he will go out of his mind.

COLM. He seems to think that the dreams and the excitement are worth the danger. For the matter of that in the life of the cloisters, and in this life of Ireland, men go mad every hour and you do not ask them to change.

S. EILEEN. There is nothing here or in the religious life to make men mad . . . It is different in Paris.

> [*A gust of wind howls through the house.* S. EILEEN *shudders and looks round at the window.*]

COLM. Madness is caused by the killing out or exaggeration of some part of the personality, and life here has been withered away by men that are held up in contrast to the French till we are more degenerate than they are.

In Act II Colm dictates a letter to his friend in which he repeats this charge: 'When I got over here the place interested me in a way I did not expect. The old-fashioned Irish conservatism and morality seemed to have evolved a melancholy degeneration worse than anything in Paris. Everyone seemed to be taking his friends to the Asylum or bringing them back from it.'

The same typescript adds three characters, all related to Mary Costello (who dies long before the play begins): Bride's mother, Mary Costello's sister, who never appears but is the 'lady . . . walking round in the Asylum with fine shoes on her feet'; Bride's uncle, Stephen Costello, Mary's twin brother, who does not appear either but at the end of Act I shoots Colm in the shoulder because of an oath to destroy the next heir, and in Act II is sentenced to the Asylum for life; and old Pat Kavanagh, Bride's drunkard father, who appears in Act I to warn Colm of 'the avenging lunatic' and dies of old age in Act II. Not until the first one-act version (in Item 50) is the general discussion about madness crossed out, and finally in 52 'J' Synge strikes out the relationship with Bride.

In the typescript from Item 50 (the first one-act version), Colm replies, [*half to himself*] 'I hardly wonder that so ⟨many of⟩ them go mad if there are nights like this night in the country.'

BRIDE. She was a big tall woman I'm thinking, with a black shawl on her, and black hair round her face? [*She begins blowing the fire with her mouth.*]

COLM. Then you know who she is?

BRIDE. She's Mary Costello, your honour. [*She goes on blowing.*]

COLM. A beggar woman?

BRIDE [*indignantly*]. Not she a beggar woman. . . . She's a Costello from the old Castilian family, and it's fine people they were at one time, big wealthy nobles of the cities of Spain, and herself was the finest girl you'd find in the whole world, with nice manners, and white hands on her, for she was reared with the nuns, as it's likely you've heard tell from his honour, God rest his soul.[1]

COLM. If he ever spoke of her I do not remember it.[2] Why should he have told me about her?

BRIDE. It's a long story, and a sad pitiful story. I'd have a right to tell you one day maybe if the Lord Almighty keep us alive, but Sister Eileen will be coming now, and the two of you won't be needing the like of that to trouble you at all. [*She stands up and sweeps up the hearth.*]

COLM. Has she been long out of her mind?

BRIDE. A long while in and out of it. It's ten years she was below in the Asylum, and it was a great wonder the way you'd see her in there, not lonesome at all with the great lot were coming in from all the houses in the country, and herself as well off as any lady in England, France, or Germany, walking round in the gardens with fine shoes on her feet. Ah, it was well for her in there, God help her, for she was always a nice quiet woman, and a fine woman to look at, and I've heard tell it was 'Your Ladyship' they would call her, the time they'd be making fun among themselves.[3]

COLM. I wonder if I ever saw her before. Her face reminded me of something, or someone, but I cannot remember where I have met it.

BRIDE [*going up to the portrait over the fireplace*]. Let you come and look here, your honour, and I'm thinking you'll see.

COLM [*going over*]. Yes, that is the woman. But it was done years ago.

¹ In Notebook 26, in speaking of his uncle Colm says, 'What a life he has had. I suppose it is a good thing that this ⟨Anglo-Irish⟩ aristocracy is dying out. They were neither human nor divine.'

BRIDE. Long years surely, your honour, and it's time the whole thing was forgot, for what call has any man to be weighing his mind with the like of it and he storing sorrows till the judgment day?

[*She goes over to window.* COLM *takes down picture and looks at it closely in the lamp-light.*]

BRIDE [*looking out*]. Sister Eileen's coming now, and I'll be going off to my bed, for I'm thinking the two of you won't be needing me, and it's a right yourselves would have to be going to rest, and not sitting here talking and talking in the dark night, when people are better sleeping, and not destroying their souls, pausing and watching and they thinking over the great troubles of the world.

[*She goes out, and in a moment* SISTER EILEEN *comes in quickly from the door ⟨which leads⟩ into the open air. She is pleased and relieved when she sees* COLM.]

SISTER EILEEN. You have come back? I was afraid something had happened.

COLM. I have been in some time.

SISTER EILEEN. I thought I would hear the wheels, and I went right down to the lake the night is so beautiful. . . . You have arranged everything?

COLM. I sent a number of telegrams, and waited for answers. He is to be buried on Friday at Glan-na-nee, and the coffin will come down tomorrow.[1]

SISTER EILEEN. When the storm broke I was sorry you had gone; you must have got very wet on the road across the mountains.

COLM. It rained heavily on Slieve na-Ruadh, but I am nearly dry again.

SISTER EILEEN. I was out for a little while getting flowers for your uncle's room, but I did not find many they were so broken with the rain.

COLM. Then you saw what a change the rain has made among the trees.

SISTER EILEEN. It has ended the spring. I was just thinking what a difference there is since I arrived here three months ago, with the moonlight shining everywhere on the snow.

¹ In the two-act versions of the play, Act I takes place on a stormy winter's night, Act II on a 'clear evening in June', 'the first night of summer'.

Earlier drafts stress Colm's sense of the mortality in life and nature. The typescript in Item 50 retains a great deal of the following speeches developed in Act II of Item 51:

COLM. There is an anguish in this splendour of June. One feels one's mortality . . . The furze bushes are withering already, and the hawthorn is decayed.

S. EILEEN. What would you do if you had been sitting all the evening by a death-bed as I have. [*The light begins to get low.*]

COLM [*talking slowly*]. It is natural for old men to die. This pageant of blossoms that fades in a few hours is far more terrible. Don't you realize the irony of beautiful life? Diamonds and rubies that do not feel are beautiful for ever, but women and flowers fulfil their task of propagation and wither in a day. It is sadder than death.

Later in the same act:

COLM [*moodily*]. Death is always terrible. . . . The last few nights—I suppose because I am not strong—I have been haunted by that appalling sensation in which we realize the gulf of annihilation we are being whirled into . . .

Both earlier drafts also contain the following exchange:

S. EILEEN. You are easily overcome.

COLM. If you had been brought from Paris to find yourself at the foot of a desolate mountain between a dead man and a nun with vague madness and risk about you you would feel what I mean. We are at an ultimate climax of desolation, yet . . . through it all it is possible to find a strange impulse of joy.

² Earlier versions of the play have a portrait of Colm's uncle over the fireplace and under the dead man's pillow is discovered a notebook containing a drawing of Mary Costello as a young girl together with instructions concerning 'a letter to be read by my heir'. The letter reads in part:

'I have never known you or wished to know you, but as you will live in my house, I want to leave you a word that you may not live in it as I did.

'My life has gone to ruin because I misunderstood love and because I was scrupulous when I should have been strong. I treated women as if they were gods and they treated me as if I might be damned for their amusement.

'When I was a young man I read Goethe and Heine, the men who were most prominent in literature at that time, and I learned things from them that made the women of my country avoid me because they were pious, and the men because they were stupid.

'If you love a woman subdue her. You will not love a woman it is not lawful to love. No man of our blood has ever been unlawful. If you live in the country live with the country and find a woman who will understand with you the mysteries of growth and life. Let her know as you will know the two twilights and the quietness of the night. Neglect nothing, for God is in the earth and not above it. In the wet elm leaves trailing in the lane in autumn, in the deserted currents of the streams, and in the breaking out of the sap, there are joys that collect all the joy that is in religion and art. . . .'

COLM. It seems like three years since you telegraphed for me, we have made such a world for ourselves.[1]

SISTER EILEEN [*changing the subject*]. What have you got there?

COLM. It is the picture from that corner. [*He turns it round to her.*] I saw her tonight at the graveyard of Glan-na-nee.

SISTER EILEEN. What took you out there, surely that was not your way?

COLM. I went wrong coming home, and this woman put me right. ⟨Do you know anything of the woman?⟩

SISTER EILEEN. I have heard a good deal about her, perhaps more than you have.

COLM. Bride has been telling me that she was a long time in the Asylum, and that she was connected in some way with my uncle.

SISTER EILEEN. He wanted to marry her although she was beneath him, but when it was all arranged she broke it off because he did not believe in God.

COLM. And after that she went mad?

SISTER EILEEN. After that. And your uncle shut himself up. He told me it was nearly twenty years since it happened, and yet he had never spoken of it to anyone. I do not think he would have told me if it had not been for his dislike of religious orders and the clothes I wear.[2]

COLM. You mean he told you as a warning. . . . And yet I suppose you take her as an example to be followed.

SISTER EILEEN. She did what was right. No woman who was really a Christian could have done anything else. . . .

COLM. I wish you had seen her tonight screaming and crying out over the bogs.

SISTER EILEEN. I do not want to see her. . . . I have seen your uncle for three months and his death today. That is enough.

COLM. It is far from enough if it has not made you realize that in evading her impulses this woman did what was wrong and brought this misery on my uncle and herself.

¹ In all two-act versions, and apparently in the version in Item 50, they argue a great deal. (See Appendix D, pp. 279–80.)

SISTER EILEEN [*giving him back the picture*]. We cannot argue about it.[1] We do not see things the same way. . . . Has she changed a great deal since that was done?

COLM. Less than he has. [*He hangs picture up again.*] He was right in thinking that their story is a warning. . . . At that time they were about the ages we are tonight, and now one is a mad woman, and the other has been tortured to death—[*Some one knocks.*] Come in!

[BRIDE, **half rolled in a shawl, as if she was not fully dressed,** *comes in with a telegram.*]

BRIDE [*giving it to* SISTER EILEEN]. That has just come for you now, Sister Eileen. It came into town after Mr. Colm had gone away, and they gave it to an old man was driving out west with an ass and cart.

[SISTER EILEEN *takes it and reads it left.* BRIDE *takes* COLM *right.*]

BRIDE [*whispering*]. I heard from the old man he seen Mary Costello coming in great haste over the hills, so let your honour not be afeard if you hear her singing or laughing, or letting a shout maybe in the darkness of the night.

COLM. Is there nothing one can do for her?

BRIDE. Nothing at all your honour. It's best to leave her alone. [*She goes towards the door.*]

SISTER EILEEN [*turning to her, in a low voice*]. Can some one drive me into the town tomorrow? I must go to Dublin by the first train in the morning.

BRIDE. We can surely, Sister Eileen. And what time will we send to meet you coming back?

SISTER EILEEN. I am not coming back.

BRIDE. Well the Lord speed you Sister Eileen, and that the Almighty God may stretch out a holy hand to preserve and prosper you, and see you safe home. [*Turning to the door.*] It's lonesome you'll be leaving the lot of us behind you, and you after bringing a kind of a new life into this house was a dark quiet place for a score of years, and will be dark again maybe from this mortal night. [*She goes out left.*]

¹ The two-act versions of the play, in which Sister Eileen stays on to nurse the wounded Colm, provide a more satisfactory explanation for this summons: 'I have heard from the Superior. She is short of nurses, so she wrote to Dr. Burke to know when I would be free. He answered that you were nearly well, so I am to go tomorrow.' Draft 52 'J' includes the direction [*with an unconscious gesture like* COLM's].

² In the earlier drafts (including a variation in 52 'J') Colm's plea for the fullness of life and defence of nature's law is developed through their argument over religion:

'I salute all my sensations even those that are beggarly or half insane, you will not recognize any that do not come to you in the livery of the saints. You have ceased to be human and now your soul is as unnatural as the toe of a Chinese princess.

S. EILEEN [*half turning away*]. I do not even know what you call a natural person.

COLM. I mean a person who has contrived a hierarchy of all his moods and passions. . . . If you were natural you would feel the glory of this moment. Death has passed near us. We are lost in a wilderness of branches. Yet this room with the old oak chairs and books is exquisitely beautiful. . . . You will not answer completely. You are asking yourself if it is right to sit up with me. Parasitic ideas are holding you back from the ecstasy of freedom.

⟨·   ·   ·   ·   ·⟩

Yet if men are born clean the excitement of life forms round them in a clear atmosphere where no parasite with thick leaves can flourish. . . . The only calm of importance is the calm of the man who feels the vortex of passion and death straining beneath him and is able to deride it. . . . The world is a mode of the Divine exaltation and every sane fragment of force ends in a fertile passion that is filled with joy. It is the infertile excitements that are filled with death. That is the whole moral and aesthetic of the world.

S. EILEEN. You would say that prayer is not fertile yet it is not filled with death.

COLM. Prayer is the veiled cry of power before the shadow of its own annihilation. No emotion is simple, and we can find the whole range of exaltation at any moment of rapture.

⟨·   ·   ·   ·   ·⟩

The worst vice is slight compared with the guiltiness of a man or woman who defies the central order of the world. . . . The only truth a wave knows is that it is going to break. The only truth a bud knows is that it is going to expand and flower. The only truth we know is that we are a flood of magnificent life the fruit of some frenzy of the earth. . . . The European races may be swept away, humanity itself may die out, but a turmoil of life is within us. It has come from eternity and I suppose it will go on for eternity.

S. EILEEN. It is simpler to believe in God.

COLM. I will believe in millions of them if you like, but I have no doubt they care as little for us as we care for the sorrows of an ant-hill.

³ Earlier drafts read, 'You will not forget Kilgreine. A day will come when you will mourn over your own barrenness. . . . I do not blame you. I only blame the creed that has distorted the nature God made for you in the beginning.'

COLM [*with a change in his voice*]. What is this talk of your leaving me tomorrow?

SISTER EILEEN. Someone has told the Mother Superior your uncle is dead, and she ⟨telegraphs⟩—as she puts it—that she is short of nurses and will need me for a new case tomorrow.[1]

COLM. Cannot you stay a little longer?

SISTER EILEEN. I am afraid not possibly. . . . [***Looking up at the clock***.] I must soon go and pack up.

COLM. Telegraph to the Mother Superior that you cannot leave me till the funeral is over. . . . Then I will have you three days more.

SISTER EILEEN. I cannot. . . . There is no use talking about it.

COLM. We must talk about it till I make you decide with your whole mind whether you will obey the earth, or repeat the story of the mad woman and my uncle.[2]

SISTER EILEEN [*severely*]. If you say what I think you are wishing to say, I will have to leave you and not speak to you any more. That is all you will gain.

COLM [*sternly, locking door*]. You shall not go till I have said what I have to say. Then if you are weak enough to give up your share of what is best in life, you may go where you will.

SISTER EILEEN [*piteously*]. I wish you would not spoil the last night we are together.

COLM. It may not be the last. . . .

SISTER EILEEN [*goes over and lights candle*, ***picks up bow of crepe***]. Please open the door, and let me go to bed. I have been very wrong to allow you to talk to me as I have done, but I will go back to my true life tomorrow, and I will ask to be forgiven.

COLM. And you think that you will forget this place[3] and what has been said here?

SISTER EILEEN. It is only those who do the will of God who are happy; that is all I know.

[*A burst of hysterical laughter is heard outside, and then a sob and a scrap of singing. A moment afterwards the door is pushed open and* MARY

¹ The version in Item 50 has Mary singing the Cuilfhionn, then seeing Sister Eileen and Colm: 'A nun too [*comes over and looks at her very carefully*]. You're a fine woman God bless—I talk the way they do now [*with a much more cultivated accent*]. You must excuse me I've had ⟨a⟩ great deal of trouble [*falling back to the country language*]. You're a fine woman, God bless you though it's a nun you are itself' etc.

COSTELLO *comes in, dazzled with the light, and goes over left without seeing* COLM *or* SISTER EILEEN. *She goes over to the bureau in the corner and sees that one of the drawers is open and pounces on it.* **She finds a ring case, and takes out two rings and puts them on her fingers, making the stones sparkle in the lamp light; she finds a bundle of white linen,** *takes out a silk dress and makes a movement as if she is going to throw it over her head. Before she does so she looks round stealthily, and sees* COLM *and* SISTER EILEEN. *She drops the dress on the floor with a cry, picks up her shawl and runs to the door, then stops, and turns towards them.*]

MARY. ⟨A nun is it?⟩[1] What right have the like of you to be walking out through the world and looking on us when it isn't any harm we're doing? What right have the nuns I'm saying to be meddling with the world? [*She recognizes* COLM.] I seen that man tonight, God bless him, and he driving round on the roads. [*She goes up to him.* SISTER EILEEN *has involuntarily drawn close to* COLM. MARY *looks from one to the other with a peculiar smile.*] You're a fine handsome woman, God bless you, a fine beautiful woman I'm saying, and let you not mind them at all. [*She puts her hand pleadingly on* SISTER EILEEN's *arm.*] Sure you won't mind them, Sister, tell me out you won't mind them at all?

SISTER EILEEN. Who shall I not mind?

MARY [*throwing up her hands, and then clasping them together and turning half round with a shriek of laughter*]. 'Who shall I not mind?' says she. 'Who shall I not mind?' It's a long while since I was in school Sister, yet it's well I know the like of that. It's well I know you've no call to mind what the priests say, or the bishops say, or what the angels of God do be saying, for it's little the like of them knows of women or the seven sorrows of earth. [*With anguish in her voice. She sinks her head and sees the bow of crepe in* SISTER EILEEN's *hand.*] . . . Who is it is dead, Mister, if that's the token of death?

COLM. My uncle, Colm Sweeny.

MARY [*indifferently*]. And a long rest behind him, why would that trouble me now? I was afeard it was my little children [*she looks up to* COLM, *and speaks piteously*]—for if I was never married your honour, and have no children I do be thinking it's alive they must

¹ Earlier drafts treat this idea more directly in Colm's speech to Sister Eileen, 'Yet I know you have a passionate instinct for children. Far down in below the level of your creed you know that motherhood, the privilege that lifts women up to share in the pain and passion of the earth, is more holy than the vows you have made', and in his letter to his friend O'Neill in Paris, 'The interest of the present moment is to know whether she will give up her religion and remain with me . . . or add another to the unhealthy women of Ireland who scorn the rules of life and the beauty that is possible and only possible within them.'

² In draft 52 'J' Mary Costello leaves the room, Colm reads his uncle's letter to Sister Eileen, and Mary Costello returns to repeat her final warning to Sister Eileen.

be if I never had them itself. . . . [*Raising her voice to a plaintive cry.*] ⟨I do see them sometimes when my head's bad and I do be falling into my sleep. . . .⟩ There are five children, five children that wanted to live, God help them, if the nuns and the priests with them had let me be [*swaying herself with anguish*][1]. . . . They're always nice your honour, with clean faces, and nice frocks on them and little sticks in their hands. But I wouldn't like them to begin to die on me, for I'm not like all the rest of you [*covering her face with her hands*] . . . and it's queer things I do be seeing the time the moon is full. [*She bends her head sobbing piteously.*]

SISTER EILEEN. Don't mind them now, Mary, there isn't anything to frighten you here.

MARY [*still sobbing*]. Oh, my head's perished with the night wind, and I do be very lonesome the time I do be going the bog road, with the rabbits running round on it and they drowned with the dew. [*She looks up piteously at* SISTER EILEEN, *sees the little cross she has hanging round her neck; she takes the cross in her hand.*] Will you give me the little cross you have Sister, for I've lost the one I had and I do be wanting the like of it to sit and hold in my hand. [SISTER EILEEN *gives it to her.*] . . . May the Almighty God reward you Sister, and give you five nice children before you die. [*She gives her the rings.*] . . . May his blessing be on them rings, and they going on your hand, and his blessing be on your hand and it working with the linen when the time is come. [*She looks at the crucifix in her hand.*] . . . This will be a quiet thing to be looking on, and it'll keep me still the long evenings when the moon is low, and there do be white mists passing on the bog, the time the little children I have do be lepping, and crying out to each other, and making games in the dark night, and no Christian waking but myself only, and the white geese you'd hear a mile or maybe two mile and they making a great stir over the bog. [*She moves towards the door.*][2] . . . I'll be going now I'm thinking, for I've a long way and this will be keeping me company in the dark lane through the wood. God save you kindly the two of you. There's great marrying in the world but it's late we were surely, and let yourselves not be the same. Let you mind the words I was saying, and give no heed to the priests or the bishops or the angels of God, for it's little the like of them, I was saying, knows about women or the seven sorrows of the earth. [*She goes out.*]

¹ Synge tried several different scenes with Mary Costello. She first appears in Notebook 28, while he still planned a two-act form with Stephen Costello shooting Colm:

MARY [*bringing over the dress and laying it at* S.E.*'s feet*]. There's a fine dress, Sister, will go well upon you, for it has been upon me—one while only—and it's the same size we are. [*She picks it up.*] It's cut low in the front Sister and shows out a bit of your neck but it's a fine neck you have, Sister, though who'ld know it at all and you covered round in black as if it was an old widow you were or the ⟨thing⟩ they put scaring the crows. [*Taking the rings.*] And here are the rings, Sister, rings made for myself and I think it's on your finger they'll go. [*She takes* S.E.*'s finger to fit on the rings. To* COLM.] Fit them on her your honour, my hand is trembling, I do be ill the dawn does come—and it is on this finger they should go. [COLM *fits the ring on the finger that* MARY *holds out on* S.E.*'s hand.*]

MARY [*stands up and takes off* S.E.*'s veil*]. It isn't the like of that thing you'll be wanting now. Now I'll be going and I'll have this thing to be keeping me company when the night is ⟨over⟩. [*She stands up holding the bow in her hand.*] Now may the Almighty God reward and prosper you and give you five nice children before you die. May his blessing be on the rings, and they going on your hand and his blessing be on your hand [*she bends her head and crosses herself*] and it working with the linen when the time is come.

CURTAIN

Item 50 offers a different exit for Mary:

[*Clock strikes the four quarters and two o'clock.*]

M.C. I'll go now and God save you, I have a long way to go before morning. God save you kindly there's great marrying in the world now but it's late we were surely. [*She goes out.*]

S.E. She is talking quite quietly again. I think she will find her way all right.

C. I suppose she came to see the body and did not remember what she wanted—

S.E. I suppose so. [*She goes over and folds up the baby linen very slowly.* COLM *looks at her and then goes to the window.*]

C. It is a very wonderful night.

52 'J' incorporated both these versions, adding the final scene as in the text.

² The typescript in Item 51 reads, 'Why will you worship the mania of Saint Teresa? Your own beauty, your own expression of the divinity of woman is holier than she is.' In this version Sister Eileen reads from an old copy of St. Teresa's works.

³ This sentence is all that remains of one of the basic themes running through the two-act versions of the play and still implied in many of the arguments in the final text. Act I of the typescript in Item 51 begins with Sister Eileen's reading from a page of Colm's manuscript:

'Every life is a symphony and the translation of this sequence into music and from music again, for those who are not musicians, into literature, or painting or sculpture, is the real effort of the artist.

'The emotions which pass through us have neither end nor beginning, are a part of eternal sensations, and it is this almost cosmic element in the person which gives all personal art a share in the dignity of the world.

'Biography, even autobiography, cannot give this revelation, for the deeds of a man's lifetime are impersonal and concrete, might have been done by anyone, while art is the expression of the abstract beauty of the person. . . .'

Later in the first act Colm tries to explain the passage: 'If you saw it with the context you would find it simple enough, but it is not easy to explain to you in fragments. . . .

[*Note 3 continued on p. 176.*]

[SISTER EILEEN *goes over and puts the linen and other things back into the drawer.*][1]

COLM. Another voice has cried out to you. In a few years you will be as old as she is. There will be divine nights like this night and birds crying in the heather, but nothing will reach you, as nothing reaches my uncle at the other side of the hall. [*He goes over to her.*] I am not a woman and I cannot judge of all your feelings, yet I know you have a profound impulse for what is peculiar to women. You realize that the forces which lift women up to a share in the pain and passion of the world are more holy than the vows you have made. [*She stands before him motionless; he speaks more tenderly.*] Before this splendour of the morning you cannot lie. You know that the spirit of life which has transfigured the world is filling you with radiance. Why will you worship the mania of the saints when your own existence is holier than they are.[2] People renounce when they have not power to retain; you have power and courage. . . . I implore you to use them.

SISTER EILEEN. I don't know what to do. . . . You are giving me such pain and yet. . . .

COLM. There is the first note of the birds. . . . When the sun comes over that ridge I will ask you to be my wife. . . . You cannot refuse. The trees might as well refuse to grow fragrant and green when it is May, or the birds to sing before the dawn. . . . There are the larks, and the wrens. . . . You have half an hour. . . . I will not touch you. . . . I will not try to persuade you. It is quite unnecessary. The world will persuade you. **The breath that drew out this forest of leaves and sent quivering voices to chant in them, is making of you also a beautiful note in the world.**[3] **. . . There is the willow warbler, you have a quarter of an hour. Will you go and put this dress about you. I am not in a humour for blasphemy.**

[SISTER EILEEN *takes the green dress and goes out without looking at him. He looks out for an instant, then packs the rest of the papers into the bureau drawer. He goes back to the window. In a moment* SISTER EILEEN *comes in behind him in a green silk dress which is cut low at the neck. She reaches the window just as the red morning light sweeps into the room.*]

SISTER EILEEN [*in a low voice*]. **Colm, I have come back to you.**

Note (cont.), p. 175.

Music is such a direct expression of the human personality that if we know music it is not easy to take up any point of psychology without finding some strange likeness to the things music has expressed. In these notes on the symphony I am trying to point out that this supreme "form" of art is a reflection of the sequence that each person, and, in a sense, all humanity tends to pass through in life. The two subjects on which all our glory is constructed are the facts of love and death. . . . After dealing with the first movement that is filled with passion and excitement I go on to the next. [*Reading*] "The position of the slow movement after the climax of the opening is also wonderfully suggestive. This sigh of beautiful relief, which comes as an explanation rather than a mere cessation of an excitement that is always pain, is the last utterance of man. A cycle of experience is the only definite unity, and when all has been passed through, and every joy and pain has been resolved in one passion of relief, the only rest that can follow is in the dissolution of the person."'

(As late as draft 52 'J' Synge retained this speech by Colm: 'Death should pass us like the dead march in a symphony, where a turn of the hand can wake a new movement of life. . . . It has done so tonight.')

In Act II of the typescript in 51, Colm applies this philosophy to their argument over Sister Eileen's belief in Christianity:

'The world is an orchestra where every living thing plays one entry and then gives his place to another. We must be careful to play all the notes. It is for that we are created. If we play them well we are not exorbitantly wretched. . . . No one pretends to ignore the bitterness of disease and death. It is an immense infinite horror, and the more we learn to set the real value on the vitality of life the more we will dread death. Yet any horror is better than the stagnation of belief. . . . There is stagnation in everything that has been once mature. . . . The world orchestra has been playing its oratorio for two thousand years and the thing has become effete. Now the players have gone out to gain new powers in lonely exaltation. The people who rebel from the law of God are not those who are essaying strange notes in the dark alleys of the world but the fools who linger in the aisles droning their withered chants with senile intonation. . . . I mean that in the Christian synthesis each separate faculty has been dying of atrophy. The synthesis has fallen. The imagination has wandered away to grow puissant and terrible again, in lonely vigils where she sits and broods among things that have been touched by madmen and things that have the smell of death on them and books written with the blood of horrible crimes. The intellect has peered down into the tumult of atoms and up into the stars till she has forgotten her complements in the personality and the instinct for practical joy has taught anarchists to hate in the passion of their yearning for love . . . . In the end men will grow human again with a more wonderful manhood. Every passion will unite in new discords resolving in what are to us inconceivable harmonies.'

Finally, as he waits for Sister Eileen to return to him, Colm stands alone at the window:

'[*speaking slowly with wonder in his voice*]. Every life is a symphony. It is this cosmic element in the person which gives all personal art, and all sincere life, and all passionate love a share in the dignity of the world. . . . If art is the expression of the abstract beauty of the person there are times when the person is the expression of the beauty that is beyond the world. . . .' (See also Oxford *Prose*, p. 3.)

¹ Earlier versions add the words, 'It is far more painful and noble to break through the creeds into life than to go down with them into the pit of abnegation.'

COLM [*turning towards her*]. You are infinitely beautiful, and you have done a great action. It is the beauty of your spirit that has set you free, and your emancipation is more exquisite than any that is possible for men who are redeemed by logic.[1] You cannot tell me why you have changed. That is your glory. As a moth comes out to a new sphere of odour and colour and flight, so you have come out to live in a new sphere of beautiful love. . . . Listen to the tumult the birds are making in the trees. That is our marriage hymn. Without love this world would be a loathsome sandhill, and a soul without love is not a great deal better. . . . Speak to me. I want to hear you, your voice will have new cadence from today.

SISTER EILEEN. I have left my veil in the room where your uncle is lying. . . . I seem to be in a dream that is wider than I am. I hope God will forgive me. I cannot help it.

COLM. How many people ask to be forgiven for the most divine instant of their lives. Let us be wiser than they are. [*He takes up one of the rings.*] Here is the ring that was the sorrowful heirloom of my uncle. Give me your hand. I, the male power, have overcome with worship you, the soul of credulous feeling, the reader of the saints. From our harmonized discord new notes will rise. In the end we will assimilate with each other and grow senseless and old. We have incarnated God, and been a part of the world. That is enough. [*He takes her hand.*] In the name of the Summer, and the Sun, and the Whole World, I wed you as my wife. [*He puts the ring on her finger.*]

CURTAIN

UNPUBLISHED MATERIAL

PART TWO

SCENARIOS, DIALOGUES, AND FRAGMENTS

(1894–1908)

I

PLAN FOR A PLAY

The following scenario from Item 50 was written in German, according to Synge's custom of writing as much as possible in the language he was studying at the time. Synge lived in Germany from 29 July 1893 to 12 June 1894, and returned for a two-month visit at the end of that year before moving to Paris on 1 January 1895. A diary entry for 25 April 1894 reads, in German, 'Plan for a play', and that for 12 May of the same year, 'Began writing a play'. The following translation was prepared for E. M. Stephens during his work on the biography of Synge, and has been revised by Paul F. Botheroyd.

23.4.93 Würzburg
Act I

Scene 1. Hero alone, a clever young gentleman who is fed up with the vanity of London life and wishes to enjoy nature and art on his estate in Ireland. His agent comes to him and tells him that a farm has just been rented to a widow and her daughter etc.

Scene 2. Cabin of the widow, she with the daughter in it. To them the hero, they tell him of the son of the house, who is said to be very clever. He, the hero, falls in love with the girl and goes.

Scene 3. Entrance-hall of a house where a big party is being given. The brother comes rather late and at the door recognizes his coachman as his brother, soon he goes in and is introduced to a lady who is the only sister of the hero.

Act II

Little wood near the widow's cabin. Hero, the girl soon to him. He reveals his love and at last gains an assurance from her. They then go to the cabin and talk with the mother about it. In the meantime by chance his sister appears in the background, looks at the couple in amazement and soon follows [them into] the cabin, which opens onto the stage. After much talk she rushes away in anger. The hero at once names a definite day for the wedding and goes after her.

Scene 2. Cabin evening of the wedding day, the widow and soon to her her son, who inquires about everything. Room of the poet brother who is in it; soon to him his brother who inquires about the wedding.

Act III

Room of the hero, who sits alone in it in a sad mood, to him his wife, who imagines that he is dissatisfied with her although it is much more with himself that he is dissatisfied. To them the brother who is a young poet. They talk together about humanity etc and the hero is encouraged somewhat by this. Now a letter arrives from the sister which announces forgiveness and her arrival soon.

Scene II. Another room, poet alone, to him the sister with whom he is in love.

Scene III. Widow's cabin, she and her daughter in it, to them the scoundrel brother and afterwards the poet.

Act IV

Room of the hero, who is chatting with the poet, to him the scoundrel; as he is leaving the ladies meet him at the door and are frightened. Hero and his wife off and the poet declares his love in vain.

Act V

A wild area near the house, the poet, who has just received the news of his brother's death, sits in the foreground. Behind him comes his love and listens to him for a time without being observed. Then she comes to him and consoles him with a promise of love. Soon the hero and his wife come to them and rejoice in the union. The hero declares that what he had been lacking was a broader view of mankind and that he had learnt so much from the two brothers that from now on he can live striving for higher things.

simple underlining = English in the original
broken underlining = crossed out in the original
[ ] = words left out in the original and here restored

II

A RABELAISIAN RHAPSODY[1]

In his diary for 14 November 1896 Synge records having read The Imitation of Christ *by Thomas à Kempis; he returned to it frequently during the next two years and his hero of* Étude Morbide *quotes from the work (see Oxford Prose, pp. 30–31). There are also references to Rabelais in his diary for February, September, and October 1898.*

W. B. Yeats in his essay J. M. Synge and the Ireland of his Time *states that Synge had planned a complete version of* The Imitation of Christ *in the language of his 'Translations'. However, in Synge's notebooks there exist only variations on the following dialogue. The first draft appears to be four heavily emended manuscript pages in Notebook 15. A further variation appears in manuscript in Item 22, and Item 50 contains two typed pages with manuscript alterations based on part of the material in 22. Later still, Synge apparently planned to incorporate the dialogue in the lengthy discussion-novel between Costello and another (22A). The theme bears a strong resemblance to the arguments presented in the two-act version of* When the Moon Has Set.

The following text is based on 22 and 50, with additions from 15 indicated in bold type. Editorial emendations are indicated by brackets.

THOMAS.[2] **Rabelais!** How you must thank the Almighty that he has found a place for **even** you among the saved!

RABELAIS. **Why?** Mercy is his peculiar glory! **If all were pious this mercy would ⟨remain⟩ unfulfilled.**

THOMAS. **Could you lend me an old copy ⟨of⟩ Gargantua?** I **have angelical sore throat and have some time to read.**

RABELAIS. **All are sold for a fancy price! The sum shortened my Purgatory by centuries. And the Imitation?**

THOMAS. **No demand in Hell.** Do the angels know of Pantagruel?

---

[1] This title is taken from a statement later modified in 22A: 'Here is my Rabelaisian rhapsody. I believe in gaiety which is surely a divine impulse peculiar to humanity and I think Rabelais is equal to any of the saints.'

[2] Synge varied between 'Thomas' and 'St. Thomas', in one draft giving simply the initials 'T' and 'R'.

RABELAIS. More than of the Imitation.

THOMAS. The sad but passionate ecstasy I wrote in has little to attract them, or indeed any but few upon the earth.

RABELAIS. You had all the poor and the vanquished who having nothing on the earth looked for treasure in Heaven.

THOMAS. Better thus than to feed the gross, the gluttonous!

RABELAIS. In my book there is health and laughter and activity, the true worship of the Almighty.

THOMAS. Your book is as a great flood that bears along with it dead dogs, and swine and dunghills, to cast them out in the end like carrion on the wayside. My book is like a well of water, with ferns round it and the fragrance of the earth.

RABELAIS. My book is like the great sea that will drink up all the ordures of the world, and remain yet with clean lips and pure jubilant voice. Your book is a puddle, and marred forever did but an innocent cow look backward over it.

THOMAS. You cannot drink of the sea.

RABELAIS. Nor wash in your pool. If the weather be but hot enough, you will find there a cake of mud only with frogs that breed about the centre.

THOMAS. **Alas Rabelais would you still jest so dirtily in Heaven!** If the Lord should understand you.

RABELAIS. Is the Lord a child or female? **He** who created me, Saint Rabelais, the Jester?

THOMAS. **St. Rabelais—!**

[JACOB BOEHME *passes talking to himself.*]

BOEHME. Some men love the devil who is nature and animals and children and women; these are the poets, for the poet sees the idea of God within the forms of the world.[1] Some men love God and the

---

[1] An intermediate version of this speech (22) adds the clause, 'some men love the idea of God in woman or symbol as Dante who is both a poet and a dreamer'.

angels and men; these are the philosophers who see the forms of the
world within the Lord. Life is a chain;

                    God
                    The Angels
                    Men
                    Women
                    Children
                    Animals
                    Nature.

And woman is the link between the earthly and the divine. She
laughs and weeps continually, and in the one the godly comes down
to earth and in the other the earthly goes up to God. [*Exit.*]

RABELAIS. When will Gabriel have ended his asylum?

THOMAS. He may understand, yet when the limbs lie asleep and the
soul creeps out like a white flower to the sound of harmonies that no
reveller could conceive of we feel the inner and synthetic mood near
which all others are partial and of small importance.

RABELAIS. At a fair also with ale and the sound of fiddles and dancers
and the laughter of fat women the soul is moved to an ecstasy which
is perfection and not partial.

THOMAS. **He who thirsteth desireth drink yet are some drinks
more than others.**

RABELAIS. **More indeed but who shall decide? I knew a girl with
green sickness who thirsteth ⟨for⟩ whey more than ⟨for⟩ wine
or brandy.** [*Exeunt.*]

FRA COSIMO.[1] **All the good ⟨end⟩ we desired was as the longing
of the waves to be the sea only. There was no good spirit in
earth drawing against a spirit of evil. No one has understood
motion therefore no man has understood the condition of life,
for life is motion and sorrow and turmoil are the condition
of life as are joy and tranquillity their opposites whom they
create and by which they are themselves created. All is relative
except the All.**

[1] In Item 15, from which this speech is taken, Synge contemplated including Manon,
Petrarch and Laura, Paracelsus, and Nicolette.

⟨22A⟩

D. Gaiety is a divine impulse peculiar to humanity. Is not Rabelais equal to the saints?

C. The gaiety of life is the friction of the animal and the divine. A life given to the search of gaiety is restrained by the sorrow that exists with it on the same plane and creates the opposite ecstasy of pity.

D. Is there not an antinomy also in the idealist between his life that remains human and his exaltation.

C. Ordinary life grows up into some mysticism as roots grow into a tree. Gaiety and pity are essentially in coexistent conflict. A man who lives in amusement reminds me of a man lighting a fire in the rain.

D. I suppose you are right. . . .

III

MAGNA SERENITAS
(THE WAY OF PEACE)

This scenario from Item 50 appears to have its origin in an incident Synge relates in Part IV of The Aran Islands (*see Oxford Prose, p. 156*), *describing his fourth visit to the islands from 21 September to 9 October 1901. There does not appear to be any other reference to the plot in his notebooks, although various details relate to his description of life on Aran.*

> Brigit Costello (very old woman—doting in third act)
> Mike Costello (her son, middle-aged man)
> Maurya Costello (his wife, woman of forty)
> Kitty Costello (his daughter, girl of eighteen)
> Tim Costello (son, twenty-two)
> Phil Costello (son, twenty)
> Biddy Costello (Tim's wife)
> Young children of Maurya
> A family of Sheehans
> A stroller
> Suitor of Biddy's
> Neighbours

Act I

Aran cottage kitchen, Brigit Costello and little boy. Dialogue on unhappy state of the house. Patch Sheehan comes in and borrows a kelp knife, sharpens it. Little boy asks what is he sharpening the knife for. He says to kill your father with. The others come. Boy tells his father and he sharpens knife. Various items of flirtation. Phil talks of going to America. Men go out to cut kelp etc. Women quarrel and go after them. Curtain.

Act II

By the sea. The men come in and begin quarrelling. Women come. Men go out in curaghs. Flirtation, news of big quarrel out at sea. Crowd rush in with the news of deaths of Costello men. Tumultuous curtain.

Act III

Fine summer day. Bright light village street. Public ⟨house⟩ on right, chapel on left. Monuments to dead men on back. Boy spelling out the names of the departed. Old woman passes. Noise in public ⟨house⟩. Then many couples come out and go into the chapel. The old woman and children talk outside. Marriage dance of the Costello woman who ⟨has⟩ married again. Old woman crying in background. They ⟨say⟩, 'She's mad surely crying over her sons and they nine months in their grave.' Curtain.

IV

A VERNAL PLAY

*There are three references to this play in Synge's diaries: 27 March 1902,
'Finished (?) Vernal play in verse'; 13 April 1902, 'Revised verse plays';
18 January 1903, 'Verse plays'. The two extant passages, both typescripts
with manuscript emendations, are undated but there is evidence that at least
thirteen more typewritten pages were destroyed by Synge. Scene divisions are
added here, but the list of persons is taken from a page of manuscript. The five
typescript pages identified as Scene One are taken from Item 52; the two typescript pages of Scene Two and the list of persons are taken from Item 51. The
text here varies slightly from that of the Oxford* Poems *(pp. 69–73).*

Cermuid
Boinn (his wife)
Etain
Niave   (two girls)
Orba
Luctaine   (two pipers)
Old Man

⟨Scene One⟩

BOINN. I hear girls laughing by our morning pool.

CERMUID. Their like come often when May nights are cool
To meet the Glen Cree shepherds. [*He looks out.*] Two come here
With half a sheaf of garlic, buds of fern,
Anemones, and blue-bells.

[ETAIN *and* NIAVE *come in behind without seeing the others.*]

ETAIN.   Shall we turn
Here east for Glenasmoil?

NIAVE.   The stream is near:
You made great talk this morning of the way
And now you've missed it surely.

ETAIN.   We can lay
  Our ferns among the bushes and creep through
  This oak-scrub till we find the paths of sheep,
  For in this wood, I'm saying, young men sleep
  When they're out herding when young lambs are new. . . .

                [*They see* BOINN *and* CERMUID.]

ETAIN. Look there's a mountain woman with her herd.
  They'll know the pathways, find some civil word.

NIAVE [*to* CERMUID]. I think the rain is ceasing. After three
  Or four days with rain falling gods decree
  A soft kind morning on the hills.

BOINN.   The glens
  Are finest then, you'd have a right to go
  Southwest today, to Clash or Drumnamoe
  To smell the quiet opening of young green
  And purple leaves.

ETAIN.   We heard a crook't boreen
  Led through these bushes to the Glenasmoil,
  And left Bla'cliath when the grey cock crew
  To pick these things we've here. [*Showing flowers.*]

NIAVE.   I picked the blue,
  Herself the white and yellow.

BOINN.   Some man stole
  Your word off you you'd come out here today
  But birds and younger women find a way
  To hide their hoping when it's love they seek.

CERMUID. And yet you've badly chosen for this week
  The shepherds are gone west to Killnahole.

ETAIN. We knew it, shepherd, and came here for peace
  To gather violets and stained hearts-ease,
  And in the shelter of ⟨this⟩ hawthorn tree
  We'll sit a short space with you.

BOINN.   Sycamores
  And larch and birch and sallows breathe new stores
  The time the rain is falling and it warm
  The way it's falling this day.

[*An* OLD MAN *begins to come in unseen.*]

CERMUID.   After storm
A light is in these hill turns [*He stops.*]—Who comes east?

OLD MAN [*comes in*]. By your good leave until the rain has ceased
I'll shelter with you, if there's a stone or stick
To let an old man sit.

BOINN.   My cloak is thick
I'll put an end beneath you. When men grow
Thus old as you do, with your kind owl's eyes
And hair like white clouds in a grey sunrise,
They are as nice as children.

NIAVE [*to* OLD MAN].   You've come down
From Glenasmoil?

OLD MAN.   See how my hood's as brown
With water as tuft⟨s⟩ of turfy moss
Beside two stones in rivers where winds toss
Their sprays about.

ETAIN.   Are none left through the glen?

OLD MAN. There are none old as I.

BOINN.   Nor married men?

CERMUID [*looking out*]. There is a little break behind that ring
Of cloud, and here two larks begin to sing,
So patience, girls.

OLD MAN.   Have patience, all that glen
Is filled with love.

NIAVE.   Your like of bird-eyed men
Would make it brimful surely.

OLD MAN.   I'm friend of love,
I think bad of men dying and death bends
When men make talk of love.

CERMUID.   Two rainbow ends,
Tilt downward now behind the west above,
East Kilmashogue.

ETAIN.   Who last has come should tell
  Who's in those hill⟨s⟩ at night.

OLD MAN.   You see a bell
  Of grey-touched cloud beyond the low'r Glen Dubh
  That blows to th'east and leave⟨s⟩ a tract of blue,
  Among the green-tipped beeches?

                    ⟨Scene Two⟩

ETAIN [*keening*]. All young girls must yield to rage,
  All firm youth must end in age.

BOINN [*keening*]. I call the lambs that browse with fright
  To mourn the man who died tonight.

              [ETAIN *and* ORBA *go out.*]

NIAVE [*keening*]. Every eye must fade and blear,
  Every bone bleach bare and clear.

            [NIAVE *and* LUCTAINE *go out.*]

BOINN [*keening*]. All must rise from earth and clay,
  All must end in green decay.
  They all are gone. My verse is hardly ended,
  But I will rest a little, for this hour
  I have had pains about me.

CERMUID.   With your lips
  You women rhyme the death-rhyme, yet your eyes
  Still say the songs of love.

BOINN.   The evening light
  Shines from Glencullen and Glen Dubh; the swifts
  Cry with the swallows for the end of day.
  No night like this night woke since first we left
  The marsh that ends the sea. From Kilmashogue
  Across Slieve Ruadh all the hills have wrapt
  New blueness from the raining. Hills as these
  Young men in dreams have walked on.

CERMUID.   On the sea
  The long-sailed ships sail from the east and south.

BOINN. I see the yellow moth that meets the night
Before the clouds are red. The air is weighed
Nor can with all its sweetness wind between
The boughs where we are standing. Let us climb
A little higher where the heath is bare
And while the sun is setting watch the clouds
That crown the western sea.

CERMUID.   I will throw
My oldest cloak about the old dead body.

[*When they have pulled the cloak over the body they walk up the scene.*]

BOINN [*breaking down a flowering branch*]. What fragrance, twist it in
my hair that I
Through all the night may dream of flowery hills.

[*While he crowns her she throws her arms round him.*]

Oh, Man, I would live ever lone with you,
Where every bough and hill-turn breathes with joy. [*They go out.*]

[*When they are gone for a little time two carrion crows come down and
perch on the rock above the* OLD MAN.]

V

LUASNAD, CAPA AND LAINE

Synge's diary for 17 March 1902 notes 'Keating/Play etc.' Other references occur on 29 March 1902: 'Revised Luasnad, Capa & Laine'; 13 April 1902: 'Revised verse plays'; and 18 January 1903: 'Verse plays'. What might be a hasty reference occurs on 2 January 1903: 'Typenuad'. The only surviving fragment of Luasnad, Capa and Laine *consists of twenty-four hastily scribbled and heavily emended manuscript pages in Notebook 26, which was in use at the time he was revising* When the Moon Has Set. *Several pages are torn out of the notebook, and it is likely that some of the pages torn from Item 51 belonged to this play also.*

Synge first read Geoffrey Keating's The History of Ireland *in September 1900, while on Aran, but it is likely that he was reminded of the passage by the publication by the Irish Texts Society of Volume I, translated by David Comyn. Synge's review of this edition was published in* The Speaker, *6 September 1902. The tale of the three fishermen occurs in Book I, Section V of Keating's History, pp. 140–1 of Comyn's edition, during a discussion as to the first inhabitants of Ireland:*

II. Some others say that it is three fishermen who were driven by a storm of wind from Spain unwillingly; and as the island pleased them that they returned for their wives to Spain; and having come back to Ireland again, the deluge was showered upon them at Tuaigh Innbhir ⟨'Ancient name of the mouth of the Bann'. Comyn⟩, so that they were drowned: Capa, Laighne, and Luasad, their names. It is about them the verse was sung:—

> Capa, Laighne, and Luasad pleasant,
> They were a year before the deluge
> On the island of Banbha of the bays;
> They were eminently brave.

A fragment from Luasnad, Capa and Laine *was published in the Oxford* Poems *(p. 76 and illustration) which varies somewhat from the text reproduced here. Punctuation has been added only where absolutely necessary; passages in parentheses are uncertain and may have been marked for omission; the bold type on p. 204 indicates conflation of passages.*

LUASNAD. The rain is over. Perhaps with the cold of dawn
New winds may come and blow all these clouds away
Across the sea.

CAPA.   I see a star, Luasnad.

LUASNAD. There are no stars, the stars are all washed out
As dew-drops perish.

CAPA.   Look where the teals are crying
Here to the westward.

LUASNAD.   Do you rave again
Or are my eyes blasted with all my weeping?
Is it I who am made blind to hope?

CAPA. Where is Laine?

LUASNAD.   He is fast asleep. I left him
Bent down beneath a boulder with his wife.

CAPA. Look, look! the clouds have parted ⟨to Arcturus?⟩!

LUASNAD. I can see it Capa. It is certain
That now the rains will cease.

CAPA.   There are The Seven
And there the Pole-star.

LUASNAD.   There look we had lost the North.

CAPA. The wind comes from it, and in this isle of Banba
North winds are dry.

LUASNAD.   We may walk through forests
In twenty days, then we will build a curagh
And let this north wind drive us home to Spain.

CAPA. I hear the birds upon the eastern peak.
There is new hope among them for they know
That all these rains are weary.

LUASNAD.   If they sing
The dawning cannot linger.

CAPA.   In the east
The mist⟨s⟩ are purple.

LUASNAD.   Yesterday
How many mountains could we count at dawn?

CAPA. I marked them out with knots along my belt—
Seven we saw. [*A cry of women's voices.*] Your wife is still in labour?

LUASNAD. When women do good things they choose a time
That makes it silly. Here the child will die.

[*Enter* LAINE.]

LAINE. This woman's cry has roused me and the water
Had reached my ankles!

CAPA.   See the sky
Is turning blue above us, we shall live
In spite of all this deluge.

LUASNAD.   Let us measure
The movement of the night.

[*They go down to the brink and look at some marks on a stone.*]

CAPA.   The rise out-passes
The width of both my hands—It ⟨has⟩ passed
So high above my scoring I can only
Make guesses at its measure.

LUASNAD.   It is light
And we will clamber up against the sky
To number all the hill-top⟨s⟩ that are bare.

LAINE. Pick stones Capa, the hares are hid so thick
Above us in the heather they will starve
And if they starve we perish.

CAPA.   All the goats
Will swim straight over from the eastern peak
For it will soon be covered.

LAINE.   Look, the sun
We have not seen for near two score days
Is rising.

LUASNAD. Let us feel this warmth, stand quiet.

CAPA. Something moves across the red-gold pathway.
Look on it Laine, I have looked so long
I see green moons about me.

LUASNAD.   The sea is filled
With limbs of trees the Liffey broke to pieces
Before the sea engulfed the lakes and streams.

LAINE. I see it Capa, it is high above
The red sea's level.

CAPA.   I think it is the curagh
That we first came from Spain in, for the prow
Is bending backward like a man's closed hand.

LUASNAD. The east peak is between us; it will stop there.

CAPA. Some god is guiding it for it creeps on,
Half turned against the wind.

LUASNAD.   The gods but toy
And make their sport to urge our sightless hope.

[*The cry of a child is heard on the other side of the peak.*]

LAINE. Your child is born Luasnad, and it lives.

CAPA. It is the first man's child has cried on Banba.

LUASNAD. It will be the first dead human body.
Count the hills.

LAINE.   Lugdubh,
Craigmoira, Tonagee and Inchavor.

LUASNAD. Three are covered?

LAINE.   And the rest are sinking.

CAPA [*looks round from the summit*]. Our curagh lies against the eastern peak
And all the birds are flashing round about us.

LAINE. Their peak will soon sink under.

CAPA.   In the west
The rains continue.

⟨WIFE OF CAPA.⟩   Your wife is dead Luasnad
And I have brought your infant. See, a boy.

LAINE. If the goats swim over from the eastern peak
Their milk will feed him.

⟨WIFE OF CAPA.⟩   I have wrapped him warm
With your dead wife's green mantle. Are we saved
Now that the rains are over and the air is warm?

CAPA. It was late winter when the rains began,
Now it is early summer. Winds may rise—

[*Wild cry on the hill.*]

WIFE OF CAPA. It is the wife of Laine who laments
The wife of Luasnad.

CAPA.   Goats are swimming and
Our curagh floats here westward with the tide.

LAINE. It will reach us if no north winds waken.
There is a ripple on our left hand side,
The prow is turning. Come down and we may reach it.

WIFE OF CAPA. I leave your child Luasnad, it is sleeping
And I would wail its mother. [*Puts it down beside* LUASNAD *and goes down.*]

CAPA [*below*].   The goats have seen us
And passed on in the sea.

LAINE.   The wind is gaining,
The prow is turning down against the south—
[*Runs down into the water, falls and climbs out again.*]
The water is not salted, taste it Capa. [*They drink.*]

LUASNAD. The gods are jesting with them.

[*Crying from the women.*]

CAPA.   Still it rises.

LUASNAD. I think it is the end of all men's life
For I am sick with hoping. While they talked
I saw two great green wood-birds flown from Spain
Pass from the eastern peak.

[LAINE *and* CAPA *pass, chasing hares.*]

CAPA.   Strike it Laine.

LUASNAD. And in the foam while Capa gaze⟨d⟩ at sea
I saw a sick man's crutches girt with hide.

LAINE. The wind is rising—there is spray around
The eastern peak—

LUASNAD.   What was the eastern peak.

LAINE. Before this white sun and this dry north wind
These waters cannot linger.

LUASNAD.   In a storm
These rock⟨s⟩ would tumble.

CAPA.   There is no sign of storm.

LUASNAD. You did not hear the gannets all last night
Fly past us from the north?

LAINE.   I dreamed of Spain
And of the first grey morning when we saw
These hills of Banba.

CAPA.   I dreamed nine babes
Were born in one bearing by my wife.

[*The two women carry in the dead body of* LUASNAD's *wife.*]

WIFE OF LAINE [*sings*]. We steered with star of Spain
To come with worlds that wane

WIFE OF CAPA. Where winds are wailing.

WIFE OF LAINE. We left the scent of Spring
Upon your grave to sing

WIFE OF CAPA. Where clouds are sailing.

CAPA. The wind is turning west.

LAINE.   The sunlight scorches,
There is no shadow on this spire of stone.

[*A gust of wind carries the cloth from the face of the dead woman into the
sea.*]

LUASNAD. The winds increase.

WIFE OF LAINE.   Are you frightened, Luasnad?
  I think the seas will lessen day by day.

LUASNAD. You hope our bones may win a space to bleach?

CAPA. He is gloomy for his wife has perished
  And his man-child may follow.

[*A wave breaks on the rock.*]

LUASNAD.   There is no gloom
  Beyond this gloom that hems the shroud of all men.

WIFE OF LAINE. Is there a war among the gods and have
  The sea gods conquered?

LUASNAD.   There is no war.
  The gods work only to gain peace from prayer.

[*Another wave breaks.*]

CAPA. Speak no more evil Luasnad, it may harm us.

LUASNAD. I have ceased to pray, and there is nothing
  More apt than prayer to anger.

WIFE OF LAINE.   Say to them
  If they will take this water from the earth
  That we will cease to call them when we labour
  Or ask them means of joy.

CAPA.   Speak it Luasnad,
  You are a wizard and know secret tongues.

[*The baby cries.*]

LUASNAD. All this life has been a hurtful game
  Played out by steps of anguish. Every beast
  Is bred with fearful torment in the womb
  And bred by fearful torments in life-blood.
  Yet by a bait of love the aimless gods
  Have made us multitudes.

WIFE OF CAPA [*keens*].   You have born a child
  In rain mists dark and wild

WIFE OF LAINE.   And weeping perished.

WIFE OF CAPA. Your dead breast is dry
  And your dark babe will die

WIFE OF LAINE. Unloved, uncherished.

LAINE. Come women, quit the dead.
  When once these wind⟨s⟩ have fallen earth will dry.

WIFE OF LAINE [*stopping ⟨and⟩ turning as they are going out*].
  Come Luasnad, bring your infant. You will perish
  If you stay dreaming—

LUASNAD.   Do not linger in your grieving
  For he will perish though I dream or wake.

[*She goes out.*]

I thought to build upon this isle of Banba
A tower of kings—

[*Another wave breaks and a stone rolls down from the head of the
mountain and strikes the infant.* LUASNAD *unfolds the green mantle.
Wind and waves.*]

                The gods have pitied him,
We cannot reach the morning. All mankind
Will cease with dusk, and leave a sightless world
Where waves winds fish, wild forms that crowd the sea
Will please the curious fancies of the gods.

[*A large wave breaks. Cries.* WIFE OF LAINE *runs in.*]

WIFE OF LAINE. Look Luasnad, all the others are washed out
  And drowning. As I climbed towards them came a wave
  Curling across the boulders where they sat
  That took them all as I would take some feathers
  And threw them out to sea.

LUASNAD.   Our time will come.

WIFE OF LAINE. I am so frightened, Luasnad.

LUASNAD.   All things die;
  I think the gods are grown old or sick
  And for some bitter envy blast the world.

[*A wave dashes over them.*]

WIFE OF LAINE. Hold me Luasnad, I will fall and drown.

[*They cling to each other.*]

LUASNAD. Behind this rock we may sit thus till dawning.

WIFE OF LAINE. Where is your infant?

LUASNAD. A stone rolled down and killed him.

WIFE OF LAINE. Then bind your wife's green mantle round us both
  The night is growing very cold and dark.

LUASNAD. I think a moon will waken if the night
  Should let her light slip towards us.

[*Comes down and binds the mantle round them.*]

My wife and her dead baby have been washed
Out with the last great ebbing. We remain
Alone in the world of night.

WIFE OF LAINE.   It would make
  A strange new life if we came through this tempest
  And lived like Eve and Adam building up
  A new mankind.

LUASNAD.   Perhaps the gods have purpose
  To fill the world with a new race more fit
  Than man has been to bear the rage of life.
  But woman they will kill us, man must die. . . .

WIFE OF LAINE. There is the moon Luasnad, and three stars. . . .
  But in the other life, whence ghosts have wandered
  Shall I find Laine out and Capa's wife
  And talk about this tempest?

LUASNAD.   We are like
  These crowns of foam that gleam and flash with gold
  And when our storm of passion has died out
  A few old gods will just remember man.

WIFE OF LAINE. Hold me closer Luasnad, I am trembling—
  I do not like to vanish and let live
  The sea and stars without me.

LUASNAD. I can feel
Your heart beat and your blood-warmth underneath
Your thick wet habits.

WIFE OF LAINE. All the clouds have broken.
How white the waves look racing towards the sun!
And how deep black the troughs! Perhaps the gods
Have felt a little pity for my youth?

LUASNAD. There is no pity in the aimless gods
And they would mock me with your kind warm voice.

WIFE OF LAINE. It is hard to die.

LUASNAD. Women know more pain
When they give birth to children.

WIFE OF LAINE. I am young
And I have never yet conceived with child. . . .
Why would the gods who made us now destroy?

LUASNAD. The gods have never made us. They have gotten
Our first grey seed upon the slime of earth
And have dealt with us as we deal with kine
Who know the one brother. We are one
With all this moon and sea white and the wind
That slays us. And our passions move when we die
Among the stars that wander or stand quiet
In the great depths of night.

WIFE OF LAINE. Take your hand
Down from my bosom Luasnad.

(LUASNAD. I love you woman.

WIFE OF LAINE. You would not shame the love of our dead consorts?)

LUASNAD. The great west boulder of our peak has fallen
And with the next high river of the tide
Our death will reach us. There is not any hope.

WIFE OF LAINE. In this white moonlight perhaps the wind ⟨may
die?⟩.

LUASNAD. You the fairest of all women, turn your lips.
The last strong man must perish,
Let me flash a last red flame of love
Across the brink of death, and shout defiance
Up to the aimless gods.

WIFE OF LAINE.   **Look on the eastern side,
A moonbeam has burst through and touched the sea.**

LUASNAD. There is some shape behind the eastern dark,
A vessel all roofed over smeared with pitch.

WIFE OF LAINE. Are men within it?

LUASNAD.   I think the gods have brought
From the dead country where the seas have end
Some new wild race to populate the wreck
Of this dead world.

WIFE OF LAINE.   (It may be Luasnad)
The craft of some wily prophet of the east
Has built up there a little band of men
To make mankind eternal.

LUASNAD.   If men steer,
The gods will guide this vessel with their hate
Till all her beams float down the endless sea.

WIFE OF LAINE. The clouds have come again and veiled the moon
And I can only hear the howl of waves.

LUASNAD. Maybe our frightened passions forged for us
This shadow on the waves.

WIFE OF LAINE.   Does day come on
For I am very stiff and cramped with cold.

LUASNAD. Cling closer, I will warm you with my breath.

WIFE OF LAINE. Remember Laine and the dead cold smile
That curled his (lip).

LUASNAD.   Dead men pass. There lives
One only life, one passion of one love,
One world wind sea, then one deep dream of death.

WIFE OF LAINE. I think that I will love you if earth dries,
But I am very fearful of the gods
And Laine in this tempest.

LUASNAD.   Man's last high mood
Can pass above this passion of the seas
That moans to crush him. In each man's proper joy
The first high puissance that made live the gods
Lives on the earth and asks each stone for worship.

[*Wave passes over them.*]

WIFE OF LAINE. I am falling Luasnad!

LUASNAD.   In this peril
The force that slays us is our own high glory.

[*Wave sweeps them round and leaves them again beside the boulder.*]

WIFE OF LAINE [*crying out*]. Oh Luasnad, must man perish? Spare me,
gods!

LUASNAD. Heed not the gods. In this high passionate sea
Mere gods would perish—

WIFE OF LAINE.   Ah! See the dark black vessel.

[*They are swept off.*]

VI

AUGHAVANNA PLAY ⟨?⟩

*In his diary for 27 January 1903 Synge entered the words, 'Wicklow Play';
a week later, on 3 February, he added, 'Aughavanna play'; there is no
further reference. Since Aughavanna, a valley in County Wicklow, might
serve as setting for* The Tinker's Wedding *and* When the Moon Has Set, *and material for both plays occurs in the same portion of the same notebook, the
assignment of this title to the following dialogue is conjectural only. However,
by 1903 Synge had already settled on specific working labels for all his other
projects, and it could well be that the birth of Christy Mahon later in the same
year caused Bartley to remain stillborn in Wicklow. The only other possible
connexion is with the heroine of a novel on which Synge was working in the
mid-nineties, who stands watching the shadow of a young violinist playing in
the window opposite.*

The following passage occurs in Notebook 30, in use in 1903:

*Scene: street in country town in South of Ireland and large window with a
faint light seen behind blind is in the middle of stage; it is night, with faint
moonlight.* MARY *and* BARBARA, *two country girls, come in and come along
the street under the trees.*

MARY. Is it that house Barbara?

BARBARA. It is surely, and it is in that window where there is a kind of
a light that she does be doing her hair.

MARY. There is often a lad below of ⟨a⟩ fine night and I would be
there by ⟨the⟩ fire with my hair down combing it out, but they'd
hardly look on me, though it's fine hair I have for I've heard two
gentlemen say it.

BARBARA. With the like of himself it is another thing altogether for he
was always a quiet man who wouldn't lift himself up to look at
anything you can see.

MARY. What is it he'd look at if it wouldn't be a thing you can see?

BARBARA. He would be looking out in the dark nights and out walking
around the time there'ld be a thick mist down on the earth.

MARY. I hear⟨a thing⟩ below maybe that would be him.

[*They listen.*]

BARBARA. It is not, but he'll come now in a little while surely for there's the light in her room.

[*A strong light is seen behind the blind and a woman's figure is seen behind it mov⟨ing⟩ to one side or the other.*]

MARY. Is there no other way he might go?

BARBARA. No way and that's how ⟨he⟩ seen her at first and all the trouble's come with himself as if he was touched with the moon and I losing a fine man like him. I was to have married tomorrow.

MARY. There he is.

BARBARA. There he is, surely.

[BARTLEY *comes in, a net on his shoulder.*]

MARY. Good evening, Bartley.

BARTLEY. Good evening kindly. [*Looking closely.*] Is it Barbara it is.

BARBARA. Who else would it be?

[*He puts his net under the tree and sits down on it with his face to the window, the shadow inside has sat down and is combing her hair with graceful gestures.*]

BARTLEY [*talking with a moving expression*]. It is time now you went home Barbara. You'll ⟨be tired⟩ standing in the coldness of the night.

BARBARA. It's yourself will be tired sitting there and you with no tea taken and—

VII

THE LADY O'CONNOR
.

Synge first heard the story of O'Connor and his lady from Pat Dirane, the old shanachie of Inishmaan who had given him the plot for In the Shadow of the Glen. *He published a prose version entitled 'A Story from Inishmaan' in the* New Ireland Review *for November 1898, and later revised it for inclusion in* The Aran Islands, *Part I (see Oxford* Prose, *pp. 61–65). However, he apparently did not consider dramatizing the material until he was already at work on* The Well of the Saints, *during the winter of 1903–4.*

Synge apparently worked on this plot for some time although never getting beyond Act II of the scenario, for in addition to a full scenario (from Item 50), there exist two manuscript pages of Act I in Notebook 28 (late 1903), five manuscript pages of scenes from Act II in Notebook 16 (early 1904), and three typescript pages revising the material from Notebook 16 in Item 50 (1904). After these attempts in verse, Synge apparently then considered a prose version, one manuscript page of which exists in Notebook 32 (September? 1904). The latest drafts of each scene are given below; punctuation has been added where necessary, and the names are given in full for the sake of consistency. Passages in parentheses are uncertain and may have been marked for omission. The two scenes in verse from Act II were published in the Oxford Poems *(pp. 74–75) with slight variations; the scenario and prose narrative were published as Appendix C of the* Poems.

A similar tale concerning the bride's dowry being worth her weight in gold is recorded in 'The People of the Glens', told to Synge about one of his own ancestors by an old man in Wicklow (see Oxford Prose, *p. 221).*

Scenario   ⟨Item 50⟩

Fair day. Big scales. Old man and his son, son asks ⟨for⟩ wife. Girl and her father come in with baggages. Girl and gold weighed, girl heaviest, girl goes. Old Connor goes, little man comes to O'Connor and gives him gold. Girl comes back and weighs again. Gold heaviest. Girl won. Act I.

Act II. Castle on Clare coast

O'Connor and wife talk in fog, hear noises, see ship wrecking on the rocks. Servant tells that the captain and crew are coming up with silk, enter Captain. Silks shown, table laid, feasting begins. Messenger, O'Connor says he must go. Exit Lady. O'Connor and Captain talk, bargain made. Scene ii. Bedroom, captain bribes servant, enter Lady, captain steals ring.

Act III. Cliff near castle

Room as in II. Return of Connor. Captain shows him ring. Connor throws wife into sea out of the window.

Act IV

Captain and little man, saved by Lady O'Connor then enter Captain and explanation.

Scenario ⟨development of Act II⟩

Lord and lady looking out of their window on Clare cliff. News of shipwreck. Captain comes with silk, and a monk along with him.

<table>
<tr><td>⟨Act I⟩</td><td>⟨Notebook 28⟩</td></tr>
</table>

[*Fair green after fair, hay and straw scattered about, large scales at centre. Rough houses at back distant.* O'CONNOR *and* DAN O'CONNOR. *They have a bag of money.*]

O'CONNOR [*counting money*]. We made great bargaining this day.

DAN O'CONNOR. That's no lie.
  Yourself's a terror when young lambs is high.
  But what at all is gold—(and you)
  And you I'm saying, single, growing old?
  And not let choose your wife?

O'CONNOR.   Well? Who'd you choose?

DAN O'CONNOR. Moira Burke.

O'CONNOR.   God help me, Dan, them screws
  Would cheat the hide from living starving beasts
  And have you broke with dowries paying priests—
  And—

DAN O'CONNOR. Let you whisht, but leave me what you've there
  And I'll soon settle.

O'CONNOR.   Glory, will you swear
  You'll not ask more all your living life?

DAN O'CONNOR. I'll swear by God and by my hope to wife!

O'CONNOR. Here they come.

[BURKE *and* MOIRA *come in.*]

DAN O'CONNOR [*going towards them*]. God bless you, Moira.

MOIRA.   God
  Bless you kindly.

DAN O'CONNOR. Every ⟨*illegible*⟩
  But's growing rightly with the warmth and rain.

BURKE. It's true.

DAN O'CONNOR. I'm asking if you think to gain
  A better than myself to wed with her,
  For I've not got all fortune.

BURKE.   Would it sit
  Her off the earth and she within them scales?

MOIRA. God save us all!

DAN O'CONNOR. We'll see and if it fails—

        [*He puts gold bag into the scales.*]

BURKE. Now, Moira.

DAN O'CONNOR.   With her boots and shawl!
  Ah, you're a schemy rascal, drop them all.—

⟨Act II. Scene i⟩   ⟨Item 50⟩

[*Scene: room in castle on cliffs of Clare. Window looking out on the sea
and* LADY O'CONNOR *at it.* O'CONNOR *looking intently at a shrine
or sacred picture in the corner.*]

LADY O'CONNOR. The fog is down again. I cannot see
  Where the ship vanished. [*She to* O'CONNOR] West by Knock-na-
  lee
  The waves are louder. Do you hear them, Connor?

o'connor. I hear them surely. [*He comes over.*] I'm thinking how
    poorly God's honour
Is slighted here where man's hard set to spare
A little thought from these high seas of Clare
To think on his soul's weariness and to taste
The joys that Holy Church lets almost waste
Among these wild men here.

LADY o'connor [*looking eagerly from window*]. Was that a cry?

o'connor. Some scald crow straying on the northern clift
Or lonesome seal this tide has washed adrift. [*He looks out too.*]

LADY o'connor. If even birds and fish are lonesome here
It's I'm in dread what we'll grow year by year,
Where scarce a person comes save tinkers only.

o'connor. Where God is, Lady, no soul is truly lonely.

⟨Scene ii⟩   ⟨Notebook 16⟩

SERVANT.   There's two could swim,
The stranger captain and a monk with him.

LADY o'connor. And where are these?

SERVANT.   They're washing out the salt
From both their eyes, and the captain drinking malt
To clear his tongue, says he; the other's praying
Fine words in Latin the like I've heard none saying.

[*Enter* CAPTAIN *and* MONK.]

o'connor. My thousand welcomes to you Lord and friar
And let you two sit up against the fire,
You should be perished with the waves and water.

CAPTAIN. We thank you kindly Lord and this your daughter—

o'connor. My wife, good friends—

CAPTAIN [*bowing low*].   Then the more honour to her.

o'connor. You see this, good father, there are fewer
Of your like than I'd wish in County Clare.
We live like fish in rivers, hawks in air,
And never turn unto the Lord Almighty
Till years and sin have ⟨made⟩ us weak and flighty.

MONK. Your words there sound a tone I'm often hearing
From men who in their youth let interfering
Spirits of Satan tempt their souls to sin.

O'CONNOR. And I have sinned?

MONK.   And made confessions after?

O'CONNOR. Never.

MONK.   Then your sin's black, and the laughter
Of Hell is whistling round you.

O'CONNOR [*doubtfully*].   Maybe tomorrow . . .

MONK. What? Would you chance the death will maybe borrow. . . .

[*They go aside and whisper.*]

⟨Act II. Scene ii⟩   ⟨Item 50⟩

LADY O'CONNOR. I'm thinking it's well for you all your life,
Walking the world while I, when the wet clouds lift
Look only all the day on the seas and clifts.

CAPTAIN. Yet you have silky pillows for your bed,
And golden combs, I'm thinking, comb your head,
It's roasted hares you'll eat and dearest wine,
And lay your feet on mats of Persian twine,
While we live shut in ships that roll and pitch,
We eating salt till our shin marrows itch,
And drinking filthy water from a barrel
Our crew half naked through their ripped apparel. . . .

⟨Notebook 16⟩

LADY O'CONNOR. It's small good women get from wines or mats.
I'd liefer stray like tinkers through the flats
Leinster's Aluin, or the bogs of Meath,
Than sit reckoning up the sighs I breathe.

CAPTAIN. Your Lord's a gallous talker and with him—

LADY O'CONNOR. He's half a monk—

CAPTAIN.   Oh, ho!

LADY O'CONNOR.   I say he'll skim
The goat's milk in the morning, eat the cream,
He talking all the while of Jacob's dream.
And when he takes a rag to skim his spoon
You'd think to hear him that he owned the moon.

[*They pass on.*]

⟨Act II. Scene iii⟩   ⟨Notebook 16⟩

MONK. You've sinned an ugly sin has earned the fire,
The Lord Almighty's sacred purifier.

O'CONNOR. How long then are you thinking it should take. . . .

⟨Prose Version.   Act II. Scene i.⟩   ⟨Notebook 32⟩

LADY O'CONNOR. I can't see the ship any more. The fog has closed in.

O'CONNOR. If they saw the cliff they may get away. But the tide's running strong in the Bay.

LADY O'CONNOR. I've a great wish to go out in those ships do be crossing back and forward through the big world. Isn't it a queer thing you've never set your foot abroad among the kingdoms of the Eastern World and you a rich free man till you were a score and ten years.

O'CONNOR. The world is a big strange place maybe, but if it is itself are not God and the Devil as near to Ireland as they do be to Jerusalem and Corinth, and what is there any man would think on a great while but God and his own sins and the fear of Limbo.

LADY O'CONNOR [*scornfully*]. There are many men do think on other things surely.

[*There are cries under the window.*]

O'CONNOR. The ship is on the Black Head. Oh God have mercy on their souls.

LADY O'CONNOR [*at the door*]. Padraic and Shawn and Bartley, let you run down and see if you'd be able to save any from the boat that is on the rocks.

MEN [*outside*]. We will your ladyship.

o'connor. Isn't it a strange thing that the whole lot of men do be sailing on ⟨the⟩ sea don't be thinking at all on God, or the Heaven of God or anything at all but the sins of flesh and the proudness of the world?

lady o'connor. Are the lot of them like that?

o'connor. They are mostly. When I was a young man in the city of Dublin I would meet with captains and mates and the great sailors of the world and there wasn't one of them had sins enough at the back of him for the damnation. . . .

VIII

BRIDE AND KATHLEEN: A PLAY OF '98

Synge appears to have planned a play on the rebellion of 1798 at the request of Frank Fay. Writing to Synge after the Irish Players' triumphant visit to London in March 1904, Fay says, 'Will you try the '98 play I was talking to you about. We must try to get an intelligent popular audience in Dublin. The people who might support us at sixpence a head are a good ⟨deal⟩ afraid that we are irreligious and politically unsound. We must do something to get them to believe in us. The same people come to show after show. . . . If you could give us a drama of '98 as much alive as *In the Shadow of the Glen* and *Riders to the Sea* showing what the peasantry had to endure. I believe there were whole districts in which there was not a woman unviolated. I think Yeats in *Cathleen* has pointed out the right road for plays of that time. The leaders only give you melodrama; it is a picture of the smaller tyrannies that their followers had to endure that we want.' *Doubtful of the wisdom of Fay's nationalist bait, Synge replied early in April 1904,* 'By all means have '98 plays—I will do one if I can—but *strong* and good dramas only will bring us people who are interested in the drama, and they are, after all, the people we must have.' *In his essay* J. M. Synge and the Ireland of his Time *and in his* Autobiographies, *Yeats gives an amusing account of the company's reaction to the scenario Synge finally produced.*

Only two fragments exist in Synge's notebooks, the scenario in Item 50 and four pages of dialogue in Notebook 16. Neither fragment of manuscript shows any sign of re-working.

SCENARIO FOR PLAY OF '98

[*Scene a Wicklow wood. Two rebels pass over stage.*]

One says, 'The soldiers is coming surely the best we can do is run up into the hills.'

The other says, 'It is maybe but I'm thinking a power of soldiers will be running the same way, the heather's crawling with them.' [*They go out.*]

Terrified woman runs in and hides in thick bushes, muttering, 'Oh

Holy Mary! The saints defend me! If them red divils would catch me.'

Another woman runs in from the other side into the same bush.

Papist Woman, 'If the soldiers is after you let you run on honey and not get me in trouble at all.'

Protestant Woman, 'Why would I run from the like of the soldiers. Amn't I a decent godly woman' etc. . . .

Dialogue leading to violent quarrel. Then they hear footsteps and the Protestant woman runs in beside the other.

One says, 'Is it a soldier?' the other, 'Is it a rebel? I see the red of his coat.' [*She is going to cry out, the other stops her with her hand.*]

A wounded rebel runs in and falls down.

One woman, 'There's a lad wounded.' [*They creep out to look at him.*]

Rebel Woman finds he is her son.

She laments over him, Protestant Woman half triumphing over her. Woman hears Papist in despair. At last moment Protestant helps her to carry wounded man into trees. Then she comes back to put the soldiers off his track. Soldiers insult her. She alternates between abuse of them and an assurance that she is a pious godly woman like themselves.

A man rushes in to say rebels are coming in numbers. Flight of soldiers. Rebel woman comes in and offers to hide her. . . .

BRIDE AND KATHLEEN

BRIDE. Oh glory, oh the bloody rogues. Oh, oh, I'll be safe here maybe. Well is there ⟨a⟩ woman left living in decency in the barony. Well I run hard from the villain, them soldiers is no fellows for quickness of foot.

KATHLEEN [*coming in on the other side*]. There's a hole I'm thinking I'll be safe there maybe, I'm destroyed surely and I after running from Vinegar hill. There's someone before me. [*To* BRIDE] May I come in beside of you and hide myself away from the rogues of the world?

BRIDE. There's no man following your steps?

KATHLEEN [*breathless*]. No man living. The last man after me was blinded with drink and I'm after seeing him fall with his head down in the butt of a sluig.

BRIDE. Thanks be to the Lord God.

KATHLEEN. Amen, my poor woman, amen and amen. Isn't it a bad ⟨day⟩ this day for the female women of Ireland.

BRIDE. You're after coming a great way I'm thinking.

KATHLEEN. A great way, running one while then hiding, then running and lepping again.

BRIDE. It's a fool you were running from one Hell to the jaws of another.

KATHLEEN. This place isn't so bad I'm thinking.

BRIDE. Not so bad is it, and not one left from one score to two.

KATHLEEN. What's that itself when there's not one left from the crawling dirty babies to three scores and ten.

BRIDE. Isn't bloody villains is loose in the land, oh will there ⟨be⟩ place at all in Hell for the lot of them.

KATHLEEN. Oh the Almighty will find a place surely, and He stretching the walls of Hell the way you'd stretch a shawl for a child.

BRIDE. I'm axing myself if it's myself or you ⟨had⟩ the biggest escape—

KATHLEEN. It'd be hard to have a biggest than me and I with two cods calling at my heels, 'Come here you heretic!'

BRIDE. Heretic? What made them call you a heretic?

KATHLEEN. What is it they call any good Christian Protestant but a heretic now. . . .

IX

⟨DEAF MUTES FOR IRELAND⟩

*Synge appears to have written the following two scenarios at the same time,
while at work on* The Playboy of the Western World, *possibly during the
attacks on his plays by the* United Irishman *in January and February 1905, or
perhaps in December 1904. They occur on three consecutive pages of Notebook
28, after the* O'Connor *dialogue and before the* National Drama *farce.
There are no other references to either plot.*

SCENARIO

The Gaels have conquered. A Pan Celtic congress is being held in
Dublin. A large prize is offered for any Irishman who can be proved to
know no English. A committee is sitting to try them. They bring in
each man in turn, throw a light on him and say 'God save Ireland' and
'To Hell with the Pope'. Men are detected again and again. One is
found at last who baffles all tests. In delight the congress is called in in
glorious robes; the victor is put up to make a speech in Irish, he begins
talking on his fingers—he is deaf mute and advocates a deaf mute
society as only safeguard against encroaching Anglo-Saxon vulgarity!

POSSIBLE SCENARIO

Gaelic having proved useless to withstand English vulgarity Ireland
does not know whether to choose to be deaf mute or blind.

An American Nerve Doctor is investigating epidemic of deaf-muteness in Ireland 2000 A.D. He reads out tract which he has found:

About the year 1920 it was discovered that the efforts of the Gaelic
League to withstand the inroads of Anglo-Saxon vulgarity, American
commercialism, French morals and German free-thought ⟨had been
unsuccessful, therefore⟩ the executive of the Gaelic League and the
United Irish League decided that drastic measures must be taken without delay if the sacred entity of the Irish and Celtic soul was to be
saved from corruption. At a crowded meeting it was resolved that as
Ireland could not speak Irish rather ⟨than⟩ us⟨ing⟩ the filthy accents
⟨of⟩ England she would be speechless. Young and intelligent organ-
izers were at once secured, and before long they had touched the saintly

and patriotic hearts of the sweet-minded Irish mother⟨s⟩. From their cradles the future hopes of the Gaels—and indeed of Europe and the civilized world—heard no more dirty English stories, no more profane swearing, and their innocent ⟨hearts were⟩ delighted only by the inarticulation of those divine melodies which are the wonder and envy of all nations. A sympathetic conservative secretary was easily induced to force deaf-muteness on the Board of National Schools and in a few years the harsh voice of the National schoolmaster was heard no more. In a little while the degrading tourist traffic ceased entering. A gang of cattle maimers from Athenry broke into Trinity College on ⟨St.⟩ Patrick's Day and cut out the tongues of all the professors, fellows and scholars, the students had become so engrossed with football that they were not regarded as human enough to require this mark of Nationality.

X

NATIONAL DRAMA: A FARCE

In a letter to Synge from Coole on 9 September 1905 Yeats wrote, 'Bring if you can, or have sent to me, the MS of the Tinkers. I want to see if it would do for SAMHAIN, if you don't object, and also to see whether we can discuss it for our winter session. We are rather hard up for new short pieces, and you have such a bad reputation now it can hardly do you any harm. But we may find it too dangerous for the Theatre at present. Also bring the Satire on your enemies, and indeed anything you have.' *The fragments of* National Drama *occur in Synge's notebooks after* The Lady O'Connor *and during the early drafts of* The Playboy of the Western World (*January–February 1905*), *and it seems likely therefore that this is the 'Satire' Yeats refers to. However, in his notes to the executors after Synge's death, Yeats wrote:* 'To be used at discretion of biographer. (1) National drama a farce (I remember origin of this at time of Playboy).' *It would appear that in his haste Yeats confused the row over* The Playboy of the Western World *in January 1907 with the earlier attacks on Synge by Arthur Griffith, editor of the* United Irishman, *which began over the first performance of* The Shadow of the Glen *on 8 October 1903, and were renewed from 7 January to 11 February 1905. The references in the farce to a definition of 'Irish Drama' and 'Ephesian Drama' substantiate this assumption. Unfortunately the executors did not accept the offer Yeats made in another memorandum:* 'I remember the circumstance that made him write this, and could give it to his editor, or write a note myself if it seem important enough.'

Two drafts of National Drama *exist among Synge's papers, both incomplete. The earlier draft, which is also longer, is in manuscript in Notebook 28, with a great many jottings and stray speeches which he apparently intended to incorporate into the finished dialogue. The six typescript pages set aside by Yeats (perhaps typed out by Synge in response to the request of September 1905), now among the papers in Item 52, appear to be a revision of the first half of the manuscript draft. In the margin is pencilled* 'J.M.S. worth keeping'. *The following text is based on the sheets from Item 52, followed by an additional scene from Notebook 28. Synge's manuscript additions are indicated in bold type.*

Scene: a national club room, simply furnished. Portraits of patriots, a map of Ireland and Hungary. A harp without strings, and the head of a pike. A book-shelf at back with volumes bound in green. FOGARTY *and* MURPHY *come in.* FOGARTY *is a country upper class Catholic, with strong patriotic principles, and a considerable thirst; he is large, red-faced and full-blooded. Has already been in Mooney's.* MURPHY *is pale and slight; he has been some years in London, and has learned to talk of the three styles of Rossetti etc. in his moments of leisure. He has papers under his arm.*

MURPHY. The members have not come in yet, will you take a book Mr. Fogarty, I want to look over the notes I have made for the debate.

FOGARTY. Very well I won't disturb you. [*He goes over to book-shelf.*] The Whole History of Hungary for Beginners, by an Eminent Writer. The Re-afforestation of the Sea-Shore. The Five Parts of Father O'Growney, being the complete Irish course needed for a patriot. How to be a Genius, by a Gaelic Leaguer. The Pedigree of the Widow of Ephesus. The complete works of Petronius and Boccaccio, unabridged. The Plays for an Irish Theatre, abridged and expurgated by a Catholic critic. Controversial Ethics for the use of Editors, by a Doctor of Louvain. Fairy Tales for all Ages. The Dawn of the Twilight, and The Autumn of Spring. The Encyclopedia Celtica, a brief statement of the facts of the Universe for Irishmen, being very useful for all who are awaiting the foundation of a University of Orthodox Science and Art. . . . What at all will I read Mr. Murphy? You've no novels.

MURPHY [*jumping up, and looking at his watch*]. They'll be coming now in a moment I think. They've only gone to the Tivoli for the first performance, and it must be over now.

FOGARTY. If I'd only known. Was there great dancing on? High-kicking?

MURPHY. I don't really ⟨know⟩. I never go. If you want Music Halls you must go to London, Mr. Fogarty.

[*There is a noise on the stairs, and the members come in, salute and shake hands with* FOGARTY *and* MURPHY.]

CHAIRMAN [*sitting down at head of table*]. Now gentlemen, let us get to work. [*He takes out his watch and puts it on the table.*] The subject for debate this evening is the Possibility, Origin, and Future of an Irish National Drama. But before beginning the debate two motions are to be carried unanimously calling on the National Bank and the National Gallery and the National Trust Society to leave off sailing under false pretences. I call on you Mr. Murphy to start the debate which I beg to say is to be conducted in a national informal manner.

MURPHY. Will I stand?

CHAIRMAN. Keep your seat Mr. Murphy. Will you make yourself at home for the love of the Lord God, and leave bowing and bending.

MURPHY. Well, Mr. Chairman, and gentlemen. I would ask first of all what is an Irish Drama. . . . [*With emphasis.*] What is an Irish Drama?

CHAIRMAN. Very good indeed, Mr. Murphy. We'll discuss that first.

MURPHY. An Irish drama gentlemen is a Drama that embodies in a finished form the pageant of Irish life, and shines throughout with the soft light of the ideal impulses of the Gaels, a drama in short which contains the manifold and fine qualities of the Irish race, their love for the land of their forefathers, and their poetic familiarity with the glittering and unseen forms of the visionary world. For us then the problem is merely the election or invention of an adequate dramatic form into which to pour out, or distill the fullness of the soul, this priceless heritage of the Gael. Now for the discovery of this form we must look first if in any foreign literature such a form is to be found, which can contain as a vial the violet tincture of a national soul. [*Applause.*] Take Molière, for instance, is Molière a national dramatist?

FLAHERTY. Not a bit of him, wasn't he always making fun of his own country, till the holy bishop wouldn't take his corpse when he was dead.

MURPHY [*continuing*]. Take Molière and ask ourselves if the man who wrote plays which display chiefly misanthropy, avarice, hypocrisy, and unruly desires, is, or is not a national dramatist?

BYRNE. He's not I think because a national drama must exhibit the virtue of its country, as a nation lives by its virtues.

MURPHY. Let us be liberal, Mr. Byrne, and take a wide view. I do not consider Molière a national dramatist in the sense that he might serve us as a model, and yet if we look closely we see that France is a decadent country, and that it is not unnatural that its national dramas should be occupied with vices that have caused its ruin, but the Irish national drama must be very different as the Irish nation is not decadent and is still living by its virtues.

JAMESON. There are 27 lunatics per thousand in Ireland, the highest figure on the earth.

FOGARTY. Will you not be talking. Isn't that the influence of Westminster law?

CHAIRMAN. Order, order. That point has been settled. If we can't have Molière as a model who'll we have?

MURPHY. Shall we take Shakespeare?

VOICES. He's English.

MURPHY. In considering the Shakespearian form it must not be forgotten that he is only one of an immense herd of playwrights, and that his work, and much more the work of the others, is infected with the plague-spot of 'sex'.

BYRNE. That's truth surely; it was a heretic age.

FOGARTY. The National Drama of Catholic Ireland must have no sex. That's certain sure, Mr. Chairman.

JAMESON. With the help of God we'll make Ireland in this matter a glorious exception from the Catholic countries of the world.

CHAIRMAN [uneasily]. Couldn't we pass on Mr. Murphy?

MURPHY. Take Ibsen. It will require little deliberation I think to convince us that this delineator of the livid realities of the north can be only a harmful influence to writers who must draw out their materials from the pearly depths of the Celtic imagination, and leaving the naked truth perhaps a little on one side.

[Cries of 'to hell with truth, let you make haste!']

MURPHY [turning pages uneasily]. Or take the Greeks?

FOGARTY. Is it more Ephesian Drama you want?

JAMESON. Christian culture should be a poor thing if it hasn't taken us beyond the need of heathen examples from the Eastern world.

FOGARTY [*leaning back and scratching his head*]. Talking of the plague spot of the Elizabethans, Mr. Chairman, I'm after hearing a great story below in the office of the Holy Patriot News. There was once a—[*He leans forward with a wicket grin.*]

CHAIRMAN. Hish, hish, hish. . . . You can tell us that bye and bye when we go out for refreshment, Mr. Fogarty.

FOGARTY. Please yourself, Mr. Chairman.

CHAIRMAN. Come on now Mr. Murphy, and be speedy for the love of God. . . .

MURPHY. I think in our review of the Drama of Europe it is pretty evident that in our sense of the word there has never been a national drama that can serve us for a model. Perhaps if we turn to the Sanscrit, and the drama of the Seventh Dynasty of Egypt—

FOGARTY [*breaking out*]. What the hell do you know about Egypt? Were you ever there?

MURPHY. Mr. Chairman, these interruptions are not endurable.

CHAIRMAN. I know that Mr. Murphy as well as you do. But—[*He lifts his little finger.*]—we must make allowances. It's a drouthy time. The Vartry's empty I've heard them say. [*He leans over to* FOGARTY.] If you go on delaying these proceedings, Mr. Fogarty,

(**To conclude. They all crowd round** FOGARTY **who begins telling his story in a whisper. They roar laughing some one says, 'It is a quarter to eleven' and there is a general stampede.**)

⟨SCENE⟩

JAMESON. In short you think that the Irish drama should hold up the mirror to the Irish Nation and it going to Mass on a fine springdayish Sunday morning? . . . . I have not much to say. An Irish drama that is written in Ireland about Irish people, and not on a foreign model will and must be national in so far as it exists at all. Our hope of it is that as Ireland is a beautiful and lovely country that the drama that Ireland is now producing may catch a little of this beauty and loveliness, as the Irish music has caught it ⟨without⟩ knowing or thinking, and will escape the foolishness that all wilful national⟨ism⟩ is so full of. A country like Holland promises a homely intimate and picturesque one. So the drama of modern city life is either colourless and forbidding or has the rather petulant gaiety of French plays. None of the work of the Irish National Theatre Society is like that. Again as it is near the peasants it will have some of the humour without which life is not human. A beautiful art has never been produced except in a beautiful environment and nowhere is there one more beautiful than in the mountains and glens of Ireland. Art is sad or gay, religious or heretical, by reason of accident and causes we cannot account for and the small Tuscany produced at one time Dante and Boccaccio, who are surely both national and yet we feel that Dante might have been born in Paris or Rabelais in Venice. The national element in art is merely the colour, the intensity of the wildness or restraint of the humour, but the other matters that have been suggested have nothing to do with Nationality as the word is and can only be used in the arts.

FOGARTY. Do you mean to say all art is national? That is an awful queer thing for you to say.

JAMESON. I do not say that all artistic production is national—Gaelic adaptations (imitations) of fourth-rate English poetry are not national —weak-kneed or thickhead Irish novels are not national because they are not anything. But any art work that is in any sense the product of a few minds working together, the work is and cannot help being national, in—as I said before—the only sense in which the word has any meaning in the relation to the arts. . . . Isolated imitations of some foreign form do not make national art, but when two or three people ⟨use⟩ the infinite number of influences from the ⟨past⟩ and present of the country ⟨that⟩ gives their work a local character which is all a nation can demand. If you do not like a work that is passing itself off as national art you had better show that it is not art. If it is good art it is vain for you to try and show that it is not national. In the little brotherhood of western nations that are thinking and living together everything is common that your controversialists claim for their ⟨own⟩. . . . If we get drunk a little more in public than the other nations of Europe would you have us reeling on the stage in order that we may be national? no? Then if we have a few little fragments of local virtue must ⟨they⟩ be paraded in our button holes like a Gaelic button? The essentials of all art are the eternal human elements (coat sleeve) of humanity which are the same everywhere and it is only in the attributes that make an art more or less charged with beauty, more or less daring and exquisite in form, more or ⟨less⟩ dull or shiny on its surface, that the influence of place is to be found. There is no place I think where the unusual is more beautiful⟨ly⟩ laid open to men's eyes than this Ireland where we live, no country where the trees and skies and mountains are so delicate, no coastline where stones are fiercer or no hillside where lovely country is more complete. Then I think that if the men are sent there there need be no country where art will be more replete with the divine beauty and power which it alone can seek.

FOGARTY. That's fine flowery ⟨speech⟩ Mr. Jameson, and it's a great credit to you. I'll not say a word against but. . . .

XI

IDEA FOR A PLAY: ⟨SMUGGLERS' ISLAND⟩

In June 1905 Synge and Jack Yeats toured the Congested Districts of the west of Ireland on an assignment for the Manchester Guardian, *travelling from Spiddal near Galway city to Dinish Island in Galway Bay, and up through north Mayo. In August Synge returned to the west, this time to the coast of Kerry and the Great Blasket Island. 'It is probably even more primitive than Aran and I am wild with joy at the prospect,' he wrote to Lady Gregory on 11 August. While on the Great Blasket he stayed with 'The King', Shawn Keane, and described his life in the essays later published in* The Shanachie, 1907 *(see* Oxford Prose, *pp. 247–57).*

In Notebook 40, which contains his notes on this visit to the Blaskets, Synge jotted down the following scenario, which has many resemblances to The Playboy of the Western World, *already begun two years before.*

Idea for a play.

Island with population of wreckers, smugglers, poteen-makers etc. are startled by the arrival of a stranger and reform for dread of him. He is an escaped criminal and wants them to help him over to America but he thinks that they are so virtuous he is afraid to confess his deeds for fear they should hand him over to the law that they are so apparently in awe of. At last all comes out and he is got off safely.

Little queen daughter of ferry man of Dinish Island in play.

XII

SCENARIO: THE ROBBERS

In Notebook 34, dated 1905–6, occurs the following scenario, which does not appear to have been further developed. It is immediately followed in the notebook by a draft of Synge's review of A. H. Leahy's Heroic Romances of Ireland, *published in the* Manchester Guardian *on 6 March 1906.*

The only other reference to St. Kevin of Glendalough occurs in Synge's diary for 24 March 1895, 'Wrote St. Kevin. 1–110', when he was evidently contemplating a narrative poem he later destroyed.

SCENARIO. THE ROBBERS

Young monk and boy before St. Kevin's cell. Boy speaks of the danger of robbers and tells of the atrocities they have done. Y⟨oung⟩ M⟨onk⟩ says God is their shelter. Famine. Robbers come in and claim food. Young Monk withstands them and reproves them for their bad deeds working them across stage and at last off abashed. He comes back radiant with the success of his faith, the boy greets him as a hero. St. Kevin comes out. Boy runs to him and tells how God has helped Brother and how brave he has been. Saint reproves him and sends boy to call back robbers, reproves young monk and prays God to soften these *four* sinners. Robbers come back astonished. Young Monk kneels and asks their forgiveness. Change in robbers then monks go into cell and leave the robbers ⟨to⟩ their talk, they go over and tap at door. Saint comes out, they ask him to take them into his order, they kneel down and he prays for them all—Curtain
Point all, robbers and monks, are equal before God.

3 Robbers {
1 Run-away monk
2 Usurping prince kicked out
3 his poet, or beggar

XIII

⟨SCENARIOS FOR THIEVES⟩

Notebook 34 contains two other ideas for plays, one following the other after the draft of 'The Vagrants of Wicklow' which Synge published in The Shanachie *in the autumn of 1906. Neither plot was developed further.*

A.

9:40 p.m. Feb. 20/1906
Quarrelling couple of thieves fail in murder or similar undertaking and then love each other. Inner subject *the love that grows out of pity.*

B.

Thief woman scorns thief man. He reforms. She pities him, falls in love with him, and runs away with him. II or III.

XIV

⟨COMEDY OF KINGS⟩

The same notebook, Number 34, contains the following drawing and scenario for a comedy. They appear to be somewhat later then the scenarios for thieves, as they are followed by a late draft of Act II of The Playboy of the Western World (*autumn 1906?*).

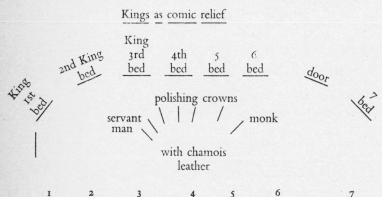

The hawker, horseman, houndman, boatman, Harper, storyteller, and gravedigger

They discuss the comrade⟨ship⟩ of the kings and the coming of the monk, decide that it would be dangerous to let the kings know of their monk's mission. Monk comes. Ossianic dialogue, servants on pagan grounds hoot at monk. Kings' heads appear through curtain. Monk sees them, they draw back as men turn. Monk put out, kings get up. Stately when the horsemen see them, childish on the sly, scratching their heads, making faces at each other etc. Servants go, kings romp. Enter statesmen etc. kings bored, they intrigue to get monk in. Exeunt statesmen. Monk comes and preaches to them, servant comes in as they are converted. Climax

XV

LUCIFER AND THE LOST SOUL: A MYSTERY

Notebook 48 contains the following dialogue, probably written in January 1908:

LUCIFER. You were a fine lad one time.

LOST SOUL. I was, your reverence.

LUCIFER. And what brought ⟨you⟩ this place?

LOST SOUL. The way of the world, your reverence.

LUCIFER. Bad company.

LOST SOUL. The worst. In Maynooth I was with all nice little priests, talking ever and always of the deadly merits. I run from that.

LUCIFER. It was drink then maybe?

LOST SOUL. It was your reverence, a pint of warmed milk I got every night for my mother. I run from that too.

LUCIFER. And from that you went racing?

LOST SOUL. I did not your reverence. I went writing pages for the Catholic Young Man.

LUCIFER. What kind were your pages?

LOST SOUL. They were—mighty flat your reverence.

LUCIFER. That's a sin. [*Writes.*] Putting out pages could make men swear oaths. Go on.

LOST SOUL.

APPENDIX A

RIDERS TO THE SEA:
WORKSHEETS AND COMMENTARY

I. DESCRIPTION OF TEXTUAL SOURCES

(Unless otherwise stated, unpublished material is in the possession of the Synge Estate.)

A. STANDARD EDITION

The Shadow of the Glen and Riders to the Sea (*London, Elkin Mathews,* *1905*); *Vigo Cabinet series no. 24. Further editions in 1907 and 1909.*

Item 90 contains the following letter to Synge, dated 3 May 1905 and signed by Elkin Mathews: 'I am sending herewith half a dozen copies of "The Shadow of the Glen" etc. It is my intention to publish as soon after Monday May 8th as possible together with some others.

'I should be greatly obliged if you would see some of the principal Dublin booksellers and ascertain how many copies I may send them either as out and out orders or on sale or return. It would be a great help.'

Copy 1 of this edition in the Berg Collection has the following note in pencil on the verso of title page: 'I hereby certify that this the first edition was published by me on the 8th May 1905. Elkin Mathews Vigo Street W.3.'

The edition published in The Works of John M. Synge, *Volume I (Dublin, Maunsel, 1910) follows the Vigo edition.*

B. OTHER EDITIONS DURING SYNGE'S LIFETIME

In Samhain: An Occasional Review, *ed. W. B. Yeats, Number Three (September 1903), pp. 25–33.*

Synge's own copy of Samhain *includes alterations to the play in his hand, apparently for the Vigo edition; fastened to the copy is a typewritten page giving particulars of the first performance.*

2. In Poet-Lore, *Volume XVI, Number 1 (Spring 1905), pp. 1–11. Published in Boston in March 1905, and advertised with Douglas Hyde's* The Twisting of the Rope *as 'Two Irish Plays from the Gaelic Originals'. Closely follows the* Samhain *edition.*

C. EXTANT MANUSCRIPTS/TYPESCRIPTS

1. *In Notebook 28, one page in ink with pencil emendations. 1900–2?*
2. *In Notebook 17, one page in pencil. 1900–2?*
3. *In Notebook 31, twenty pages in ink and pencil. Spring–summer, 1902.*

4. *In Notebook H, thirteen pages in ink and pencil, heavily emended. Summer–autumn, 1902.*

5. *In Box File E, sixteen typescript pages; pp. 3–5 and 13–14 prepared for the printer; pp. 1–5 and 13–14 read* Maura *and* Cailteen, *other pages read* Maurya *and* Cathleen; *a note in Synge's hand on page 1 reads,* 'In small type version Cailteen is the old woman Maura the elder daughter.' *Apparently made up from at least three typescript drafts, based on an even earlier draft (in small type); in all extant earlier versions the old mother is named* Bride. *1902–3.*

6. *In Houghton Library, Harvard University, seventeen uncorrected typescript pages, with the characters indicated only by initials; title-page gives only four characters:* Maura, Bartley, Cailteen, Nora. *Wording, especially in the stage directions, differs occasionally from TS. in Box File E. Possibly the copy referred to by Lady Gregory in her letter postmarked 13 February 1903, telling Synge of Arthur Symons' offer to send it to the* Fortnightly Review: 'You should keep a copy—as the Fortnightly sometimes keeps things a long time—And if you are typing it again I think you should put the full names in—N and M are so like each other that children learning the catechism are not sure which belongs to what.' *1902–3.*

7. *In the Berg Collection, New York Public Library, nineteen typescript pages with occasional manuscript alterations and compositors' signatures(?) spaced throughout the copy; on title-page in Lady Gregory's hand are the words* 'Signed & sent me by Synge A. G.' *Verso of last page (18) reads* 'From J. M. Synge 4 Handel Street Brunswick Sq. W.C.' *The London address is struck out and Synge has added* '31 Crosthwaite Park Kingstown Co. Dublin'. *Text apparently typed out after Lady Gregory's letter of 13 February 1903 (Synge lived in London from 9 January to 18 March 1903) and used for the Samhain edition, which it resembles more closely than do the earlier typescripts.*

II. DRAFT MANUSCRIPTS

(Synge's deletions and alterations are copied from the original manuscript, with his alternative wording indicated between the lines in italic.)

A. *The following passage from Notebook 28 appears to be the earliest dialogue for* Riders to the Sea. *It is written in ink, with pencil emendations, on the inside cover of a large blue notebook used by Synge over a period of some years and containing also early drafts of the* National Drama *scenario, dialogue for* When the Blind See (The Well of the Saints), *the unpublished play* (When the Moon Has Set), *and* The Playboy of the Western World, *and notes about his visit to County Kerry. The only date referred to is September 1903, but the flyleaf has the following inscription:* 'J. M. Synge 90 rue d'Assas Paris et 31 Crosthwaite Pk. Kingstown'. *(90 rue d'Assas was Synge's permanent address in Paris from mid-November 1898 until mid-March 1903.)*

                    It's nine days   and cruel

B⟨RIDE⟩ [*keening*]. Micheal is a week drowned this day and isn't a sad thing we've no news or knowledge of the body.

[NORAH *seen at the door with bundle in her hands.*]

N.

with an old woman is sickened with crying.

of the will of God

It's little use talking ~~to an old woman~~ when there is no new thing to be told.

B. *The following passage, written in pencil, seems to have been written at approximately the same time. It occurs in a small black notebook (No. 17) apparently used by Synge from the late '80s until as late as 1901 and containing notes in Italian, French, and Irish, comments on his r:ading while studying in Paris, autobiographical commentary and poems, and early drafts for* The Aran Islands. *This passage occurs in that section of the notebook dated 3 November/⟨October? 1899⟩ describing his second visit to Aran, but other passages refer to later visits in 1900 and 1901.*

there is

NORAH. I see boys running, something down at the quay.

M⟨AURA⟩ [*looking out*]. There is a mass of people coming up and there is something among them.

B. Maybe it's Micheal has been washed ashore.

M. Didn't I tell ⟨you⟩ he was found in the North?

B. There do be always a power of young men floating round in the sea, and how would they know if it was Micheal they had or another man like him?

M. [*comes back from the door and half closes it after her*]. They are after sending down two bits of his clothes

C. *Notebook 31, a small black jotter notebook, contains early dialogue for* The Tinker's Wedding, Fool of Farnham (The Playboy of the Western World), The Well of the Saints, *several 'invented' expressions, and the following dialogue for* Riders to the Sea. *The only date in the notebook is 4 May 1903; the bulk of the pages are untouched, but the notebook appears to have been in casual use from 1902 until at least 1904.*

1. *The following passage begins at one end of the notebook and continues uninterrupted through fifteen pages. Most of the manuscript corrections are made in pencil:*

hard and   when a man   the thing his mother is saying

B. Isn't it a / cruel thing ~~he~~ wont hear what I'm saying and
   she   *being destroyed*   upon
~~I~~ holding him back from ~~death and~~ destruction ~~and the danger of the sea?~~

M. What man can be here without going out every day on the sea and
an old woman
   there is no one will listen to / and she making annoyance saying
the same word every time of the
   ~~one~~ thing ~~every~~ / day.
over one thing all through the day

                      come at
P. [*to* NORA]. Is the hooker ~~coming to~~ the slip?

NORA [*looking out*]. She's passing the green head, and dropping one of
her sails.

                                    go quickly
PATCH [*standing up with the bridle*]. I'll have time now if I ~~hurry~~. I'll
   down on   *me*
   ride / the mare ~~quickly~~ and the other horses will follow. [*He goes
out.*]

                and the lord knows
B. He's gone now / when we'll see a sight of him again.

M. In a week surely.

B. He'ld be going out when the waves would open to let a ship bump
through them on the sea-sands. All the ones there is broken since
three weeks or beyond it, and I am afeard I'll not see him again and
have no son from today.

M. Isn't it sorrow enough we have without sending him on the sea
with a word after him without luck or reason. Go down now beyond
the spring well and you'll see him passing the turn and lively and
well and then you'll see with it the foolishness in your mind.

B. Maybe he'ld be cross if he saw me and call a hard word upon me.

~~NORA. He would not and if you stand down by the well he'll not know~~
~~you at all.~~

B. [*puts shawl over her head*]. Isn't there great sorrow on everyone who is
alive in this place? [*Goes out.*]

   [*The two girls stop as soon as she is out of the door.* NORA *steps up
gradually to the door watching round the doorpost.*]

NORA. She is gone surely. Open it now.

M. Maybe she'll turn round again. She's that sorry you wouldn't know what'll she'd do. Run to the thornbush and see if she's following the path. [NORAH *runs out of the door.* M. *goes up a ladder and takes a paper parcel out of the thatch. Then goes to the door.*]

NORA [*running in*]. She's gone surely. I seen her stand down by the well.

out

M. Quick now take up Micheal's shirt so we see if it's his body they've found.

NORA. What name now is on the place they found him.

on it won't stay in

M. It was ~~in~~ on the letter but it was a big long name ~~I don't rightly mind.~~

~~remember.~~ Give me a knife. The string's destroyed with the salt water and the knot's tightened on me, ~~the Devil twist it.~~

[NORA *gives her a knife.*]

M. Wherever it was it is a cruel way from this place [*pulling out a torn shirt and one sock.*]

NORA. It's his surely.

M. Whisht your talk. Aren't there many shirts the like of that one. Put down his own beside it. Is that cloth alike.

N. It is Mareen.

M. It's a queer hard thing to know certainly.

and counting the stitches].

N. [*picking up the stocking /*] It is his stocking.

M. How do you know that?

3rd

N. It⟨'s⟩ the pair ~~I first~~ pair I knitted and I put up 50 stitches and I dropped 3 of them.

M. Show me here. [*Takes the stocking and counts quickly.*] It's that number and it's no lie you're ⟨telling⟩. God help him it was him surely and isn't it a sad thing to think of ~~him there~~ floating and tumbling on the sea with no one keening him or—what's that.

NORA [*looks out*]. It's herself running.

I

M. Then quickly we must tell her some time but ~~it~~ wont tell her now

Patch

the while she's taking on about ~~Mike.~~

> [*They hide the things and sit down again carding and spinning.*]

> [B. *comes in and goes over and sits down at the corner of the fire with her back to the girls and pulls her shawl over her head rocking herself backwards and forwards and keening very faintly.*]

[NORA *and* M. *hide the parcel more carefully and then look at her wonderingly.*]

M. [*to old woman*]. You seen him riding down?

> [B. *goes on rocking herself.*]

M. Did the grey pony follow well by the mare

> [B. *gives a half-sob.*]

M. [*a little impatiently*]. God forgive you isn't it a better thing to raise your voice and tell us what you've seen, than to be always making

Patch

lamentation for what is done and gone. Did you see ~~Micheal~~ I'm saying to you?

B. I seen a fearful thing ~~and~~ My heart's broken from this day.

was it   aw

M. What did you ~~see.~~ Sure Patch wouldn't fall from the mare and ~~the~~ he wasn't yet on the sea.

B. I've seen the fearfulest thing any person has seen since the day ~~Mar~~ Nora Ruadh saw the woman was dead a week trying to carry the child.

> [*The girls stop their work.*]

M. You seen what?

B. I seen a thing is not right to be talking of.

> [*The girls go over and sit near her.* NORA *faces the door.*]

puts out her hand as to shut out ⟨*shield herself?*⟩

B. ~~Mich~~ Patch rode and the grey pony followed him / and the son of God spare us Mareen.

M. What did you see?

B. Micheal.

M. [*looks at* NORA *and puts her hand to her forehead*]. It was not Micheal you seen for his body is found now in a place in the far North and a decent burial they gave him.

         and he

B. I saw him now / ~~riding~~ riding and galloping on the grey pony, and
  and galloping before   *so*
Patch riding / ~~in front~~ of him, ~~and when~~ Patch came first I tried to say 'God speed you,' and I thinking it was some other lad was riding
                    God speed you
on the pony. But when I tried to say it / some thing choked the words in my throat and when Patch came by 'the Blessing of God on you' says he, and I could say nothing. Then I looked up and I crying at the grey horse and there was Micheal upon ⟨it⟩ with fine clothes and strong boots on his feet.

[*The girls sit looking at her with frightened faces.*]

          and lost it is likely can   coffin for me with
B. Patch will be drowned now / and ~~let~~ you make a good / white boards—[NORA *is looking from the door and starts.*]—for I wont live after them I have had a husband and a husbands father in this house and six sons and there was some ⟨of⟩ them was found but they drowned in the sea it is two of them I saw at one time carried in
      the
through ~~that~~ door.

[NORA *goes over to the door and looks out.*]

2. *Directly below the above draft, also in ink but written with a different pen, is the following poem which, though apparently set in County Wicklow, sustains the mood of the old woman's keen.*

          and I
It's a long while I was / waiting at the
          stepping stones of Ballyquinn
Waiting on my white treasure to come
          from Glenacree
It's a long while I was hearing the
          birds sing and seeing

fish leap in the pools
And seeing the fish leap up through
          the shadows on the grey pools
And then I seen and I waiting
          a great crowd coming on the path
And women and children and young men
And they hard set walking in the
          steep way with
          the two black coffins they
                    had between
                    them.

3. *The first two pages of the other end of the same notebook appear to offer slightly later versions of some of the speeches in the above scene. The page is headed, in blue pencil, 'Studies J.M.S.', but the passages following were obviously written at a later time. The first two passages are written in pencil with ink corrections; the next two passages, on the lower leaf, are written in ink. (Other passages written from this end of the notebook appear to belong to the* Fool of Farnham *period.)*

                                        speaking
Isn't it a hard and cruel thing he wont hear me talking ~~to him~~ and I holding him back from the sea—
                    he
There is no man in life but / must be going out on the sea, and who would listen to an old woman and she saying the same thing ten times in the day?

          will
An old woman / soon tire with anything she will do, and isn't herself after keening and crying making great trouble for nine days and a night?

without you sending him out with an unlucky word behind him and a hard word in his ear. Go down to ⟨the⟩ path below and say 'God speed you', when you see him passing along.

D. *In Envelope H of Box File E there is a large notebook torn out of its covers, which appears to have been in use the summer of 1902 and which contains early draft scenes of* The Shadow of the Glen *and* The Tinker's Wedding, *and the following early draft of the complete* Riders to the Sea. *It is divided into three scenes, the last scene composed before the middle scene.*

1. *The opening scene, five pages in ink, is much overwritten, many of the corrections made in pencil:*

          Scene. Island in the west of Ireland, cottage kitchen door in the middle of the room fire-place with open hearth on one side. ~~BRIDE~~

sitting by the fire MAURA *spinning at spinning-wheel at end of room opposite the fire.*

this day
B. It's a week ~~now~~ since he was drowned, and ~~to think~~ we've ~~had~~ no news or knowledge of the body.

~~after~~   *weeks*
M. It's often they do be found / two weeks and three / and five weeks after. There was Shawn Noreen ~~who~~ was found after two weeks and four days at Kilmagush, and there was Mourteen Patch Dara ~~was~~ found after three weeks and one day only at Ballynaknockeen.

The young priest is asking for you
NORAH [*comes in*] *to* B. You're wanting outside on the road.
you
is it
B. ~~Who~~ / ~~wants me?~~

NORAH. ~~The young Priest.~~

with me, with an old woman is weary
B. ~~Where is he? and~~ What is it he wants?   *with crying*

west   *so you're to*
N. He's going down to ~~the quay~~ and he said he'd not time to come in. /
go
Go out to him now quickly.

Its little is it   *be told.*
B. What ~~does he~~ want when there is no sure thing to ~~tell me~~?
          can

[*She goes out.* NORAH *follows her for an instant and then runs in with the parcel.*]

has he heard? word of the body
M. What ~~does he want~~?

He has not but
It's little he   *H*   *bundle and*
NORAH. ~~No He~~ wants ~~nothing, but~~ he's after giving me this ~~parcel,~~
          this bundle
there's a shirt in it and a stocking were found on a drowned man
in the far   *it*
~~somewhere in the~~ North ~~is written down on the inside,~~ and, says he,

'let you and Maura wait till the old woman is out and then take that
piece of a shirt and that stocking and ~~see~~ find out if it's Micheal's they
   surely   And
are ~~really~~. If they are his you may tell the old woman Micheal's
  in the sea   *let no one of you*
found / and if they aren't his say ~~nothing~~ of them the way you wont
                a word   *her death*
trouble her ~~more~~, for, says he, she'll ~~might~~ get ~~ill~~ with ~~the~~ crying and
keening. ~~she's making. if it isn't soon she will stop.~~

> mind her now or she'll get her death with the crying and lament-
> ing.

                   to look at
M. ~~Have we time /~~ now? *open it?*

    We've no time.   *to hide it*
NOR. ~~We have not~~ *He* only called her for a moment it was I'd have
                 ~~have time to~~
          for a minute while I'd put the bundle away.
time

M. ~~Where shall we hide that thing~~? Give me the ladder and I'll put it
in the thatch. [*They put the ladder against the wall and put up the parcel
in the thatch.*]

NORAH [*looks out*]. She⟨'s⟩ coming.

[M. *puts down the ladder and goes back to her wheel.* BRIDE *comes in
and goes back to the fire.*]

~~B. It's little enough he had to say. 'Let you not be crying' says he 'for~~
     ~~the Almighty~~   ~~The Son of God~~
 ~~it's the will of God done it.' God forgive him if it was himself had a~~
 ~~son lost on the sea he might talk then of the will of God and anything~~
 ~~more.~~

*It's an easy thing for them as has no children to talk of being satisfied in the
world*

                 ~~of the~~
M. ~~[to NORAH]. Card a piece more wool I'm near through with the~~
~~piece I have. [NORAH *begins to card the wool.*]~~

Put more turf round the oven Norah Patch'll need a cake if he goes out this

is   ?
B. ~~Do you know~~ where Patch is itself.
    Where is he itself?   *there*
NOR. He went down to ask ~~if there~~ would / be another hooker when
    he could send the horses instead of going today, he'll be coming in a
    minute for if he goes today they've an hour only before the tide goes
    ~~at the quay.~~

in
~~B. He wont go this day he won't go and leave me here with no son or~~
~~man in it.~~ the place. ~~B. he won't go now please God~~

~~M. If he must go there is no good in your talk.~~

[PATCH *comes in.*]   Where is the bit of new rope? ~~give~~

M. [NORAH]. give it to him. It's in the cupboard behind you
                on the nail behind those boards at the wall.

B. What is it you want with the rope?

    to make
P. ~~I want~~ a halter for the mare.

                T
PATCH. ~~It's today I must go~~ there'll be no other boat ~~bef~~ for two weeks
                will be a good fair I heard them saying below.
    or three and the fair ~~is before that time.~~

B. ~~Dont go Patch~~ for the weather's broke now and there'll be danger
    on the sea. ~~Dont go Patch~~ if it was a hundred horses you had itself.

                                hundred
[PATCH *gets down a halter and begins settling the rope.*] What is a horses
            in a house
    against a son where there is one son only?

                each   and
P. [*to* MAURA]. Let you go down ~~every~~ day ~~to~~ see the sheep ~~if~~ are not
    lepping over   garden with the
    ~~getting~~ into the / rye, and if the jobber comes you can sell one pig
    there is
    if / a good price is going.

M. I will surely.

 below
B. What will all say / if the body is washed up and there is ⟨no⟩ man ~~in~~
 the *giving a big price for the finest white boards*
 to make coffin and I after buying the finest white boards were in the
 you'ld find in any island in the world, any place in this island or out of it.
 ~~whole island.~~

P. It will not be found surely.

B. Well if it isn't found itself the wind is rising up and you seen yourself
 there was a little star up against the moon last night, and there was a
 today.
 ring round the sun and it rising ~~this morning~~.

 and wind
P. [*to* MAURA]. If east comes with the last bit of the moon let you and
 up enough of weed *of kelp that* *for it is*
 Norah get weed enough to finish the cock / we were making. We'll
 hard we'll be *for*
 be set / from this day with one man only the work.

B. We'll be hard set surely if you go out

 in the sea
B. It is if you go out and the wind rising and get drowned ~~that we'll~~ be
 ~~hard set. Dont go~~ heir of my heart, dont go Patcheen and leave an
 old woman alone

 ~~hold~~
P. [*standing up with the halter*]. I have it knotted ~~at last~~.

B. ~~Stay on the dry shore, Patch, stay on the dry shore, star of my sight,~~
 it's hard set we'll be and they children only and I an
 and dont leave me in full darkness and I an old woman looking round
 for the grave.

P. [*to* M.]. In three nights it is Martin's night and it is from this house a
 sheep must be killed. If I am in the land that day Eamon Shawn
 Pheety will be passing and let you call him in and give him the big
 knife to sharpen it and kill the sheep.

B. [*turning to the fire and putting up the shawl over her head, to* MAURA].
 Isn't ⟨it⟩ a hard and cruel thing he wont hear me and I holding him
 back from the sea.

every morning and night
and

M. There is no man but he must be going out on the sea who would listen to an old woman and she saying the same thing ten times in the day?

P. [*taking off his ragged coat and putting on a newer one, to* NORAH]. Is the hooker at the pier?

NORAH. She's passing the green head and letting fall one of her sails.

P. I'll have time now if I go quickly. I'll ride down on the mare and the grey pony will run after. [*He goes out.*]

[M. *gives him bread.*]

end Scene I

2. *This version of scene two, two pages in pencil with few corrections, appears to have been the last composed. It is followed by the early version of* The Shadow of the Glen, Dead Man's Deputy.

Scene two.

B. He's gone now and I'm afeard I'll not see him again and have no son from today.

M. Isn't ⟨it⟩ sorrow enough we have without sending him out on the sea with an unlucky word after him and a hard word in his ear. Go down now to the spring well and then you'll see him again and *know*
~~see~~ the foolishness of ~~the way~~ you're taking on, and you'll say God speed you when he goes across and he'll go ~~happier so.~~ *sail luckier so.*

B. Maybe he'd be cross if he seen me and say some hard word himself.

quickly
M. He won't surely go down now or maybe he'll be gone out of it before you'll be there.

slowly
B. [*putting a shawl over her head*]. I'll be hard set to walk ~~that bit~~ itself for my legs are weakened beneath me. [*Goes out.*]

[*The girls stop their work as soon as she is gone and watch her round the doorpost.*]

NORAH. She's gone surely. Take it down and open it now.

M. Maybe she'll turn round again, she's that sorry you cant tell what she will do.

NORAH [*looking from the door*]. She's passed the thorn bush and turned down to the spring well.

M. She'll go the whole way so. Close the door the way there will no one come in. [*She goes up the ladder and brings down the bundle.*]

3. *The final scene was composed after the opening scene. It is six pages in pencil with many interwoven drafts.*

Last scene.

       There are   in every place and
NORAH. I see boys running / there is some thing down by the quay.

               surely there is
M. [*looking out*]. There is / a mass of people coming up and some thing carried among them.

                 up   *after*
B. Maybe its Micheal has been washed I knew he'd come and I ~~praying~~
making ⟨*speeches?*⟩
to the Lord.

      you after   *is after being*   *is*
M. ~~Didn't I tell you~~ he was found in the far north and when he found
   I told you
there how could he be here ~~now~~ in this place?

B.

M. There ~~is no time but there~~ does be a power of young men floating
round in the sea, and what way would they know if it was Micheal
                       man
they had or another man like him for when a is four days in the sea
and a wind blowing on it, it is hard set we'd be know who it was
surely.

      they found
M. It was Micheal and there's no lie in it for here is two bits of his

M. [*comes back from the door and half closes it behind her*]. There are two
clothes and
bits of his clothes and you'll see yourself it is his they are surely

crosses and   It is his they are and

B. [*taking and squeezing them to her breast*]. / ~~The Lord have mercy on us~~

thing   a man   son

~~all~~ isn't it a pitiful / when there is nothing of ~~my fine~~ / who was a

one

great fisher and ~~boatman~~ but a bit of a wet rag and a ~~soiled~~ stocking.

rower

NORÁH [*who is looking out of the door*]. ~~Merciful Mary~~ it's to this house they're coming.

M. To this house? and for what?

dropping
There is ~~running~~ off it

NORAH. ~~I see~~ water / of the thing they're carrying in among them!

and leaving a track on the road.

They are carrying a thing among them and

water dropping out of

B. [*jumping up and throwing the pieces of clothes away from her*]. You see water?   *what they're carrying among them.*

[*A woman knocks at the door and comes in.*]

B. [*jumps up with a shriek and throws the clothes away from her*]. Water dropping out and leaving a track on the road to this house. The son of God assist us. [*She throws herself on a bench near the door. The girls look at her.*]

WOMAN. God help all here.

Youre bringing

B. ~~Is it~~ Patch? ~~thats drowned?~~

WOMAN. It is surely.

2ND WOMAN. God help all here.

~~Men carry in~~ / *the body of Patch laid on a board and put it on the table. Women come in cross themselves and make groups on each side of the fire. Then men carry in the* ⟨body⟩ *slowly and carefully through the small door and as they come in* B. *gradually raises herself and stands watching them with stronger feeling while they put* /.

Then

> [B. *goes over and sits down on a stool at the end of the table and leans her forehead on her arm. A few other persons crowd in round the door.*]

B. It is as good soon as late and first as last, and I knew surely it was coming.

It is the last now and if they come riding on horses it ⟨is⟩ the sons of other old women will be drowned.

he drowned

M. How was ~~so near~~ at the quay and he the finest boatman in the island?

going after   *man*

MAN. They were ~~following~~ the hooker and ⟨he⟩ and another / leaned

it a

out to hit at them black birds with his oar, and when he did ~~a~~ wave came behind them and upset them and it took Patch and washed him

and

back by the rocks ~~till~~ he was ~~quite~~ drowned. *there.*

[*One of the women begins to keen.*]

of men

M. [*taking one the towards the door*]. The priest will be back tomorrow night and maybe yourself and Eamon would make the coffin in the morning. We have ~~the~~ fine clean boards you see on the wall that

God help her

herself bought / thinking the body of Micheal would be found in the sea.

MEN. We'll make it and welcome in the morning, ~~God help you all~~.

Are there nails

[~~They go out~~.] *with the wood in this house?*

M. ~~In the truth~~ There are not we forgot the nails altogether.

MAN. Well we'll run down now for there is a curagh going with fish and they ⟨will⟩ bring them tonight if no storm rises.

M. Well do it so and God speed you. [*The men go out.*]

> [M. *sits down for a minute with her hand to her eyes. The women come over to her.*]

sheet

ONE OF W. There is a fine white / and fine candles below with Maura Leary, and maybe she'ld give them for the ~~funeral~~ burying and we might bring them up after milking the cows.

The Lord save your health.

M. God speed you. ~~Is~~ there any poteen in the island?

in the island and

2ND WOMAN. There is ~~plenty but it's~~ a high price they're taking.

[*The women go out.*]

[B. *is still sitting as before.* NORAH *comes over next* MAURA.]

M. Bring me the sheet and the fine candles along with you and I'll see for the poteen after.

and easy

NORAH. She is quiet now / ~~and~~ but the day Micheal was drowned you could hear her crying from here to the spring well. It is fonder she was of him than of Patch. Who'ld have thought that?

M. ~~It is only foolishness that you're talking~~. An old woman will be soon tired with anything she will do, and is not herself after keening for nine days or beyond it.

[B. *gets up very slowly and goes over to the corner pulls different things and then an old stocking. Comes over to the table and begins counting out money, putting it in little piles on the table by the dead man.*]

B. There's one pound, there's two pound, and there's seventeen and eleven pence. Will we have enough with that to get decent pipes and poteen?

M. We have surely.

B. Then what more can we want. What man can be living forever

III. RELATED PASSAGES FROM NOTEBOOKS

(*Unless otherwise indicated the references are to the Oxford* Prose *edition.*)

A. *THE ARAN ISLANDS*

1. 'They live here in a world of grey . . .', *p. 89; p. 72.*
2. 'Now a man has been washed ashore in Donegal with one pampooty on him, and a striped shirt. . . . For three days the people here

have been trying to fix his identity. . . . Tonight . . . we met the mother of the man who was drowned from this island, still weeping and looking out over the sea. . . . Later in the evening . . . the sister of the dead man . . . pieced together all she could remember about his clothes. . . . Often when an accident happens a father is lost with his two eldest sons, or in some other way all the active men of a household die together', *pp. 136–7*.

3. 'the burning of the kelp', *pp. 76–77*.

4. '. . . their grey poteen, which brings a shock of joy to the blood . . .', *p. 73*.

5. 'Gannets are passing up and down above the sound, swooping at times after a mackerel . . .', *p. 73. Cf. the* 'great flock of birds', *p. 181*.

6. 'When the horses were coming down to the slip an old woman saw her son, that was drowned a while ago, riding on one of them', *p. 164. Cf. p. 159*.

7. 'Their ⟨the horses'⟩ shipping and transport is even more difficult than that of the horned cattle. . . .', *pp. 78–79*.

8. 'While the grave was being opened the women sat down among the flat tombstones . . . and began the wild keen, or crying for the dead . . .', *pp. 74–75*.

9. '. . . they'll want to borrow the boards that a man below has had this two years to bury his mother', *p. 158*.

10. 'The young man has been buried, and his funeral was one of the strangest scenes I have met with. . . . the keen lost a part of its formal nature, and was recited as the expression of intense personal grief by the young men and women of the man's own family', *pp. 160–1*.

11. 'The maternal feeling is so powerful on these islands that it gives a life of torment to the women . . .', *p. 108*.

B. *IN WICKLOW, WEST KERRY AND CONNEMARA*

'The Kelp Makers', *pp. 307–9*.

C. MSS. QUOTED BY GREENE AND STEPHENS

'But at the same time we have to be satisfied because a person **cannot** live always', *p. 105*.

IV. FIRST PRODUCTION

By the Irish National Theatre Society at the Molesworth Hall, Dublin, 25 February 1904, with the following cast:

MAURYA	Honor Lavelle
BARTLEY	W. G. Fay
CATHLEEN	Sara Allgood
NORA	Emma Vernon
MEN & WOMEN	P. J. Kelly, Seamus O'Sullivan, George Roberts, Maire Nic Shiubhlaigh, Maire Ni Gharbhaigh, and Doreen Gunning

APPENDIX B

THE SHADOW OF THE GLEN: WORKSHEETS AND COMMENTARY

I. DESCRIPTION OF TEXTUAL SOURCES

(Unless otherwise stated, unpublished material is in the possession of the Synge Estate.)

A. STANDARD EDITION

The Shadow of the Glen and Riders to the Sea (*London, Elkin Mathews, 1905*); *Vigo Cabinet series no. 24. Further editions in 1907 and 1909.*

See Appendix A, I.A for letter from Elkin Mathews to Synge, dated 3 May 1905. *The edition published in* The Works of John M. Synge, *Volume I (Dublin, Maunsel, 1910), follows the Vigo edition.*

B. OTHER EDITIONS DURING SYNGE'S LIFETIME

1. *In* Samhain: An Occasional Review, *ed. W. B. Yeats,* ⟨Number Four⟩ (*December 1904), pp. 34–44. Title reads* In the Shadow of the Glen. *Based on an earlier draft than TS. in Box File E.*

2. *In the Shadow of the Glen (New York, John Quinn, 1904). A copyright edition limited to fifty copies published simultaneously with* Samhain, Number Four. *Based on Texas TS./MS. According to Maurice Bourgeois in* John Millington Synge and the Irish Theatre (*London, 1913), Quinn's copyright editions of Synge were 'designed' by E. Byrne Hackett of Yale University Press. Copyright was registered 10 December 1904.*

C. EXTANT MANUSCRIPTS/TYPESCRIPTS

1. *In notebook H, seven pages in ink and pencil. Summer–autumn, 1902.*

2. *In envelope H, thirty typescript pages, heavily annotated; p. i+1–22, also loose pages numbered 12, 13, 14, 16A, and 20, and a page with alternative stage setting. One title-page reads* In the Glen; *the other reads* In the Shadow of the Glen *with the* In *struck out. 1902–3.*

3. *In the University of Texas Library, twenty-two typescript pages with occasional ink emendations; title reads* In the Shadow of the Glen; *written in ink by Synge on the back of the last page is* 'J. M. Synge 4 Handel Street London W. C.' *and* 'Permanent address 31 Crosthwaite Park Kingstown Co. Dublin Ireland'. *This typescript is prepared for the printer and appears to be based on the TS. in envelope H. 1904.*

4. *In Box File E, twenty-five typescript pages including title-page and two pages of stage setting, prepared for the printer and apparently used for the Vigo edition. Title reads* The Shadow of the Glen. *1904–5.*

II. DRAFT MANUSCRIPTS

A. *On 11 February 1905, during the revived controversy over* The Shadow of the Glen (*see Introduction*), *the following letter was printed in* The United Irishman:

> 'Sir, I beg to enclose the story of an unfaithful wife which was told to me by an old man on the middle island of Aran in 1898, and which I have since used in a modified form in *The Shadow of the Glen*. It differs essentially from any version of the story of the Widow of Ephesus with which I am acquainted. As you will see, it was told to me in the first person, as not infrequently happens in folktales of this class. Yours &tc., J. M. Synge.'

Although Arthur Griffith, the editor of The United Irishman, *neglected to print the story Synge enclosed, it is apparent that Synge refers to the story of an unfaithful wife told him by Pat Dirane, the old shanachie of Inishmaan, on his first visit to Aran in May and June 1898. Synge later published the story in a more polished form in* The Aran Islands, *Part I (see Oxford* Prose, *pp. 70–72), but there is no reference to it in Notebook 19, in which the rest of this section of* The Aran Islands *is recorded. The original version, now in Box File E, appears to be the following, written in ink on three sides of foolscap paper headed* 'P. Dirane':

P. Dirane

One <del>day</del> ^{ce} I was travelling on foot from Galway to Dublin and the night came down on me when I was out of the town I was wanting to get into for <del>to</del> pass the night. The rain was falling and it was growing <del>so</del> dark I turned <del>that</del> aside into a <del>hut</del> ⁿ old house without a roof <del>so that the</del> the walls would give me a bit of shelter. As I was looking round me I saw a light about fifty ⟨feet⟩ from me in some bushes. Thinkin' I'ld be better in any sort of a house than there I crossed out over the wall and got up against the wall to look into the window. I saw a dead man laid out on a bed and candles lighted and a woman sitting up watching by him. I felt startled like when I seen him but it was rainin' hard and I said to myself in ⟨my⟩ mind that if the man was dead he'd do me no harm. With that I knocked at the door and ⟨a⟩ woman opened to me.

'Good even' ma'am' says I

'Good even kindly stranger' says she 'come in out ⟨of⟩ the rain'

So she took me in and told me how her husband was dead and she watching by him. After she brought me into the parlour it ⟨was⟩ a fine clean house and gave me a cup of tea putting a cup with a saucer under it on the table in front of ⟨me⟩ with good sugar and bread. A while later I came back to the kitchen where the dead man was lying out on the table and when I sat down she gave me a fine new pipe off the table and a drop of spirits then says she

'Are you afeard to be alone with himself stranger'

'Bedad then I'm not ma'am' says I 'he thats dead can do no hurt'

With that she told me how she wanted to go out and say to her friends how her husband was after dyin' on her and she left me there and locked the door after her.

I smoked one pipe and I leaned out and took another off the table and was smokin' it with my hand on the back of my chair the way you are yourself in this moment, God bless you, well I was lookin' on the dead man and I thought he lifted his eyes. Then I was afeard and I looked at him still and he opened his eyes right open and looked at me.

'Dont be afeard stranger' says the dead man 'I am not dead at all in the world. Come here and help me up and I'll tell you all about meself.' So I went up to him and took the sheet off of him and I saw how he'd a fine clean shirt on his body and fine flannel drawers. Then says he

'I've got a bad wife so I let on to be dead the way I⟨'d⟩ catch her at her goings on'

Then he got two fine sticks he had to keep down his wife, and he put the two down at each side of him, and lay down again as if he was dead. In a half an hour the woman came back and a young man along with her. Well she gave him his tea and told him he was tired and would be right to go in and lie down in the bedroom. The young man went in and the woman sat down beyond me to watch by the dead man. A while ⟨after⟩ she stood up and 'Stranger' says she 'I am going to get the candle out of the ~~young man's~~ bedroom the young man will be asleep by now.'

She went into the bedroom and stayed there.

Then in a little while the dead man got up and took one stick and gave me the other and when we went in he saw them and he hit the young man with the stick so that his blood lept up and hit the gallery. That is my story.

B. *Preserved in an envelope marked 'H' and stored in Box File E is a notebook, circa 1902, its cover gone, containing early drafts of* Riders to the Sea *and* The Tinker's Wedding *and the following sketches for* The Shadow of the Glen :

1. *Four consecutive leaves in ink immediately following fourteen leaves for* Riders to the Sea :

Dead Man's Deputy—/Last Scene

D. There are their steps, mind yourself now, stranger and tell a good lie.

T. I will your Honour.

—[*Woman and a friend of hers with red hair come in.*]—

W. Was I a long time, stranger?

T. [*half drunk and half terrified*]. Middling long—Lady of the House.

W. The neighbours wouldn't come out with the rain that's falling except this man only stranger.

T. The blessing of God on him!

W. Did ever you see the like of that for a fine handsome man stranger and you walking round through the world ~~stranger~~?

T. I did not L⟨ady⟩ of the House, I never seen a man till this day with a head on him like a setter coming out of a bog.

W. [*looking at her friend*]. He's fine hair surely.

FRIEND. Put on the tea and dont be blathering, ma'am [*Playing with his watch chain with his eyes on the dead man.*] Did ever you go across to the States stranger?

T. I did not I'm not fond of the water.

FRIEND. You dont look it—
    That's easy seen—

T. I went into a bog hole a while ago and I after an old setter was settling what they call a guinea hen and she perched in a tree—from that I⟨'m not⟩ fond of setter's—of water your Honour—

                                                        stretch
W. Take a drop more stranger and then ~~lie down~~ yourself here and sleep easy. Your head's tired with walking.

FRIEND. If he gives any jaw I'll walk him out through ⟨that door⟩ as I'd walk any bloody god-damned know-nothing like him—

W. Let you not be taking offence. [*Whispering to the* FRIEND.] I wouldn't have you in it alone—he'll sleep easy let you not be afeard—

F. [*going round to the other side of the fire*]. Bring me the tea to this side.

T. [*drinking*]. Your good health Lady of the House—

W. Your health stranger, put up your feet now easy on that bench. [*She puts up his feet and covers them with an old petticoat.*]
—[*She goes round with the teapot to the* FRIEND *and pours out his tea*]—

2. *Three consecutive leaves in pencil from the other side of the same notebook, apparently written at approximately the same time as the above draft, and not much later than the early drafts of* Riders to the Sea:

We'll be going on now the soft days when / the herons do be
/ the branches on the trees
are red with the great wet and the drops do be hanging on the fir trees to the end of the branches the way you'ld be thinking it was silver bead⟨s⟩ they were hanging out of the green cloak of a queen and I'm telling you now, woman of the house, the time you're feeling the cold and the frost and the night—and the sun with it you'll not be sitting up the way you were sitting here and you making yourself old with letting the time be running on you and it passing you quick.—You'll be saying one day, it's a grand evening and the lord be thanked and you'll be saying another time it's a wild night God help us and is it soon it will pass.

Maybe it's not woman of the house I'll be calling you but woman of the hills, and you'll ⟨be⟩ listening to the herons and they calling out over the black lakes when you'ld think the stars would be lepping on the water each with each twist of the wind, and you⟨'ll⟩ be listening to the grouse and the owls and the larks and the titlarks and ~~everyone~~ it's not from one of them I'm telling you, you'll hear a talk of
It's soon you'll not be talking any more of getting ~~old~~ like Peggy Cavanagh and loosing out the teeth in your head but you'll be saying it was little I got between my teeth this day, God help me, and what at all will I be eating tomorrow when the sun goes up?

III. RELATED PASSAGES FROM NOTEBOOKS

(*Unless otherwise stated the references are to the Oxford Prose edition.*)

A. *IN WICKLOW, WEST KERRY AND CONNEMARA*

1. '"... I shouldn't comb out the hair of her poll and she dead"', '*In West Kerry*', p. 261.

2. '"... in the valley of the Lough Nahanagan"', '*An Autumn Night in the Hills*', p. 189; '*People and Places*', p. 199.

3. '"... often when I do be excited with the thunder I do be afeard I might die there alone in the cottage and no one know it"', '*The Oppression of the Hills*', p. 210.

4. 'The fog has come down in places; I am meeting multitudes of hares that run round me at a little distance—looking enormous in the mists ...', '*Glencree*', p. 234.

5. '... the three shadowy countries that are never forgotten in Wicklow—America (their El Dorado), the Union and the Madhouse', '*The People of the Glens*', p. 216.

6. '"... there was a poor fellow ... threw off his clothes and ran away into the hills"', '*The Oppression of the Hills*', p. 209.

7. '"... I got the old stocking, where I keep a bit of money ..."', '*The People of the Glens*', p. 219.

8. '... flocks of sheep I could not see coughed and choked with sad guttural noises in the shelter of the hedge, or rushed away through a gap when they felt the dog was near them', '*An Autumn Night in the Hills*', p. 192.

9. '"... wouldn't any one be glad of it in the lonesome place we're in?"', '*An Autumn Night in the Hills*', p. 188.

10. '"... it's company to see you passing up and down over the hill ..."', '*The People of the Glens*', p. 219.

11. 'We went out at once and she walked quickly before me through a maze of small fields and pieces of bog, where I would have soon lost the track if I had been alone', '*An Autumn Night in the Hills*', p. 192.

12. 'This peculiar climate, acting on a population that is already lonely and dwindling, has caused or increased a tendency to nervous depression among the people, and every degree of sadness, from that of the man who is merely mournful to that of the man who has spent half his life in the madhouse, is common among these hills', '*The Oppression of the Hills*', p. 209.

13. '"... there were many people were afeard to speak to her, for

they thought she was after coming back from the grave"', '*On the Road*', p. 214.

14. 'Here and there in County Wicklow there are a number of little known places—places with curiously melodious names, such as Aughavanna, Glenmalure, Annamoe, or Lough Nahanagan . . .', '*The People of the Glens*', p. 216.

15. '"... yet you're nowhere in the world beside the herds that do be reared beyond on the mountains. Those men are a wonder . . ."', '*At a Wicklow Fair*', p. 228 and note.

16. 'Often after these hot days . . . a peculiar fog rises in the valleys of Wicklow so that the whole land seems to put ⟨a⟩ white virginal scarf about it to meet with the stars and night', '*People and Places*', p. 199.

17. 'As the night comes on herons cry with a lonely desolate note that is echoed backwards and forwards among the hills . . .', '*People and Places*', p. 195.

18. 'As I turned away I heard the loud clap of one hand into another, which always marks the conclusion of a bargain', '*At a Wicklow Fair*', p. 226.

19. 'In Wicklow, as in the rest of Ireland, the union, though it is a home of refuge for the tramps and tinkers, is looked on with supreme horror by the peasants', '*The People of the Glens*', p. 217.

20. '. . . the vagrant, I think, along with perhaps the sailor, has preserved the dignity of motion with its whole sensation of strange colours in the clouds and of strange passages with voices that whisper in the dark and still stranger inns and lodgings, affections and lonely songs that last for a whole life time with the perfume of spring evenings or the first autumnal smoulder of the leaves . . .', '*People and Places*', pp. 195–6.

21. 'The tramp in Ireland is little troubled by the laws, and lives in out-of-door conditions that keep him in good humour and fine bodily health. . . . In all the circumstances of this tramp life there is a certain wildness that gives it romance and a peculiar value . . .', '*The Vagrants of Wicklow*', pp. 202–8.

22. 'The cottage men with their humour and simplicity and the grey farm-houses they live in have gained in a real sense—"Infinite riches in a little room", while the tramp has chosen a life of penury with a world for habitation', '*Glencree*', p. 236.

23. 'All round in the valleys geese and cattle can be heard calling in the mist, and in the sky very often flocks of golden or green plover fly round and round ⟨in an⟩ infinity of crying', '*People and Places*', pp. 194–5.

B. *THE ARAN ISLANDS*

1. '"Take a sharp needle . . . and stick it in under the collar of your coat, and not one of them will be able to have power on you"', *p. 80*.

2. '". . . then I remembered that I had heard them saying none of those creatures can stand before you and you saying the *De Profundis* . . ."', *p. 180*.

IV. FIRST PRODUCTION

By the Irish National Theatre Society at the Molesworth Hall, Dublin, 8 October 1903, with the following cast:

DAN BURKE	George Roberts
NORA BURKE	Maire Nic Shiubhlaigh
MICHAEL DARA	P. J. Kelly
A TRAMP	W. G. Fay

APPENDIX C

THE WELL OF THE SAINTS: WORKSHEETS AND COMMENTARY

I. DESCRIPTION OF TEXTUAL SOURCES

(Unless otherwise stated, unpublished material is in the possession of the Synge Estate.)

A. STANDARD EDITION

The Well of the Saints: A Play in Three Acts, *being Vol. I of the Abbey Theatre Series (London, A. H. Bullen; Dublin, The Abbey Theatre, 1905).*

The Well of the Saints. *With an Introduction by W. B. Yeats, being Volume Four of Plays for an Irish Theatre (London, A. H. Bullen, 1905) is technically the same edition.*

Lady Gregory's signed presentation copy of the first issue (now in the Berg Collection) is dated by Synge 10.11.05. In a letter to Dr. Meyerfeld dated 26 May 1905, Synge writes, 'A small edition of "The Well of Saints" was issued at the time of the performance for sale in the theatre. . . .' *On 31 July 1905 he writes,* 'The little edition of the play is nearly all gone so I could not find a spare copy of the printed text—a more expensive edition is coming out shortly with a preface by W. B. Yeats.'

Item 90 contains the following letter to Synge, dated 15 December 1905 from the Shakespeare Head Press and signed by A. H. Bullen: 'I owe you many apologies about "The Well of the Saints". The annoyance has possibly been as great to me as to you, for naturally I was anxious to have your book upon the market in good time. What has happened is that the binders—Burn of Kirby Street (the best London binders)—have contrived, *mirabile dictu,* to lose your book! Again and again I sent messenger after messenger to enquire the cause of the delay and at last the binders reluctantly confess that the quires had been mislaid. It was the grossest carelessness on their part; but I could only keep on hammering away at them. They now tell me that the sheets have been found, and that we shall receive copies immediately.'

In the possession of Mrs. L. M. Stephens is Synge's own copy of the first issue of The Well of the Saints, *with emendations in his own hand which differ from any other version of the play.*

B. OTHER EDITIONS DURING SYNGE'S LIFETIME

1. The Well of the Saints: A Drama in Three Acts *(New York, John Quinn, 1905), a copyright edition limited to fifty copies published simultaneously with the first edition in London and Dublin. It does not contain Yeats's introduction. Copyright was registered 7 February 1905.*

2. The Well of the Saints (*Dublin, Maunsel, 1905*). *Second Edition of the Abbey Theatre Series Volume I. The text corresponds to the First Edition.*

3. Der Heilige Brunnen (*Berlin, S. Fischer Verlag, 1906*). *This is the German translation by Max Meyerfeld.* (*See Section IV of this Appendix.*)

4. The Well of the Saints (*Dublin, Maunsel, 1907*). *Item 90 contains a statement of account from Bullen stating that on 26 April 1907 100 quires were forwarded to Messrs. Maunsel, Dublin,* 'who undertook to arrange with author'.

NOTE: *On 19 December 1908, Messrs. Sidgwick and Jackson, London, wrote to inform Synge that they had taken over the publication of* The Well of the Saints *from Bullen.*

C. EXTANT MANUSCRIPTS/TYPESCRIPTS

1. *In Notebook 28, roughly a dozen pages in ink interspersed with dialogue for* When the Moon Has Set *and* National Drama. *Winter 1903.*

2. *In Notebook 31, four pages in ink followed by notes for* The Fool of Farnham (The Playboy of the Western World). *May 1904.*

3. *In Box File E, over 250 typescript pages plus fragments, all heavily annotated. Spring 1903–summer 1904 and revision of III in spring 1908.*

   a. *Act I. Six drafts, the fourth one entitled* When the Blind See.

   b. *Act II. Six drafts, with many variants of the scene between Martin and Molly, and one draft entitled* The Crossroads of Grianan.

   c. *Act III. Five drafts, with an additional four pages of corrections to the 1905 edition.*

NOTE: *This revised version of Act III was published in* Plays of John M. Synge (*London, Allen and Unwin, 1932*).

4. *In the University of Texas Library, a complete typescript draft of the play, with annotations for Max Meyerfeld.* (*See Section IV of this Appendix.*) *Spring 1904, annotations July 1905.*

5. *In Houghton Library of Harvard University, eighteen typescript pages, bound by handstitching, with a title-page indicating only the character of Timmy the smith. Apparently a theatre part, yet italicized for the printer. 1904–5.*

6. *In Notebook 35, six pages in pencil of a 'translation' for Meyerfeld. July 1905.*

II. DRAFT MANUSCRIPTS

A. *Synge first records the story of a holy well which could cure blindness in Notebook 19, during his first visit to Aran in May 1898. He later revised the passage reproduced below and included it in* The Aran Islands (*cf. Oxford Prose, pp. 56–57*).

I have found a professor an old man who walked and guided Petrie, Sir William Wilde, and many others. We are already great friends. He is then one of the Aran Islanders I read of in Petrie's notes when ~~I was~~ ~~years since~~ ~~seek for~~ first touched with antiquarian passion ~~and~~ I used to wander many miles to seek the vestige of ~~a~~ some tiny church gloating on its few fragments

with more joy than I have felt since at Rouen or Amiens—He has described to me already how the epileptic and the blind have within his
own experience been restored to health by a draught from a holy well,
and how the Fairies were thrown from heaven and carry in themselves
the pain of Hell. He deplores continually my incapacity to follow his
Celtic disquisitions and his own limited ~~power of~~ English which prevent

marvel

him from imparting to me the marvels he has known. At times he recites

amorous pleasure   ~~music of~~

poetry dwelling with ~~great love~~ on the rhythm till he brings tears
almost to my eyes though there is nothing I understand. He is unique.

seeing

An accident has injured his ~~sight~~ but he is still otherwise agile and full

further

of delight in himself and all around full ~~moreover with~~ of a primitive
piety that it is of much interest to contemplate. The priest he told me
today is answerable before God for every soul that is under him hence
though all men are brothers we name him not incorrectly ~~our~~ Father
in that this responsibility is shared also by each father for the flock
housed by his own thatch.

At the church of St. Carolan which I have just visited with my old

~~still~~

guide there is a holy well remarkable for many cures. While we loitered
in the neighbourhood an old man came to us from a near cottage and
told us how it became famous. A woman of Sligo had one son who was

~~One n~~   *ed*   ~~moved with hope~~

blind. She dreaming of a well that held water potent to cure so she took

and came after long sailing and she knew the shore

boat with her son following the course of her dream and reached Aran.

~~the~~   *of this who spoke*

She came to the house of my informant's father and told what had
brought ⟨her⟩ but when those around offered to lead her to the well
nearby she declined all aid saying she saw still her way clear before
⟨her⟩. She led her son from the ⟨house⟩ and going a little up the hill

~~her~~

stopped at the well. Then kneeling with the blind child beside her she

~~then~~

prayed ⟨to⟩ god and bathed his eyes. In ⟨a⟩ moment his face gleamed

said

with joy as he said 'Oh Mother look at the beautiful flowers.' Twice

since the same story has been told to me with unimportant variation
yet ending always with the glad dramatic cry of the young child.

One night she dreamed how moved with sudden ⟨hope⟩ she took
~~with her son~~
boat and came after long sailing to a rocky island where she mounted
from the shore till a well was suddenly at her feet. There she bathed the
blind eyelids of her son and he received his sight. When she told her
                              said
dream a⟨n⟩ old man ~~told her~~ it was Aran she had seen.

B. *Included in Box File E among the typescript drafts of* The Well of the Saints *is
the following analysis of the play, drafted in Synge's hand:*

Analysis Well of Saints

Act I		
	1. Martin and Mary	Exposition of characters and psychics
	2. +Timmy crescendo narrative	comedy

	3. +girls
	     current more
	     Martin excitement	

	4. +Saint	
	5. minus Saint	
	6. quarrel	tragic
II	Timmy and Martin no current	comic
	2. Martin and Molly Love current	traPoetical

III	Martin and Mary
	   current of reawakened
	   interest	

	2. plus crowd
	     current
	        to make Martin
	           recured	

III. RELATED PASSAGES FROM NOTEBOOKS

A. *Preserved in Notebook 30, among numerous drafts of articles and scenarios including notes for* The Tinker's Wedding *and* When the Moon Has Set, *are notes in a mixture of French and English based on the monumental* Histoire du théâtre en France au moyen-âge *by Professor Petit de Julleville, whose courses at the Sorbonne Synge had attended in the spring of 1895 and the winter of 1896–7. On 3 October 1903, according to his diary, Synge recorded portions of Chapters II and III of the particular volume* La Comédie et les mœurs au moyen-âge *(Paris, 1886); the relevant pages (100–3) describing Andrieu de la Vigne's* Moralité de l'aveugle et du boiteux *(1456), based on the life of St. Martin, are reproduced below. Italics indicate the special passages noted by Synge.*

Moralités Religieuses

La moralité d'André de la Vigne s'ouvre au moment où *le saint vient d'expirer. Son corps est resté exposé au fond* du théâtre, et l'on va tout à l'heure l'emporter à l'église en procession solennelle. *Deux mendiants* sont en scène; *l'un* d'eux est *aveugle, et* ne marche qu'en tâtonnant, *l'autre* est *boiteux,* et gît au milieu de la route. Mais n'ayons pas trop grand' pitié d'eux. Ce sont deux paresseux, deux ivrognes; quoiqu'ils gémissent d'une voix plaintive; l'aveugle en disant:

> L'aumosne au povre disetteux,
> Qui jamais nul jour ne vit goutte.

et le paralytique:

> Faites quelque bien au boiteux
> Qui bouger ne peult pour la goutte

Quand ils seront sûrs qu'il ne passe personne, ils se feront leurs confidences, et nous apprendrons qu'ils sont charmés d'une infirmité qui leur permet de vivre grassement, sans rien faire. Mais, voici la mauvaise nouvelle que le boiteux apporte à son compère:

> *Un saint est mort nouvellement*
> *Qui fait des œuvres merveilleuses.* . . .

'Dieu! *si ce saint allait nous guérir, malgré nous.*' Quel plus grand malheur ces paresseux peuvent-ils redouter? *Le boiteux* en frémit d'avance

> *Quant serai gari, je mourrai*
> *De faim; car un chascun dira*
> *'Allez, ouvrez'. Jamais n'irai*
> *En lieu ou celui sainct sera.*

Fuyons donc; mais comment? Le boiteux ne peut faire un pas; l'aveugle ne peut se conduire. Une bonne idée leur vient. Le boiteux monte sur le dos de l'aveugle; l'un prête ses yeux, l'autre ses jambes; et nos gens s'en vont lourdement, au cabaret le plus voisin. Mais l'aveugle est trop chargé pour courir.

> . . . . . . Escoute.—Quoi?
> Cella qui meine si grant bruit . . .
> Si c'estoit ce sainct?—Quel esmoi!
> . . . Cachons-nous soubz quelque fenestre
> Ou au coin de quelque pourpris . . .
> Garde de choir. . . .

Mais il est *trop tard pour fuir*; la procession défile, et *le corps de saint Martin passe tout près de nos deux drôles, qui sont subitement guéris.*

Leur miraculeuse guérison ne produit pas à tous deux le même effet. *Le boiteux* jure et *tempête*, en se sentant solide sur ces jambes. *L'aveugle-né en contemplant* pour la première fois le ciel, rend grâces à Dieu, et *éclate en transports*. Le poète a-t-il voulu indiquer assez finement qu'il vaut mieux perdre ses jambes que ses yeux et qu'il n'est pas d'être assez ingrat pour en vouloir à Dieu de lui avoir montré *le monde*. En tout cas la joie du nouveau voyant n'est pas sans charme et sans poésie

> *Hellas! le grant bien ne sçavoie,*
> *Que c'estoit de veoir clerement!*
> *Bourgoigne voy, France, Savoie,*
> *Dont Dieu remercie humblement.*

Le boiteux lui-même finit par prendre assez gaiment son parti d'être ingambe; il en sera quitte pour feindre désormais l'infirmité qu'il n'a plus, et une foule d'autres.

> Homme n'aura qui ne me donne,
> Par pitié et compassion.
> *Je ferai bien de la personne*
> *Pleine de desolacion.*
> 'En l'onneur de la Passion,
> *Dirai-je, voyez ce povre homme,*
> 'Lequel par grant extorcion,
> 'Est tourmenté, vous voyez comme!'
> Puis dirai que je viens de Romme;
> Que j'ay tenu prison en Acre,
> Ou que d'ici m'en vois, en somme,
> En pelerinage a sainct Fiacre.

Ainsi finit un peu trop gaiment la représentation édifiante donnée à Seurre en 1496. Faut-il soupçonner dans la moralité de l'Aveugle et du Boiteux une pointe d'irrévérence et d'incrédulité? Nous ne le pensons pas. La croyance était si profonde qu'on pouvait, en ce temps-là, parler avec un sourire des choses de la religion, sans que ce sourire des lèvres indiquat la dérision ou l'hostilité du cœur.

B. *As early as January 1902 Synge had completed the essay 'The Vagrants of Wicklow' which was finally published in* The Shanachie *in 1906. The earliest version, entitled 'A Hundred Years by the Wayside' and preserved among the typescripts of Box File C, includes the following passage which differs slightly from the version later published (cf. Oxford* Prose, *pp. 202–3.)*

A few of these people reach an extraordinary age, though it is usually difficult to check with any certainty the stories that are told about them. One old man, however, who is usually found among the lakes in the middle of the county is said with a certain probability to have attained a hundred and one years in last December, for the oldest men in the district remember his first appearance in the neighbourhood as a man of past forty some years before the famine of 1848. This man is rather apart from his class, for he has been married several times and reared children of whom he had lost all knowledge, even, I think, of their names and sex. He was a sailor for nearly thirty years in his early life and sailed with somebody he calls 'il mio capitane', visiting India and Japan and gaining odd words and intonations that gave tone to his language.

Since he has been too old to wander in the world he has learned all the paths of Wicklow and can go the thirty miles from Dublin to the Seven Churches, without, as he says, 'putting out his foot on a white road, or seeing any Christian but the hares and moon.'

When he stops to rest by Lough Bray and the Night-jars burr and the Snipe drum over his head, and the grouse crow and the heather moves about him, he still hears in their voices the chant of singers in dark chambers of Japan, and the clamour of tambourines and the writhing limbs of dancers he knew in Algeria.

All the things he has seen have had an influence on his mind, and he is still full of scorn and humour as is perhaps right for the man who has understood more of the world than most of the people that he begs from.

A few years ago he married an old woman of eighty-five, but in the honeymoon they quarrelled, and before a fortnight was over he beat her with his stick and came out again to sleep among the trees.

The next day he was arrested and sentenced to a month in the prison of Kilmainham. He did not care anything for the plank bed or uncomfortable diet, but he gathers himself together and curses with extraordinary rage, as he tells how they cut off the long white hair that had grown down on his shoulders. All his pride, and his half-conscious feeling for the dignity of his old age, had twined itself with this long hair that marked him out from the country people of his district, and I have often heard him muttering to himself as he sat beside me under a ditch:— 'What use is in an old man without his hair? A man has only his bloom like the trees, and what use is in an old man without his white hair?'

For the last few years he is grown too old for the road ~~but~~ and ⟨lives⟩ in a nasty little cottage supported I suppose by the charity of the neighbours.

c. *Two passages in* The Aran Islands *also have relevance to the play.* (*References are to the Oxford* Prose *edition.*)

1. '. . . sometimes when I go into a cottage I find all the women of the place down on their knees plucking the feathers from live ducks and geese', *p. 163*.
2. '. . . I heard a fierce wrangle going on between a man and a woman near the cottages to the west, that lie below the road. . . . I stopped for a few minutes at the door of our cottage to listen to the volume of abuse that was rising across the stillness of the island', *pp. 152–3*.

IV. SYNGE'S TEXTUAL NOTES FOR MAX MEYERFELD

In the spring of 1905, Synge entered into correspondence with Dr. Max Meyerfeld, who applied for permission to translate The Well of the Saints *into German. In his letter of 26 May 1905 Synge replied:* 'I should be very glad to have it translated into German but—as you will see—it will not be easy to render adequately a great part of the dialogue which depends for its effect on the peculiar colour-quality of the dialect I have used. I imagine in the German "Volkslieder" one would get a language that would be pretty nearly what is needed. . . .' *To Dr. Meyerfeld's request for 'an English transcript of the play' he answered on 10 July:* 'I am afraid I can hardly promise to make a version into ordinary English of the whole play—just at present, at least, it would not be possible—but I can do a few pages at first and then any particular passages that you find difficult. I do not think you will find the general language hard to follow when you have done a few pages, as the same idioms are often repeated, and the purely local words are not very numerous.' *By September 1905 Synge was able to report his delight with the completed translation, adding as usual only a few comments on interpretation and phrasing:* 'Sometimes in the translation there is an inevitable loss of terseness, which does not signify in a reading version, but I dare say when the play goes into rehearsal a few words or speeches will have to be cut out here and there. Indeed in our own performances here I made a very few cuts and changes, which I will point out to you when the time comes.'

The German version of the play was eventually produced by Max Reinhardt's Deutsches Theater in Berlin in January 1906, together with Oscar Wilde's A Florentine Tragedy, *but was not, apparently, a success. The correspondence, now in the possession of the National Library of Ireland, was translated by Meyerfeld and published in the* Yale Review, *July 1924.*

In addition to the suggestions and answers to particular queries throughout the letters, Synge as promised attempted a 'translation' into standard English. Two scenes he rewrote completely before giving up the task and compiling and annotating the remainder from early typescripts. This entire collection, including a letter to the purchaser from Dr. Meyerfeld explaining the arrangement, is now in the possession of the University of Texas.

A. *On 26 July 1905 Synge wrote,* 'I now send you a version—as you will see a rough and bald one—of the first scene and some notes on first act that I hope may be of use to you.' *Six pages of typescript are entirely rewritten. An earlier draft of the first three pages appears in Notebook 35, apparently made by Synge during his visit to the Congested Districts with Jack Yeats in June 1905, but it differs little from the Texas typescript here reproduced:*

MY. Where are we now, M.D.?

MN. Passing the gap.

MY. So far as that. Well the sun is coming out warm today although it is late in the autumn.

MN. Why would it not be warm when it is high up in the south? You were so long plaiting your yellow hair, that we have lost the whole morning and the people have passed by to the fair of Clash.

MY. When they are going to the fair, driving their cattle, with a litter of pigs, perhaps, squealing in their carts, they never give us anything at all. You know that right well, but you like to be talking.

MN. If I didn't talk I would soon be destroyed—(killed, driven mad) —by the chatter you are always making, for you have a queer cracked voice, the Lord have mercy on you, even if you are a fine looking woman.

MY. Who wouldn't have a cracked voice if they were sitting out in the rain the whole year round? It's a bad life for the voice, M.D., although I have heard it said that there is nothing like the wet soft wind that is always blowing on us for keeping a white beautiful skin —like my skin—on your neck and on your brows and there is nothing as good as a fine skin for giving great beauty to a woman.

MN. I often think we do not know exactly what gives you your beauty, or asking myself, perhaps, if you are really beautiful at all, for when I was a boy and had good sight, it was the girls with sweet voices that were the most beautiful.

MY. Dont be talking like that, when you have heard T. the smith, and M.S. and P.R.—(Patch Ruadh = red Patch, it had best be translated as Martin recognises him after he is cured by his red hair)—and many more praising my face, and you know right well they used to call me 'the beautiful blind woman' in Ballinatone.

MN. Well even if they did call you that I heard M.B. saying last night in the twilight that you were little more than an ugly old hag.

MY. She was jealous God forgive her, because T. the smith had been praising my hair. . . .

MN. Jealous?

MY. Yes—(doch)—jealous, M.D. and even if ⟨she⟩ was not jealous young and silly people are always mocking at the blind, and they would think it a fine thing to deceive us so that we should not know we were beautiful at all.

MN. I often think in the long nights that it would be a grand thing if we could see ourselves for an hour or even for a single minute so that we might know without a doubt that we are the finest man and the finest woman in the seven counties of the east, and then the
                                        below
wretched crowd of seeing people (in the village) might damn their souls by telling lies to us, and we would not mind anything they would say.

MY. If you were not a great fool you wouldn't mind them now for they are a bad lot—(des sales types)—those that have their sight, and they are glad when they see a beautiful thing to pretend they dont see it at all, and to tell fools lies, like what M.B. was telling to you.

MN. If she is always telling lies, she has a sweet beautiful voice you would never be tired hearing if she was only calling the pig or crying out after her hens in the long grass. I think it ought to be a fine rounded woman that has a voice like that.

MY. Dont mind at all if she is flat or round, for she is a flighty—(i.e. capricious, uncertain)—foolish woman you can hear when you are a long way off, laughing and making a great noise at the well.

MN. Is not laughing a nice thing when a woman is young?

MY. A nice thing? A nice thing to hear a woman making a loud braying laugh like hers? Ah, she is a great woman for attracting men and you can hear T. the smith when he is sitting in his forge getting mighty fussy if she comes walking from Grianan so that you can
(or better) while he is sitting there
hear his breath going (and you can hear him) wringing his hands.

(when she is
MN. I have heard him say many times she is nothing at all when she is *compared with you)*
seen beside you, and yet I have never heard any man's breath getting uneasy when he was looking at you.

MY. I am not like the girls that are always running round on the roads, swinging their legs, and twisting their necks out to be looking at the men . . . Ah there's great wickedness in the world M.D., among those that are always wandering about with their staring eyes and their sweet words, although they have no sense in them at all. (NB it is the gadding women, not the words that have no sense in them)

MN. It's true perhaps, and yet I have heard that it is a great sight to see a young girl walking on the road.

MY. You would be as bad as the rest of them if you had your sight, and I was right certainly not to marry a man with his sight—scores would have been only too glad to have me if I had wished—for the seeing people are a queer set, and you would never know what they would do.

B. *On 31 July 1905 he wrote,* 'I have gone over one of my old manuscripts and written in explanations where they seemed necessary. I am sending you this version today. One scene—the 2nd of Act II—I have rewritten for you in full and put into its place in the MS.' *This 'rewritten' scene came to five pages of type-script:*

⟨MARTIN⟩. When we have our sight we have to see many raw nasty days and dark mornings and shabby-looking fellows but we have one fine thing and that is to be looking on a fine white handsome girl like you, and every time I see you I say a blessing on the saints, and the holy water and the power of the L. ⟨Almighty⟩ in heaven above us.

M.B. I have heard the priests say that it isn't by looking at young girls that most men learn to say their prayers.

M. Most men have not been living as I was, hearing your voice and not seeing you at all.

M.B. That must have been a queer time for an old wicked coaxing fool like you, when you were sitting there with your eyes shut and never seeing girls or women passing on the road.

M. If it was a queer time still I had joy and delight when I used to hear you speaking when you were going by to Grianan, for your voice would make a poor blind man think of many fine things, and the day that I heard your voice it would never go out of my head.

M.B. I'll tell your wife if you talk to me like that . . . You have heard perhaps that she is picking nettles below—(là-bas)—for the widow O'F. who took great pity on her when she saw both of you fighting, and you mocking her at the cross roads.

M. Can no one speak a score of words to me or even say 'God bless you,' without reminding me of the old woman, and that day at Grianan?

M.B. I thought it would be a good thing to remind you of the day that you called the grand day of your life.

M. Grand day, indeed? Or a bad gloomy day, when I was roused up and found I was like little children that listen to the stories of an old woman and then dream afterwards in the dark night that they are living in fine golden houses with speckled—(i.e. varied, beautiful) horses to ride, and then awake again in a little while perished with the cold, and find their little room with rain dripping from ⟨the⟩ thatch, and a starved ass braying outside in the yard.

M.B. You have great romance in your talk today, M.D. Were you up drinking whiskey at the still last night?

M.D. I was not M.B. but I lying down in a little rickety shed, lying down on a sheaf of straw and thinking to myself that I was watching you walking along, and hearing the sound of your step on a dry ⟨road⟩, or hearing laughing and talking in a high room with dry timber lining the roof. For your voice has a grand sound in a room like that and I think I am better off lying down like that,—as a blind man is lying always—than I am sitting out here in the grey light and hearing the hard words of T. the S.

M.B. You have queer talk although you are a little old shabby lump of a man.

M.D. I'm not so old as you hear the people saying.

M.B. You are old I think to be talking like that to a girl.

M.D. Perhaps you are right for I have lost long years of the world feeling love and talking love to the old woman when I was made a fool of the whole time by the lies of T. the S.

M.B. It's a nice way you want to pay T. the S. . . . . . You are not making love to his LIES today, Martin Doul.

M.D. I am not M. but to the good looks of yourself—(I have altered the text here)—for even if I am getting old I have heard that there are lands away in C.I. and the R. of C. with warm sun and fine light in the sky, and light is a grand thing for a man that ever was blind or a woman with a fine neck and a skin like yours, so we should go off today so that we can have a fine life walking through the towns of the south telling stories r singing songs in the fairs.

M.B. Well it is a queer thing that when your wife has gone away from you because you are an ugly fright you would talk like that to me.

M.D. It is queer perhaps, for all things are queer in the world, but there's one thing I can tell you, if my wife went away from ⟨me⟩ it was not because of seeing me—although I'm no better than I am—but because I was looking at her with my two eyes when ⟨she⟩ was getting up, and when she was eating her food, and combing her hair, and lying down to sleep.

M.B. Would not any married man do the same?

M.D. I think by the mercy of God few men see anything but those that are blind for a while: few men see the old women rotting for the grave, and few see women like yourself though you are shining like a high lamp would draw in the ships from the sea.

M.B. Keep off from me, M.D.

M.D. You would do right I tell you not to marry a man who has been ⟨looking⟩ out for a long time on the bad days of the world, for how could anyone like that have fit eyes to look at yourself, when you rise up in the morning and come out of the little door you have up in the lane, when it would be a great thing if a man could see you for an instant and then lose his sight so that he would have your two eyes facing him when he would be going along the road, and shining above him, when he would look up into the sky, and springing up from the ground when he would lower his head instead of the filth that men with their sight see everywhere spread on the ground.

M.B. You hear talk like that from a man who is going out of his mind.

M.D. It would be little wonder if a man near a woman like you should go out of his mind. Put down your can now and come along with me, for I see you today, and see you perhaps as no man has seen you in the world. Come on now, I say, to the lands of I. and the R. of C. where you won't put down the width of your two feet, and not be crushing fine flowers and making great smells ⟨in⟩ the air.

M.B. Let me go, M.D. Let me go, I say.

M.D. Come along now: Come along the little path through the trees.

M.B. T. . . . T. the Smith. (   ) Did you ever hear that those who lose their sight lose their senses along with it, T. the Smith?

C. *Included with the typescript which Synge annotated for Meyerfeld is the following page in manuscript, perhaps the 'notes on first act that I hope may be of use to you' which he sent with his letter of 26 July:*

Grammatical Notes

What way? = Why? or How?

Lost *on* us = we have lost (there is no verb 'to have' in Gaelic hence these idioms).

They do be driving ⎫ idioms from the Gaelic tense of habitude—
I do be thinking ⎬ I do be thinking = 'I think often' or 'I think
They did call me ⎭ continually.'

Dark woman = blind woman.

⟨page⟩ 6) power = 'many', 'a great deal of' (like our use of 'force' in French).

Note the constructions with 'and you' 'and he' etc.

e.g. p. 18 how you'd look *and you* a saint etc = how you'd look if (or when) you were a saint of the Almighty God.

p. 19 bell-ringing with the s. of G. *and he* wedded with myself = How could he be bellringing with the saints of G. when he is wedded with me.

There is also another form which occurs often for instance 'I saw a man and he smoking his pipe' = I saw a man smoking his pipe. The idiom, of course, is a Gaelic one, and it has shades of meaning that cannot be rendered in ordinary English.

On p. 22 insert 'we' at end of first line 'and we not tidied etc'. Will he mind the state we are in when we are not tidy or washed clean at all?

D. *In his letters of 12 and 21 August Synge included the following guides to pronunciation; the page numbers refer to the 1905 edition:*

Doul, 'ou' as in 'out'. Byrne like 'burn'. Simon long English 'Ī'. Bállinatone, 'Grīanan', Annagolan = annagóulan the 'ou' as in 'out'. Laragh the gh is now usually mute otherwise it is a guttural.

p. 51, l. 20 Cahir (kăhĭr) = city of Iveragh. The nominative is on page 54, here it is genitive, pronounced ēe-v'ráu and ēevráu-ig the 'au' as in caught.

V. FIRST PRODUCTIONS

A. *By the Irish National Theatre Society at the Abbey Theatre, Dublin, 4 February 1905, with the following cast:*

MARTIN DOUL	W. G. Fay
MARY DOUL	Emma Vernon
TIMMY, a smith	George Roberts
MOLLY BYRNE	Sara Allgood
BRIDE	Maire Nic Shiubhlaigh
MAT SIMON	P. Mac Shiubhlaigh
A WANDERING FRIAR	F. J. Fay
GIRLS and MEN	

The scenery was designed by Pamela Colman Smith and Edith Craig.

B. *The play was revived on 14 May 1908, with a revised third act, with the following cast:*

MARTIN DOUL	Arthur Sinclair
MARY DOUL	Sara Allgood
TIMMY, a smith	Ambrose Power
MOLLY BYRNE	Maire O'Neill
BRIDE	Eileen O'Doherty
MAT SIMON	J. M. Kerrigan
A WANDERING FRIAR	J. A. O'Rourke
VILLAGERS	Maire Ni Gharbhaigh, Fred O'Donovan, S. J. Morgan

Costumes and a new setting were designed by Charles Ricketts and executed in the Abbey Theatre workshop.

APPENDIX D

WHEN THE MOON HAS SET:
WORKSHEETS AND COMMENTARY

I. DESCRIPTION OF TEXTUAL SOURCES

(All unpublished material is in the possession of the Synge Estate.)

A. FINAL TEXT

This play has never before been published. The text for this edition is a conflation of two one-act versions labelled 'J' and 'K' in Item 52.

Version 'J', thirty-one typescript pages with manuscript emendations, is the one referred to by Yeats in his Memorandum (see p. 155 note 1) and which Lady Gregory also read after Synge's death, judging it 'but of slight merit' (Our Irish Theatre, p. 125). This is probably the version Synge refers to in his diary for 23 May 1903: 'Finished (?) one act Play When the Moon Has Set (?).'

Some time later Synge took up the play again, producing version 'K', twenty-two typescript pages with manuscript emendations, which ends just before Sister Eileen leaves to put on the green dress.

Both 'J' and 'K' are labelled 'Rejected Version' in Synge's hand. This suggests that, as neither Yeats nor Lady Gregory records having read the play more than once during Synge's lifetime, Synge himself was still dissatisfied with it in its one-act form. However, he retained it among the papers to be reviewed for publication by Yeats after his death.

B. EARLIER TWO-ACT VERSION

Stored in a green clip binder (Number 51) with Synge's Crosthwaite Park address and signature on the cover page, is a complete two-act version of the play with versions of Étude Morbide, Vita Vecchia, and a fragment of the Vernal Play, all evidently retained by Synge as of some value. (He lived at 31 Crosthwaite Park from 1890 until 10 October 1904 and again from 15 February 1905 until 6 February 1906.) This version, forty-three pages of typescript with manuscript emendations, is in the small type that was on Synge's typewriter when he bought it in about 1900, and is apparently the version read and rejected by Lady Gregory and Yeats at Coole in September 1901.

C. RELATED TYPESCRIPTS AND MANUSCRIPTS

1. In Notebook 15, ideas and snatches of dialogue. 1896–8, Paris.
2. In Notebook 22, reference to subject in autobiographical sketch. 1896–8.
3. In Notebook 21, dialogue and incident in autobiographical sketch. 1898.

4. *In Notebook 17, fragment of dialogue on one page. November 1899.*

5. *In Notebook 26, scenario notes for Acts I and III. Spring 1902.*

6. *In Item 52, references among twenty-four typescript pages stapled together and marked in Synge's hand,* 'Early fragments. mostly rubbish J.M.S. XII 1908'. *1902?*

7. *In Notebook 28, several scenarios for play in two acts, including curtain scene in rough draft. January 1903.*

8. *In Notebook 30, rough draft of two-act scenario. Spring 1903.*

9. *In Item 50, six typescript pages with ink emendations and four manuscript pages, all stapled together, rough draft of play in one act, incomplete. Spring 1903.*

II. DESCRIPTION OF EARLY DRAFTS

A. *Notebook 15 contains a rough dialogue between two men in Paris: one is reading his manuscript on aesthetics to the other,* 'Costello', *a violinist. It is headed* 'Chap. I Flowers and Footsteps', *and contains the following excerpts which are the earliest (1896–8) indications of the themes expressed in the play:*

All emotions have neither end nor beginning, they are part of a long sequence of impulse and effect. The only relative unity in art is that of a whole man's lifetime. Hamlet though seeming complete is but the link from Romeo ⟨to⟩ Lear, as Shakespeare is the link from Chaucer to Byron, and modern literature from classical to what we are approaching. . . .

Real art is always a suggestion, an intangible emotion lurks behind the things that we produce as life lurks within the body.. . .

The human joys and human pities are the two feet of the human being on which he moves in the limited human life. The divine ecstasy is above both, yet it may be for a man it will retain the power of his feet though he dreams as often as he can rest from his walking. The unlimited ecstasy is found only through art or through religion and is bound to sensual love in the lower forms of art and to sentimental love in the lower forms of religion. Sensual love is unlimited because it has no pity and low religious hatred is unlimited because it also has no pity. All art is perhaps an expression ⟨of⟩ a trebly refined and purged growth of the joy of sensual love or the sorrow of desire as all religion in so far as it is an ecstasy rather than a philosophy is a growth of the sensual love nourished in the sentiments. Although of course we have seen religious arts and artistic religions and the ultimate effort of both is a perfect union which will be the last great task of humanity.

B. *Notebook 22, in use about the same time as Notebook 15, contains a bundle of notes stitched together which include passages later used for* Vita Vecchia. *Again, the dialogue is spoken by a violinist named Costello, who says, after references to a story '⟨which⟩ I have partly told in verses I call Vita Vecchia' and 'the study I call the Vale of Shadow',*

At this time I began a long poem in blank verse about a nun who was set free from her bondage by the influence of the statues in the Vatican and met and married a person who represented myself.

These pages conclude with the following statement:

From this time I turned away from the ordinary life, and never wrote wildly of the things that happened to me but out of their impulses and meaning.

C. *Notebook 21, containing the autobiographical sketch written in 1898 (see* Oxford Prose, *p. 7), includes references to the afternoon he and his cousin Florence Ross spent in the woods while their families attended a relative's funeral, and the following speech later woven into the first full-length version of the play:*

Every life is a symphony and the translation of this sequence into music and from music again, for those who are not musicians, into literature, or painting or sculpture, is the real effort of the artist.

D. *Notebook 17, containing Aran notes dated 3 November 1899, has this comment scribbled on one page, and later incorporated into the two-act version of the play:*

To the little Irish pigs that have eaten filth all their lives that I might wander in Paris these leaves are dedicated with respect ⟨and⟩ sympathy.

E. *Item 51 contains the typescript of* A Play in Two Acts, *completed by September 1901. This incorporates material from Notebooks 15, 22, 21, and 17 and draws a great deal on the autobiographical sketch (see* Oxford Prose, *pp. 3–15).*

Act I takes place during the winter, Act II three months later in June. Six characters are introduced on stage: Columb, Sister Eileen, Bride, Mrs. Byrne, Bride's father Pat Kavanagh, and Sister Dora. Four other characters affect the action but do not appear: Columb's uncle who dies just before the play begins, the madman Stephen Costello who shoots Columb, Bride's mother who is in the asylum, and Murphy a servant who will marry the pregnant Bride after her father dies in Act II. Reference is made to another character long since dead, Bride's aunt Biddy, the woman who rejected Columb's uncle many years ago and whose 'injury' lingers on in the disturbed mind of her brother Stephen Costello. Both acts include much argument about religion and references to

Columb's manuscript on aesthetics; Columb was apparently once a musician; a letter from his strange friend in Paris makes use of passages from Vita Vecchia *and* Étude Morbide. (*See* Oxford Prose, *pp. 16–38*.)

F. *Notebook 26 contains the only projected outline in three acts. Synge records the following entries in his diary for 1902: 16 March 'Finished Act I of play'; 28 March 'Revised Act I'. Evidently he returned to the play while working on the two verse plays.*

Act I contains eighteen numbered pages of dialogue between 'A' and 'B' (the nurse), mainly a discussion of religion, with references to Thomas à Kempis, Rabelais, and Boccaccio. 'A' contributes the following arguments:

Take a crowd of faces all moved by the same emotion and throw a coloured light on them and you have the faces of Christian literature. Take away the special light and you have one mood still such ⟨is⟩ religious literature. Take a crowd in the market place and you have literature in general—the literature I read.

.   .   .   .

Any one would be dismal here with the rain and the old people and their mournful intonations. There is no one in the house under seventy except ourselves there are no girls or children in the district. Death is in the air I breathe. My family is dead and the country is dead. The turf bogs are stripped and the timber is cut down—why shouldn't I read of life and amusement.

.   .   .   .

Once men thought water was an element, a thirsty man must have water but he need not continue to believe that water is an element because he continues to be thirsty. A spiritual man—I mean a man with fine instincts and perceptions must drink of the exquisite things of the earth but he need not for that reason continue to believe the effete philosophy of Christ. You are like people who live in a church and look out at the hills and river through quaintly stained rose windows. What you see is beautiful you are sheltered from the rain and winds every morning you see Christ appearing in the east. But there is another world the real world which we are learning to look at with white light and in it we have rain and wind and snow but we see all things and experience all things and to wonder at sunsets and to lose ourselves among the lustrous heather on the hills. This life is more than yours. . . . I won't send my soul into the workhouse while I have power to sustain it.

The heading 'Act II' is followed by five blank pages.

Act III follows, with three pages of pencil manuscript. In this act time has elapsed. 'A' is now a grey-haired lay nurse converted by 'B' to atheism; 'B' is dying. A servant Moira enters briefly; the scene breaks off, with the next two pages of dialogue torn out.

G. *The fragments of typescript in Item 52 appear to have some connexion both with the notes for Act III of Notebook 26 and the early autobiographical notes. The dialogue now occurs between 'Myself' and 'My grey wife', who are sorting papers written much earlier by 'Myself'. Fragments are read from* Vita Vecchia, *the correspondence included in the two-act version of the play, and the autobiography, interspersed with comments from 'My grey wife'. From marginal notes it seems that Synge also contemplated adding passages from his essays on the tramps of Wicklow.*

From the comments there appears to be an attempt to balance sections from 'town documents' *with* 'documents from the country'. *As with the two-act version of the play, there is an emphasis on* '⟨playing⟩ all the notes; it is for that we are created'.

H. *With Notebook 28 Synge returned to the two-act form. The notebook contains two scenarios, the first following a simplified version of the action as developed in 51 and a draft of the concluding scene with the madwoman. A later draft, however, is still further simplified, the action following the one-act draft, but Stephen Costello, the madman, still retained as a character.*

Synge's diary for 2 January 1903, reads 'W.T.M. is set', *the first use of a title.*

I. *Notebook 30 appears to have been in use about the same time as Notebook 28. The scenario is again in two acts, but Stephen Costello disappears and Mary enters for a few minutes at the end of Act I. This draft follows an early scenario for Act I of* The Tinker's Wedding.

J. *Ten pages stapled together in Item 50, six typescript pages followed by four manuscript pages, contain the first draft of the one-act form. It still relies heavily on the two-act version: the setting is given simply as* 'Library etc.'; *Bride's father is discussed and her mad mother mentioned, then that portion of the dialogue is crossed out in pencil; Sister Eileen waits tea for Columb; Columb later pours out wine for them both; the scene with Mary Costello is not written out in full; and the draft breaks off before the final scene.*

K. *TS. 'J' from 52 follows directly from the draft in 50. There is no mention of Bride's father, and the relationship between Bride and the madwoman is again struck out. The incident with the wine is also crossed out, but the play still opens with a conversation between Bride and Sister Eileen, as in all earlier versions. Mary Costello makes two entrances, repeating her warning to Sister Eileen.*

III. RELATED PASSAGES FROM NOTEBOOKS

(*Unless otherwise stated, all references are to the Oxford* Prose *edition.*)

A. '. . . a single woman with all the whims of overwrought virginity ⟨has⟩ perhaps a more utter, if higher sort of misery', '*The Oppression of the Hills*', p. 210 note 1.

B. 'The desolation of this life is often of a peculiarly local kind, and if a playwright chose to go through the Irish country houses he would find material, it is likely, for many gloomy plays that would turn on the dying away of these old families, and on the lives of the one or two delicate girls that are left so often to represent a dozen hearty men who were alive a generation or two ago', '*A Landlord's Garden in County Wicklow*', p. 231 *and note 1*.

IV. FIRST PRODUCTION

This play has never been produced.